Hush

Sign, Storage, Transmission

A series edited by
Jonathan Sterne and Lisa Gitelman

Hush

Media and Sonic Self-Control

Mack Hagood

DUKE UNIVERSITY PRESS *Durham and London* 2019

Designed by Matthew Tauch
Typeset in Minion Pro by Westchester Publishing Services

Library of Congress Cataloging-in-Publication Data
Names: Hagood, Mack, author.
Title: Hush : media and sonic self-control / Mack Hagood.
Description: Durham : Duke University Press, 2019. | Series:
   Sign, storage, transmission | Includes bibliographical
   references and index.
Identifiers: LCCN 2018037348 (print) |
   LCCN 2018047134 (ebook)
ISBN 9781478004479 (ebook)
ISBN 9781478003212 (hardcover : alk. paper)
ISBN 9781478003809 (pbk. : alk. paper)
Subjects: LCSH: Mass media—Social aspects. | Mass media—
   Influence. | Noise (Philosophy) | Noise—Physiological
   effect. | Headphones—Health aspects. | Noise control—
   Equipment and supplies. | Communication and culture—
   United States. | Information technology—Health aspects. |
   Popular culture—Effect of technological innovations on.
Classification: LCC P94 (ebook) | LCC P94 .H345 2019 (print) |
   DDC 302.23—dc23
LC record available at https://lccn.loc.gov/2018037348

Cover art: Design including Frederic Leighton,
Orpheus and Euridyce, oil on canvas, 1864, Leighton
House Museum, London.

Duke University Press gratefully acknowledges the
support of the Department of Media, Journalism,
and Film, Miami University, which provided funds
toward the publication of this book.

Contents

───────

Acknowledgments

Hush would not exist without the words, actions, inspiration, and generosity of many people—so many, in fact, that I dread the inevitable glaring omissions I will find once these hastily written words of thanks are in print. This book began as a PhD dissertation for Indiana University's Department of Communication and Culture, so I want to begin these acknowledgments by expressing gratitude to those who let a graduate student into their homes, workplaces, support groups, trade shows, storage spaces, and archives so that he could learn from them. I thank the people associated with Marpac (Gertrude Buckwalter, Liz Heinberg, Mac McCoy, Jimmy Sloan, Dave Theisen, Gordon Wallace, and Janet Zimmerman) and Sound Oasis (Troy Anderson), who shared the history and business of sound machines with me. Chris Newby of Lightning Bug, Adam Terranova of Amadeus Consulting, and Todd Moore of TMSoft provided an invaluable education on the world of sound app development.

I am also grateful to the many family members, friends, fans, and associates of Irv Teibel who shared stories and information with me: Miriam Berman, Robert Carlberg, Tony Conrad, Craig Eley, Daniel Emanuel, Lou Gerstman, Steve Gerstman, Lou Katz, Mark Levbarg, Rosanne Levbarg, Linda Lloyd, Mike O'Neil, Tom Roudebush, Laurie Spiegel, and Hans-Ulrich Werner. Special thanks go to Irv Teibel's daughter, Jennifer Ballow, who shared the Syntonic Research Inc. materials with me. One of the great pleasures of doing this research has been seeing Jennifer bring SRI back to life with a new website, downloadable recordings, and even an *environments* app. It has been rewarding to play a small part in this resurgence, and I want to congratulate Darren Richard and Jonathan Een Newton for their success in getting it done.

I am also indebted to the researchers and clinicians who provided me with insights into tinnitus and its treatment through interviews or observation of their practices: Nathan Amos, Jennifer Gans, Steve Hallenbeck, Pawel Jastreboff, Erica Koehler, Karen Libich, Jill Mecklenburger, Jill Meltzer, Jeanne Perkins, Michael Piskosz, and Robert Sweetow. Thanks to GN ReSound in Glenview, Illinois, and North Shore Audio-Vestibular Lab in Highland Park, Illinois, for allowing me to do observations at their facilities. I am grateful to Joel Styzens for sharing his story with me and to Joel, Nathan Amos, and Robert Hillman for welcoming me to the hearing and tinnitus support groups they lead. My deep thanks also go to the many people with tinnitus and hearing impairments who shared their stories with me but whose names I will not mention in order to protect their privacy.

Many sound machine images were acquired from the retail catalog collection at the Browne Popular Culture Library at Bowling Green State University. Thanks to my friend Hsin-wen Hsu and his students Mei-chen Chen and Wen-chun Lin for their research assistance on the *nianfo ji*. I am also grateful to Christiaan Virant of FM3 for discussing his Buddha Machine with me.

Next, I wish to thank the many academic mentors, staff, and peers who helped me when this book was in the dissertation phase. First and foremost, I thank my PhD advisor, Mary L. Gray, whose knowledge, patience, support, inspiration, and generosity have far exceeded any reasonable expectations. The foundations of this book were built in the graduate seminars of Mary and my other PhD committee members at Indiana University's Department of Communication and Culture: Stephanie DeBoer, Ilana Gershon, and Jane Goodman. I am so grateful to each of them. I thank my outside dissertation reader, Norma Coates, for generously sharing her time and knowledge with me over the years. Jonathan Sterne was also kind enough to offer feedback, advice, and encouragement to me as a sound studies newbie (and has continued to do so over the decade since). I would also like to thank Rayvon Fouché, Ted Striphas, and my anonymous readers at *American Quarterly* for their invaluable feedback on the dissertation. Props to the incredible Kathy Teige and Sabrina Walker for guidance with the administrative details of doing fieldwork and getting a degree. My brilliant fellow graduate students at CMCL supplied critical intellectual and emotional support—Eric Harvey, Andrea Kelly, and Travis Vogan were especially helpful in the Inspiration and Maintenance of Sanity departments.

The second phase of *Hush's* creation, the metamorphosis from disserta-tion to book, took place entirely at Miami University, where I have been an assistant professor for five years. I can't imagine a more supportive place to work than Miami and its Department of Media, Journalism, and Film. At MJF, Richard Campbell has been an exemplary chair, Ron Becker has been the most generous of mentors and readers, and my colleagues have been the best workmates a new professor could ask for. Sara Christman, Susan Cof-fin, and Kim Hensley have been patient with me in the management of my research accounts and paperwork, and Steve Beitzel and Ringo Jones have been my trusted advisors in audio hijinks. My student research assistants Claire Stemen and Laurel Wilcoxson were most helpful in putting together the manuscript and art.

Led by Tim Melley, the Miami University Humanities Center has been another center of support for this research. In particular, the Humanities Center's 2015–16 John W. Altman Program on the Senses, led by Altman Fel-lows Charles Victor Ganelin and Elisabeth Hodges, was an enriching experi-ence and a space for trying out some of the ideas in this book. I am grateful to Elizabeth Stockton for keeping the Altman on track that year and to all of my fellow Altman Scholars for their ideas and energy. Thanks also go out to all my friends across the College of Arts and Science for their support, espe-cially my partner in the *Phantom Power* podcast, cris cheek, who is helping me keep the sound in my sound studies.

This book was made all the more possible by my appointment to the Robert H. and Nancy J. Blayney Professorship. I wish to extend my deep-est gratitude to the Blayney family, Provost Phyllis Callahan, Dean Chris Makaroff, and Associate Dean Renée Baernstein for this great honor and financial support.

Beyond Miami, there are a number of people whose close reading and feedback at various stages made this book much better than it would have been: Ashley Hinck, Kristopher Holland, Eric Jenkins, Steve Jones, Danielle Kasprzak, Dylan Mulvin, Greg Seigworth, Nandita Sheth, Ben Tausig, Fred Turner, and my anonymous readers at Duke University Press and the Uni-versity of Minnesota Press. Particular thanks go out to one repeat anonymous reader who has greatly improved *Hush* through their extensive and perceptive comments and suggestions.

Eric Jenkins helped me understand the roles of modes in Spinoza, while David Howes suggested the terminology of "intra-modal" and "cross-modal" sensory effects that I use in the book. Tarleton Gillespie supplied me with helpful resources on patents. Dave Novak supplied thoughts on the onomatopoeia of the word *hush* and encouraged me to go with my gut on chapter order. I have been fortunate to test my ideas at the conferences of a number of scholarly societies while writing this book: the American Anthropological Association; the International Communication Association; the International Association for the Study of Popular Music; the Society for Cinema and Media Studies; the Society for Ethnomusicology; and the Society for Literature, Science, and the Arts. I am grateful to each of these organizations and to all of the amazing people I know through them.

Working with Duke University Press on this book has been highly gratifying. Courtney Berger has been a perceptive and patient editor, helping me sort out my sometimes tangled ideas over time. Sandra Korn has been excellent to work with during the production process. And I still can't quite believe my book is now part of my favorite academic book series—Lisa Gitelman and Jonathan Sterne's "Sign, Storage, Transmission." A special shout-out to Jennifer Lynn Stoever of *Sounding Out!* for taking an interest in my work and introducing me to Courtney.

Thanks also go to the many good friends I've made while living in New Orleans, Taipei, Chicago, Bloomington, and Cincinnati (Northside!). Books mean nothing without friendship.

Finally, I thank the people who have supported me the longest—the people who believed in me even when I provided them with little evidence to go on. Thanks to my family, especially Anita and Skip Capron, who taught me the ethics of listening—and how to listen through the ears of others. James Lopez, we've been brothers for my entire adult life and my futile efforts at keeping up with your intellect have made me an accidental academic. Paul Preissner, our friendship will soon be counted in decades—may the snarky iMessages never cease! I couldn't possibly have married into a better family than I did with Liz, Art, and the Scotts, and I'm grateful to be a part of it.

Bridget, there is no way this book would exist without your incredible love, patience, and example. Abe and Theo, thanks for the cries, squeaks, giggles, belly laughs, questions, musings, poems, and songs. Some noise is joyful indeed.

Introduction

Hearing What We Want

Hear What You Want. This is the tagline of one of the most culturally resonant television ad campaigns in recent years, produced for headphone
maker Beats Electronics. In these commercials, which first began airing in
the United States in late 2013, star athletes are portrayed using smartphones
and Beats Studio Wireless noise-canceling headphones to shield themselves
from the verbal abuse of opposing teams' fans or the insulting interrogations
of reporters. In one ad, San Francisco 49ers quarterback Colin Kaepernick
peacefully strides through a gauntlet of deranged, insult-hurling Seattle Seahawks fans outside their National Football League (NFL) stadium. Though
shot years before the athlete's national anthem protests, the ad eerily fore-
shadows his impending status as political lighting rod. Kaepernick walks
through a near-riot of hatred—all directed at him—yet he barely hears it,
his face displaying an equanimity derived from noise cancellation and the
ego-affirming sounds of Aloe Blacc's song "I'm the Man" (figure I.1). The
"Hear What You Want" campaign, in the words of one reporter, "went beyond marketing and actually became part of pop culture," generating millions of views online and sending Blacc's song to the top of the iTunes singles
chart (Beer 2015). The crescendo reached new heights in May 2014, when

Figure I.1 An athlete besieged in Beats' "Hear What You Want" ad campaign.

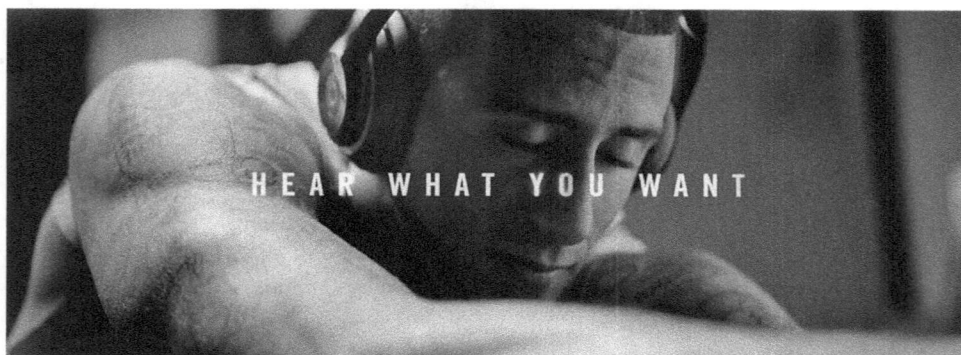

HEAR WHAT YOU WANT

Figure I.2 Kaepernick displaying sonic self-control.

Apple acquired Beats Electronics for $3 billion, confirming the ascendency of headphones in the global electronics marketplace.

Despite the campaign's popularity, however, there is something curious about the heroism these ads depict. We see no game, no team protecting Kaepernick, no field where he vanquishes his opponents, nor any spectacular display of physical prowess, joy, or celebration. There is only the lone man, protecting himself from the scrutiny and invective of "haters" through an act of sonic separation, getting himself into the mental zone necessary for success. As Kaepernick finally enters the stadium, a victorious grin forms on his lips. His victory is over the maddening crowd, which has failed to touch him. We last see him alone, stretching before the game, headphones on, at peace: in the end, the mastery he has displayed is a mastery over himself, a *hush* cast over his own senses and emotions (figure I.2).

ORPHEUS - *3. Orpheus als Argonaut.*
LIEBIG PRODUCTEN vergemakkelijken de keuken.

Figure I.3 Orpheus fighting sound with sound to create a safer space.

Media devices that provide control and customization of individuals' sonic environments are proliferating. Generating billions of dollars in revenue, these technologies include not just noise-canceling headphones, but also white noise machines, smartphone apps designed to make a noisy office or bedroom sound like the seashore or a rainy country field, wearable sound generators to suppress the sound of tinnitus, and new in-ear smart devices ("hearables") that filter, alter, and hush the sounds of the world. In Greek mythology, the musician-priest Orpheus heroically drowned the Sirens' fatal, mind-captivating voices in sound waves of his own, singing and playing his lyre to create a space of safe passage for the Argonauts as they returned with the Golden Fleece (figure 1.3). Similarly, what I call "orphic media" promise to help users, as represented by the Beats-wearing Kaepernick, remain unaffected in changeable, stressful, and distracting environments, sonically fabricating microspaces of freedom for the pursuit of happiness. Hear no evil, fear no evil.

Until now, neither consumers nor scholars have seen the disparate devices discussed in this book as a singular and prevalent type of media technology, but I argue that they should. The hush fabricated by white noise machines, nature sound recordings, noise-canceling headphones, and sound-filtering digital apps and devices reshapes our engagement with self, other, and world. As Natasha Dow Schüll writes in her study of video machine gambling, "Although interactive consumer devices are typically associated with new choices, connections, and forms of self-expression, they can also function to narrow choices, disconnect, and gain exit from the self" (2012, 13). Indeed, the freedom not to choose something, not to connect, not to attend to unwanted aspects of self and world, is a powerful form of choice in itself. The orphic dynamics I describe in this book involve much more than just the experience of sound and silence—orphic media foreground a deep desire for control as freedom, a desire that motivates the use of nearly all electronic media today. Studying these technologies reveals how media function as a controllable interface between subject and environment—and as an interface between a society's ideological imperatives and the personal poetics of its citizens' self-making, self-defense, and self-control.

Understanding orphic mediation—the control of how we allow ourselves to resonate, especially where the vibrations of others are concerned—has important sociopolitical potentials. It provides a sensory and material framework for our often-abstract debates about public and private spheres, media echo chambers, urban noise, online noise, fake news, trigger warnings, and safe spaces. Central to all of these controversies about physical and digital spaces are our beliefs about how—and how much—we should affect and be affected by one another. When we use mechanical or electronic sound to reshape space, the blueprints are these often-unexamined beliefs about what self, freedom, and society should be. Intuitively, using the tools the market provides, we build the acoustic architecture of the future, but we do so piecemeal, individual by individual.

One of the risks associated with the unprecedented choice our new media tools offer is an ever-increasing need to literally and figuratively "hear what you want," fostering intolerances both sensory and political. But at the same time, new media's din of mediated voices—diverse and democratic, yet overwhelming and often hateful—makes guarded listening a necessity for sensory and emotional self-care. In this context, auditory freedom of choice is a self-reinforcing necessity: both personal and political, "sensitive listening," with all the ambivalence that term implies, becomes a central issue of our time.

In *Hush*, I argue that addressing the literal and figural problem of sensitive listening begins with changing our notions of what media are and what they do, thinking, as John Durham Peters puts it, "beyond messages" to understand media as "our infrastructures of being, the habitats and materials through which we act and are" (2015, 14–15). Drawing on the philosophy of Baruch Spinoza (1970) and subsequent theorists, I argue that the real essence of media use is not the transmission of information but rather the attempted control of *affect*, the continually changing states of bodies that condition their abilities to act and be acted upon. Subjectively speaking, affects are the immediate impacts that other "bodies" (defined broadly as composites of moving or resting material relations) make upon our bodies (Spinoza 1994, 128). Although affect can be transmitted through representation, it operates nonrepresentationally, overcoming us before we can even "read" an experience or give a name to it as an emotion, as in the moment a loud sound startles, a musical chord overwhelms, or the sudden memory of such an event echoes through us as if the sound were in the air all over again. Affect also accumulates slowly over time, gradually conditioning the range of possibility for future action.

The word *hush* itself speaks to sound's affective power and utility. Its sound is not an arbitrary signifier or a mere carrier for a message—it is both onomatopoetic and performative, defying our Enlightenment-derived "binary separation of internal cognition from external vibration" (Samuels and Porcello 2015). *Hush* sounds like the hushed murmur of a crowd and the masking noise of its *shhh* has been soothing babies and disciplining the unruly from time immemorial—displaying controlled sound's ability to enact and enforce social and bodily states. Similarly, while Orpheus's song had words, its lyrical message was secondary to its sonic force in silencing the Sirens. And of course, any music fan can speak to the wide array of physical and emotional conditions that wordless music can bring forth. Plentiful examples such as these make sound a convenient sensory modality for understanding affective media with powers beyond effective messaging.

Like the Argonauts, we all travel through a world of things that affect us. Attempting to navigate these sometimes rough seas and atmospheres, we use media to pursue what feels enlivening and enabling—and to avoid what makes us feel diminished and disabled. In this way, we enact the same "autopoietic" (self-making) biological phenomenology that causes a single-celled organism to engulf a sensed food source and recoil from a perceived threat (Maturana and Varela 1998, 48–52). Yet unfortunately, as we use media to affectively engage the world, many of our motivating feelings and beliefs about what empowers and disempowers us are "inadequate ideas"—shortsighted, incomplete, and inaccurate (Spinoza 1994, 154–58). In fact, as Paul Roquet (2016) points out in his study of ambient music and video in Japan, autonomy-loving neoliberal cultures encourage subjects to disavow "atmospheric determinations of self" (15) even while "turning the atmosphere into a site of ever-increasing control and regulation" (11). "We need to learn to *read the air* in a way that better recognizes the forces moving through it," Roquet asserts, highlighting its potentials as a technology of self (15, emphasis in original).

But reading the air in this way provides other kinds of insights as well. Conceiving of media orphically, as the technologies of our often-misguided and ideologically driven attempts to control affectivity, dissolves the seeming paradox of recent media history: the spread of information through digital interconnectedness has fostered the retrenchment of identities and the proliferation of filter bubbles, echo chambers, trolling, and misinformation, rather than fulfilling the cultural fantasy that better communication would enlighten, cure social ills, and foster democracy (Dean 2009; Peters 1999).

To address the current impasse around listening, this book traces the modes and potentials of affective media use, identifies the ideologies that motivate it, and examines how the remediation of affect—particularly affects of fear and aversion—is designed, marketed, and monetized. While affective media practices *do* foster certain kinds of freedom and relief, they also often work against the best interests of individual and social "bodies politic" (Protevi 2009). The personal sense of control that orphic media provide often derives from the suppression of the biological, social, and material differences that make us who we are—a suppression of difference that actually makes us more compliant as subjects of the control society we inhabit (Deleuze 1992). Ultimately, the technologies I call orphic media may be designed to hush an age-old secret that is both too obvious and too frightening to contemplate: that we have never been, and will never be, in control.

Structure and Argument of the Book

Hush presents its explication of mediated self-control through the ethnographic and archival study of a half century of fighting sound with sound in the United States. Since the early 1960s, American consumers have increasingly turned to orphic media to increase their sense of personal ability as they respond to an ideological ableism that fears difference in human bodies, a postwar capitalist landscape of disrupted spatial coherence and social stability, and a neoliberal information economy that demands individualized attention and, therefore, the suppression of audible difference as unwanted noise. The book contains three parts. Each centers on a different affective modality through which orphic media fight sound with sound to pacify space for beleaguered subjects: suppression, masking, and cancellation.

Part I presents an ethnographic study of the personal experience and clinical treatment of tinnitus, a "phantom sound" of the body that is sometimes deeply disturbing to those who hear it. Tinnitus is the sound of a subject's own auditory system, yet it interacts with environmental sound, growing subjectively louder in quiet spaces and quieter in loud spaces. Due to this fact, clinicians and tinnitus sufferers often use orphic media to sonically *suppress* its aural presence, thereby providing the ethnographer an intimate opportunity to examine these technologies of the self through the experience of disability. Through tinnitus, I plumb the depths of aural suffering, showing how an affect of fear can attach to our listening at a neurological level when we feel sonic difference diminishes our ability to act. In tinnitus, sonic threat feels inescapable, presenting a heightened version of the kind of dynamic that animates the orphic media practices in the rest of the book. Tinnital sound and suffering emerge in a complex relationship between neurophysiology, sociomaterial environment, and an ideologically infused habitus of listening (Becker 2004) that hates tinnitus, fears it, and locates it exclusively in a supposedly anomalous body. Not only does this "ideology of ability" (Siebers 2008) misunderstand the nature of phantom sound—it also feeds into subjects' suffering, making tinnital suppression the most affectively charged form of orphic mediation.

In part II, I pull back from this intimate suffering to work at the larger scales of commercial and national history, surveying the evolution of white noise machines, nature sound LPs, and their digital descendants in order to isolate the cultural catalysts and repercussions of orphic mediation. This history maps the sociomaterial conditions that gave rise to these *sound-masking* technologies and examines their production, marketing, and use to discern Americans' changing ideologies about sound, space, self, and society. Marpac's noise-generating "sound conditioner," the Sleep-Mate, first domesticated and feminized noise to sonically privatize the home for sleep in the early 1960s (chapter 2). However, soon the company found itself rebranding the same device as the Sound Screen, responding to demand for an almost opposite functionality—enhancing concentration and reducing distraction in work and study settings. In both cases, I argue, consumers and producers were responding to a postwar destabilization of physical space and temporality that accompanied the increased circulation of people and capital. Syntonic Research Incorporated responded to these changes in a different way. Its *environments* series of nature recordings (1969–79) recast the phonograph as a cybernetic medium of techno-pastoral liberation, human and nonhuman interconnection, and self-development—a brief countercultural deviation from the utilitarian use of orphic media (chapter 3). However, today's contemporary smartphone apps such as TMSoft's White Noise return even more rigidly to Marpac's utilitarian sleep/concentration binary, helping users mask affective interconnection to live up to the physical and attentional demands of a 24/7 economy that disdains the limitations of the human body and conceives of even consciousness itself as information capital (chapter 4).

Part III audits the racial, gender, and class politics of fighting sound with sound in the twenty-first century. It does this by studying the social construction of the orphic mode of *phase cancellation*, used by noise-canceling headphone manufacturers to turn environmental sound into a self-canceling signal. Recounting the development, marketing, and reception of noise-canceling headphones, I ask who these media are designed to protect from sound and why, whose sounds are perceived as too noisy or disruptive, and why we have such a hard time listening to one another in a milieu of unprecedented social diversity and interconnection. Using the noise-canceling headphones currently sold by Bose (chapter 5) and Beats Electronics (chapter 6) as case studies, I analyze the differing racialized, gendered, and classed conceptions of noise promoted by these manufacturers in their products' early days. Early Bose marketing and reviews centered on the elimination of what could be called "white noise," which often included women's and children's voices, heard from a white, male, upper-middle-class point of audition. Over a decade later, the "Hear What You Want" campaign introduced Beats noise cancellation as a solution to the "black noise" of racism that threatens even the most successful man of color. Although both companies would soon diversify the representations in their advertising, these early ads show a masculinist and neoliberal problematization of listening across difference that both companies still promote.

Finally, the book's conclusion sounds a cautionary note on the future of listening, examining orphic media's miniaturization (and weaponization) as "hearables," in-ear computers designed to turn the aural world into a database of content for selective access and control, taking "hearing what you want" to a new level and potentially further atrophying our ability to listen across difference. But despite its critiques and warnings around audio technologies, *Hush* is not intended to simply condemn orphic media—nor is it a book only about sound. Rather, its purpose is to create awareness of this ubiquitous form of mediation, explain why it exists, and, through its example, encourage greater understanding of the orphic aspects of *all* media use. Reflecting on our affective entanglements and the reductive, defensive, and utilitarian ways we often remediate them is the only way to challenge our self-defeating attempts to be free of one another—and a first step toward more ethical and inclusively empowering media practices. In the remainder of this introduction, I will present the theoretical underpinnings of the book and provide a brief historical backstory of how sound became a problem in need of personal remediation.

Making Room for Self-Control

As a musician-priest, Orpheus shows how the mastery of sound (and other sensory modalities) can be used to move and unite people across differences—an affordance of affective mediation that music and the arts have long mobilized. The question, then, is why have orphic media emerged in such defensive and utilitarian configurations?

Perhaps the most intuitive answer to this question would be that people use orphic media because the world has gotten too noisy—both acoustically and in the sense of distraction and nonsense that prevents us from processing information efficiently. Acoustic ecologists such as Barry Truax and R. Murray Schafer (1994) first sounded the alarm on the issue of our degraded "soundscape" back in the 1970s, while more recent popular press books with titles such as *In Search of Silence* (Narse 2011), *In Pursuit of Silence* (Prochnik 2011), *Zero Decibels: The Quest for Absolute Silence* (Foy 2010), and even the rather resigned-sounding *One Square Inch of Silence* (Hempton and Grossmann 2009) attest to ongoing anxieties around noise both as unwanted sound and as unwanted information or informatic interference. Noise has also been a central concern in the interdisciplinary field of sound studies, with many cultural and philosophical analyses written on the topic—some of which have strongly influenced the present work.

Nevertheless, I have not found noise, in itself, to be a robust explanation for what people do with orphic media. As Hillel Schwartz explains, noise is "a register of the intensity of relationships" in a given space and time and therefore its history is fourfold. To understand noise in a given milieu, we must apprehend the ambient sounds of its sonic environment; its ways of listening and evaluating sounds; its definitions and theories of noise; and its practices of condemning, defending, reducing, and producing noise (2011, 21). As a scholar working on the present and recent past, I find that our contemporary definitions and theories of noise often make it more difficult to examine relationships of intensity. Like information—and, to a great degree, *because of* information theory and cybernetics—noise has become a sprawling and shape-shifting epistemological presence in modernity. While a skillful analyst like Marie Thompson (2017) capably combs out noise's many matted meanings and rehabilitates the term for scholarly duty, noise still remains an overdetermined phenomenon in everyday life. Therefore, I have largely excluded noise as what ethnographers call an "etic" category (an implement in the scholar's own analytical toolbox) so that I can better scrutinize the discursive and material dynamics behind its emergence as an "emic" category (one in use among the people being studied).

In other words, I treat noise as a symptom, not a cause. The historical argument in this book does not reduce to noise, but nevertheless attempts to explain at least some of its facets. Orphic media have arisen to silence a blaring contradiction in our liberal, capitalist, and increasingly "infocentric" society, which generates the imperative for a focused, free, and disembodied subject while also complicating the environmental conditions that have always negated the possibility of such a subject. The noise people use these technologies to block out is symptomatic of this more fundamental conflict, which is both societal and deeply personal at once.

A humorous early twentieth-century device called the Isolator both anticipates the use of orphic media and hints at its longer Euro-American philosophical and social heritage (figure 1.4). Invented by the techno-utopian science fiction pioneer Hugo Gernsback, the Isolator is something like a diving helmet for immersion into paper media. As shown on the cover of the July 1925 issue of Gernsback's magazine *Science and Invention*, the helmet is isolating enough to require the use of an oxygen tank, creating a sonic buffer between the author and the world outside as he writes or edits his articles and stories. Peripheral vision is also limited. In fact, the eye slits in the Isolator are so small that "it is almost impossible to see anything except a sheet of paper in front of the wearer." This attempt at disappearing the sensing body and projecting one's consciousness into the representation that one is manipulating anticipates William Gibson's cyberspace by more than sixty years. Making a claim that might resonate with both the professoriate and noise-canceling headphone-wearing business travelers, Gernsback wrote, "The greatest difficulty that the human mind has to contend with is lack of concentration, mainly due to outside influences."

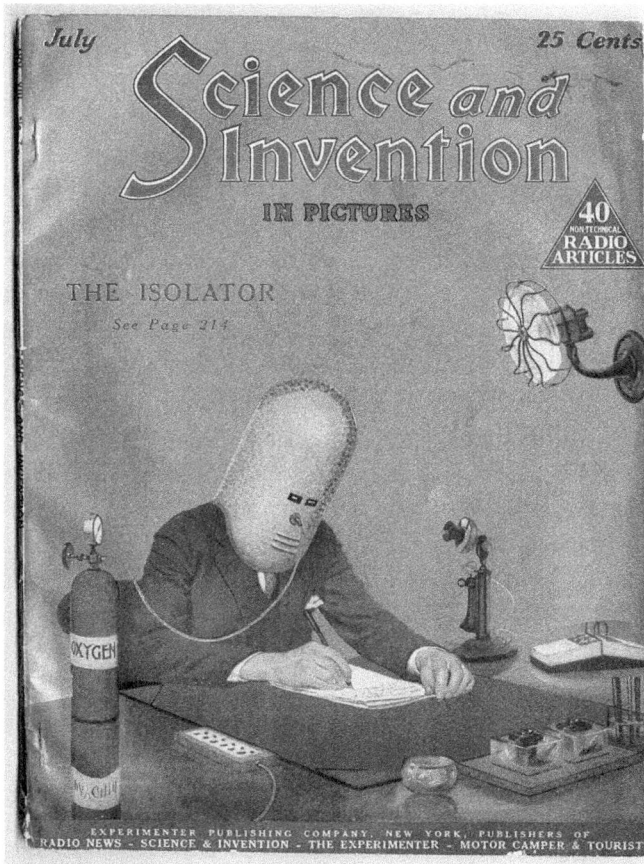

Figure I.4 Hugo Gernsback's Isolator, shown on the cover of his magazine *Science and Invention*, July 1925.

The Isolator was meant "to do away with all possible interferences that prey on the mind." Looking at the accoutrements that surround the helmeted scribe, it is possible to get a sense of the interfering conditions that make the production of silence so salient in modernity. An electric fan, a telephone, an address book, and some sort of remote control device surround him, facing him expectantly, offering up the affordances (and interferences) of electrical and informatic circulation and connection. It's only a short jump from the Isolator to a sound conditioner—or a digital app such as Freedom, which promises to prevent you from being distracted by shutting off social media and the World Wide Web. However, despite then-recent inventions such as the phonograph, radio, and Eric Satie's utilitarian "furniture music," Gernsback doesn't light upon sound generation as a less cumbersome means of controlling one's self.

By the arrival of the Walkman (1979), Discman (1984), and iPod (2001), sonic self-control came into full view and scholars began framing the personal stereo's powers of "mobile privatization" (Du Gay et al. 1997; Williams 2003) as a response to the distracting and alienating conditions of modernity and capitalism, generating a literature that perhaps comes closest to the subject matter of this book. The most prolific and accomplished analyst of the personal stereo, Michael Bull, characterizes its use through a different Greek hero—not Orpheus, but the Sirens' best-known opponent, Odysseus, who orders his men to tie him to the mast and fill their ears with wax before sailing through the Sirens' strait: "This passage from Homer is significant, in part, because it is the first description of the privatisation of experience through sound, experienced now as a commonplace in iPod culture" (2007, 19). Drawing on Horkheimer and Adorno's reading of the myth (1972), Bull writes that "the auditory self" of the iPod user "rebels at the very same time as it is seduced—this is the dialectic of iPod culture" (23). Users want to be Odysseus, the hero of their own universe, but they achieve this by binding themselves to the mast, finding cognitive freedom "precisely through a tethering of cognition to the auditory products of the culture industry" (23, 133). Scholars and critics working in this Odyssean mode of analysis mainly disagree as to whether the headphone wearer, "whose step occupies the vague threshold between zombism and activism" (LaBelle 2010, 98) is truly a hero or more of a dupe, with some emphasizing individual agency through music listening (Chow 1990; DeNora 1999; Hosokawa 1984), while others, like Bull, are more aligned with a Frankfurt-inspired, anti–culture industry approach.

A comparison between the Odysseus and Orpheus myths illustrates *Hush*'s debt to—and differences with—personal stereo scholarship. In the Frankfurt School reading, Odysseus represents the prototypical bourgeois individual, instrumental in his reasoning, with no particular concern for sound until he enters the Siren Strait of modernity. Modern capitalism gives us both the dulled senses of the workers/rowers and the instrumental listening of the managerial Odysseus. However, as Bull does note, the very existence of these Greek myths shows that the dream of auditory self-control *predates* modernity (2007, 18). Even the philosopher Seneca, after prescribing a Stoic indifference to urban noise, admitted defeat and retreated to the quiet Roman suburbs. "Why should I need to suffer the torture any longer than I want to," he wrote, "when Ulysses found so easy a remedy for his companions even against the Sirens?" (Atkinson 2015, 15). An orphic perspective, on the other hand, emphasizes that sonic entanglements are indeed ancient and multivalent. Orpheus, son of the musical muse Calliope, is aurally sensitive from birth and sonic in his everyday practices. His power comes not from wax-filled ears, but from listening to the world's vibrations, taking musical lessons from the birds and attending to the sounds of spiders spinning their webs (Wroe 2011, 15). When Orpheus encounters the Sirens, he combats their song with a song of his own, displaying the affective modes of connection and disconnection, harmony and dissonance, that sound has always afforded. The problem in modernity, then, is not that these affective entanglements are new, but rather that they are now simultaneously denied, suppressed, revealed, and multiplied, affectively ensnaring us in complex new ways.

Gernsback's Isolator serves as the perfect symbol of this contradictory state. This helmet for wranglers of representations harkens back to René Descartes's *Meditations* ("Now I shall close my eyes, I shall stop my ears, I shall disregard my senses") and technologically inscribes a cognitivist, liberal view of a rationally detached, thinking self (1951, 33). At the same time, the helmet's existence suggests how difficult it is to achieve such a disembodied, unaffected state—and to what absurd lengths we will go in the attempt. The contradiction the Isolator embodies is both naïvely idealist and naïvely materialist—on the one hand, the body is just the unimportant physical carrier of the all-important, immaterial mind, but on the other, we are desperate to perfect what we perceive as that body's disabilities (Siebers 2008, 7). Similarly, we tend to think of our environment as a transparent, idealist grid to be filled with our grand designs in one moment, while in the next, we think of it materially, a field or stockpile of matter that confounds or furthers our wishes (Lefebvre 1991, 30). The oscillation between idealist and materialist thinking powers the modern advance of science and capitalism, but it also prevents a holistic understanding of our relation to body and environment.

Thus, the orphic perspective draws on Bull's critique of post-Enlightenment instrumental reason, but also focuses more intently on its consequences for the capacities of bodies and their relations to environments. Ironically, the outputs of instrumental reason have included a proliferation of commodities, images, and voices that affect us beyond all reason, as well as scientific and sociological revelations that undermine or disprove any notion of self as a unique, coherent, autonomous, and agentive mind (Barglow 1994; Gergen 1991, 1996, 2000; Jameson 1991; Lyotard 1984). At the same time, economic and environmental transformations have required the average person to be more disciplined with her powers of attention. "At the moment when the dynamic logic of capital began to dramatically undermine any stable or enduring structure of perception," Jonathan Crary writes, "this logic simultaneously attempted to impose a disciplinary regime of attentiveness" (2001, 13). Technologies and labor practices reshaped perception, absorbing and immobilizing subjects through attentive practices aimed at production or consumption. From this perspective, "stopping our ears" looks less like a dubious act of rebellion and more like a requirement of modern living.

Examining the century preceding the advent of orphic media, one sees noise problems escalating in tandem with economic and political demands for autonomous selfhood and attentional discipline. It is no coincidence that the eighteenth- and nineteenth-century forerunners of Richard Florida's "creative class" (2014) were the loudest public noise critics of their day. William Hogarth's 1741 engraving "The Enraged Musician," for instance, which shows an angry middle-class maestro railing against the noises of the London street outside his window, portrays the sonic hindrances of the lone, urban creative (figure I.5). Over a century later, in 1862, the famed mathematician Charles Babbage blamed his inability to complete his mechanical computer, the Analytical Engine, on the "vile and discordant" sounds of London's street musicians (Swade 2001, 212). One of Babbage's contemporaries, the writer Robert Carlyle, constructed an architectural forerunner to orphic media—a literal room to think—a double-walled and windowless soundproof study for reading and writing. John Picker avers that such Londoners' noise problems stemmed from "their own fledgling and curious status as housebound professionals, workers whose place of rest doubled as their place of labor" (2000, 428). The technological and social practices of the industrial revolution were generating economic liquidity and affording a spatial and temporal proliferation of economic activity, including that of both the street musician and the genteel home worker whom he would torment. Nineteenth-century physicians and psychiatrists increasingly came to the opinion "that years spent toiling amid ever-present noise do in time take their toll, if not in nervous collapse then in a loss of mental focus" (Schwartz 2011, 343). In this era, sonic fatigue rose as a cultural concern while sleep and concentration became threatened personal and economic resources.

Then, as now, privileged individuals tended to locate the noise problem not in the structural contradiction they inhabited, but rather in the person of the noise-making other. Many have pointed to the classist and xenophobic aspects of London intellectuals' complaints about street music, the sound of which was actually quite harmless in comparison to the industrial noise that was literally deafening boilermakers and other workers at the time

Figure I.5 William Hogarth's *The Enraged Musician*, 1741. Retrieved from the Library of Congress, https://www.loc.gov/item/miller.0342/. (Accessed March 20, 2018.)

(Bailey 1996; Goldsmith 2012; Hendy 2013; Keizer 2010). Far removed from the greatest sonic hazards of the industrial revolution, Babbage decried the noise of "those whose minds are entirely unoccupied" (Goldsmith 2012, 113), while Carlyle complained of the "vile yellow Italian grinding" and "vagrant musical scamps . . . with guitars and Nigger songs" (Hendy 2013, 243–44).

From the soundproof study to the Isolator to the noise-canceling headphone to the filter bubble, we see the miniaturization, refinement, and virtualization of technologies that afford the freedom of not listening to difference. At first, these technologies were mostly *passive* attempts to block out sound, compensating for our lack of "earlids" through architecture or earplugs. Their effectiveness was limited: Carlyle found no relief in his study, as its insulation from outdoor sounds seemed to reveal all manner of noises coming from within the house. As for earplugs, while a sensitive artist such as Franz Kafka was a devotee, a combination of social stigma, ineffective and uncomfortable materials, hygiene concerns, and other factors prevented most people from using them (Bijsterveld 2008; Schwartz 2012). Like architectural acoustical treatment, the earplug would find its technological refinement and widespread adoption only in the twentieth century, although, like Carlyle's soundproof study, earplugs tended to reveal interior noise—in the form of tinnitus.

However, by the 1960s, when attention came even more under siege, electromechanical and electronic technologies emerged that *actively* mobilized the affective potentials of vibration—not merely buffering subjects, but instead fighting sound with sound. When Gernsback was working on his Isolator, a little over half the U.S. population lived in urbanized areas and the nation's rural way of life was quickly waning. Both industrialization and, later, a postindustrial economy reshaped and fragmented the spaces and temporal rhythms of work and home life, while media supplied a proliferation of new sensory inputs. With the rise of the information economy, the problem of attention found its full overdetermination. Insofar as it posits information processing as the essence of consciousness, what I call "infocentrism" may be the ultimate disciplinary discourse, placing the responsibility on each of us to control that which cannot be controlled, especially in the informatic din it has catalyzed. In this setting, an "attention complex" emerges, a network of power relations that produces the problem of attention in individuals—thus a "complex" in two senses of the word (Rogers 2014).

In response to these attentional conflicts and pressures, individuals use orphic media as "technologies of the self" (Foucault et al. 1988, 19), technologies that make them "capable of bearing the burdens of liberty" (Rose 1999, viii), in an attempt to be the kinds of individuals they think they are supposed to be. In liberal, market-driven democracies, freedom, self-reliance, and individuality are less the motives of government than its requirement (Burchell 1996, 271). On the one hand, the relationship to self becomes highly *managerial* as we are expected to maximize our own attentional potential in a marketplace of precarious labor with little in the way of a safety net (Gershon 2011). On the other hand, government's respect for private space and individual autonomy leads it to take a hands-off approach to the kinds of neighborly noise that can degrade our abilities to maximize our powers of attention (Bijsterveld 2008, 262).

In such a sonic setting, the market supplies "technologies of individuality for the production and regulation of the individual who is 'free to choose'" (Rose 1999, 232). However, the technological freedom from being affected is most often used by subjects to thrive *within* prescribed spaces of power and value. The kinds of spiritual or economic freedom they support are thus highly individualized and circumscribed. As designed and constructed today, orphic media provide freedom of choice *within* the system, not the freedom to listen carefully, reflect upon our situation, and potentially choose a different system altogether. These devices encourage us to hear *private* problems of sonic self-control and noise-making others where, in fact, a *shared* social dissonance affects us all. In order to address this social dissonance, it is important to examine the affective modes and potentials that subtend our current configurations of orphic media—modes and potentials that also offer possibilities of reconfiguration.

Sonic Space and Empty Media

The story of this book began two decades before I knew I would write it. It was 1994 or so, my workday at an educational magazine in Taipei, Taiwan, was over, and I was indulging in my frequent habit of walking for miles through the streets of that vast city. As night fell, I found myself in the narrow alleys of an old section of Taipei's Wanhua District. Somewhere up ahead, I heard the sound of a lone male voice chanting a Buddhist sutra. Pursuing the sound, I eventually came upon a conundrum: the voice came through the open and uncurtained window of a dimly lit room, but the singer wasn't there. Instead, the room was practically empty save for a small, wall-mounted altar holding flowers, incense, an electric candle, and a box of some sort that I couldn't identify. Nevertheless, the voice repeated its short, enchanting refrain over and over again until, after a few minutes, I forced myself to move on.

When I later related this uncanny case of the invisible monk to a Taiwanese friend, she told me the voice came from a *nianfo ji* (念佛機, literally "reciting—or chanting—Buddha machine"), a cheap, plastic audio device used to generate karmic merit and bring peace to its user (figure I.6). According to religion scholar Natasha Heller, the *nianfo ji* "brings forth the sound of the Pure Land," an important heavenly realm in Chinese Buddhism, "creating an environment that is both protective and efficacious" (2014, 301). Fascinated with their looped recitations on digital chips, I began purchasing these little sutra boxes, which, I learned, were found in Buddhist households across Mainland China and the Chinese diaspora. Sometimes I would turn on one or more of my chanting machines and listen, often imagining that unseen devotee in Wanhua and wondering what feeling he or she may have derived as its sound filled the small house from that otherwise empty room.

This scenario reminded me of the occasional sleeplessness of my own childhood and the soothing company I found in a late-night show for

Figure I.6 A *nianfo ji*, which "brings forth the sound of the Pure Land."

long-haul truckers on a little AM radio, which seemed to transform my dark bedroom into a safer space. Years later, I would learn that the Spinoza-inspired theorists Gilles Deleuze and Félix Guattari recognized this sort of sonic spacemaking as well:

> A child in the dark, gripped with fear, comforts himself by singing under his breath. He walks and halts to his song. Lost, he takes shelter, or orients himself with his little song as best he can. The song is like a rough sketch of a calming and stabilizing, calm and stable, center in the heart of chaos. Perhaps the child skips as he sings, hastens or slows his pace. But the song itself is already a skip: it jumps from chaos to the beginnings of order in chaos and is in danger of breaking apart at any moment. There is always sonority in Ariadne's thread. Or the song of Orpheus. (1987, 311)

In *A Thousand Plateaus*, Deleuze and Guattari refer to the child's song as a form of "Refrain," a practice that reworks the emergent relations between sound, space, and subjectivity. There is also a social dimension to this kind of mediation: "Radios and televisions are like sound walls around every household and mark territories (the neighbor complains when it gets too loud)," they write (1987, 311).[1] Sitting in the resonant territory of the sutra box and reflecting on my childhood radio refuge, I got an inkling of how sound can *pacify* a disordered space, *establish fortifications* around an already orderly space, or *open up new spaces* of possibility by breaking down such barriers—the three (de)territorializing potentials of the Refrain (312).

About a decade after my experience in Taipei, Beijing-based electronic musicians Christiaan Virant and Zhang Jian convinced a Chinese manufacturer to produce a custom version of the *nianfo ji*, replacing the sacred chanting with ambient music loops of their own design and branding the result in English as the Buddha Machine (figure 1.7). With the help of American underground music distributor Forced Exposure, the two musicians—known together as FM3—turned the Buddha Machine into an international indie hit, selling tens of thousands of units, setting the blogosphere abuzz, and capturing the attention of minimalist, ambient, and electronic pioneers Philip Glass, Brian Eno, and Throbbing Gristle. At this point, in the mid-2000s, I was back in the United States and studying popular music as a graduate student in Indiana University's departments of Folklore and Ethnomusicology and Media and Culture. Now, a happy convergence befell me: the pleasures of the Buddha Machine rekindled my interest in the *nianfo ji*, while my reading of Deleuze and Guattari gave me an initial vocabulary for analyzing how (and to what purposes) it created "protective and efficacious" spaces.

My initial question at the time was simply, *What exactly are people doing with these Buddha Machines?* My hunch was, there were material and practical commonalities between the Buddhist and secular use of these little devices. Since the mid-2000s, I have explored these commonalities by identifying other sonically spacemaking media, isolating the processes by which they operate, and trying to understand what these objects and processes tell us about human nature, culture, and politics. In this endeavor, I have drawn on the work of primarily *visually* focused scholars such as Brian Massumi (2002), Bernard Stiegler (1998), Mark N. B. Hansen (2004), and Eric Jenkins (2014), who "demonstrate the significance of affect as a force in the contemporary media landscape . . . present[ing] constant threat of danger and *manipulation*" but also "the promise of moving past old distinctions and creating new connections" (Sheppard 2017). I also join the efforts of affect-minded theorists such as Steve Goodman (2010), Christoph Cox (2011), Julian Henriques (2011), and Marie Thompson (2017) who, working in the interdisciplinary space of sound studies, similarly consider the potentials of *sound* as affective vibration.

Using sound as a way to think about media, and mediation as a way to think about sound, I present an orphic model in which media use is neither informational nor representational, but instead *relational*, the means by which differing mediated intensities suffuse the bodies, conscious states,

Figure I.7 A Buddha Machine by FM3.

and intentions of ostensibly free and rational subjects. The different uses people have made of Buddha Machines suggest the multivalent potentials of orphic mediation: through interviews and exploring reviews and online discourse, I found Pure Land Buddhists using these devices to fortify the already orderly spaces of temples, white-collar workers using them to pacify disorderly workspaces, and musicians like FM3 using them to open up new spaces of artistic and social possibility through interactive improvisation.

Yet, ironically, although religious and secular Buddha machines inspired this book, their representational complexities eventually led me not to include a chapter on them.[2] This decision has to do with a problem I perceive in the recent wave of affect-driven media and music studies: since both media technologies and our conceptions of them are so suffused with representations and codes, it can be very hard to discern the exact influence of the affective. This problem is evident in the work of Deleuze and Guattari themselves, who famously write, "We will never ask what a book means, as signified or signifier: we will not look for anything to understand in it. We will ask what it functions with, in connection with what other things it does or does not transmit intensities, in which other multiplicities its own are inserted and metamorphosed" (1987, 4).

By describing a book in this way, the philosophers attempt to strike at the heart of representationalism; yet by choosing an object so thoroughly understood as representational, they make it more difficult for the reader to tease out its affective dimensions. If words and images can be vectors for both affect *and* ideology, how do we know which modality (or admixture) is most salient in a given instance? In *A Thousand Plateaus*, Deleuze and Guattari also filter their ideas on sonic affectivity through the aesthetics of music. This forces us to contend with a tangle of affectivity and semiotics similar to that found in media studies, due to the fact that music—even the noisy avant-garde music they advocate—is, in part, a cultural code.

This problem of isolating affectivity is exacerbated by infocentrism. This prevailing cultural ideology reduces all matter and action to the flows of an often poorly defined, shape-shifting, and mystically immaterial substance called "information," creating an impression that "pattern is predominant over presence" (Hayles 1999, 19), redefining the human as "information processor," and casting nature as "information to be processed" (Bolter 1984, 13).[3] For all of the remarkable technologies and academic disciplines this idealist notion has catalyzed, transcendent, immaterial "information" may have passed its sell-by date in critical media scholarship's marketplace of useful ideas. As media scholar Nicole Starosielski writes, "analyses of twenty-first-century media culture have been characterized by a cultural imagination of dematerialization: immaterial information flows appear to make the environments they extend through fluid and matter less" (2015, 6)—a critique that could be extended to our understanding of the human beings who use media as well. Deploying an unproblematized notion of information in the analysis of media's affective and material roles in human life is not so unlike using the Invisible Hand as the basis of a critique of free market capitalism—in both cases, a tacit understanding that should be an object of critique instead roots the analysis.[4]

Therefore, the use of affect theory in media and music studies by scholars who still maintain tacitly informatic and representational conceptions of media technology can lead to a lack of concreteness in analysis. As Lawrence Grossberg puts it, affect often becomes "a magical term," allowing scholars to reference nonrepresentational effects without doing "the harder work of specifying modalities and apparatuses of affect" (2010, 315). As a result, despite affect theory's huge popularity in the humanities, affect still too often feels like an also-ran to semiotics or a ghost in the informational machine of our media and music technologies.

The study of orphic media is intended as a methodological intervention in affect studies because it brackets representation to a large degree, easing "the harder work" by identifying technologies that clearly defy informatic and representational logics. Answering the question *What other kinds of work do media do besides information work?* pushed me to "de-center media radically to see what else is in the picture" (Gray 2009, 17), observing people's practices of mediation and eventually coming to study some devices that don't fit our received notions of media at all. Whereas the words of a Buddhist sutra or the notes of a musical loop from a Buddha Machine are representationally complex, the orphic media presented in this book foreground media's material and affective dynamics because they are more or less "contentless."[5] The monotonous rainfall sound of the website rainymood.com is impossible to pay attention to for long—and this is its very utility. The sound of a white noise app carries no representations, yet it is meaningful in people's lives.[6] These technologies do not tell stories, entertain, or inform. Instead, they offer people the nonrepresentational utility of using sound to control their relations to their surroundings, and in so doing, to control themselves.

Lisa Gitelman writes, "the success of all media depends at some level on inattention or 'blindness' to the media technologies themselves (and all of their supporting protocols) in favor of attention to the phenomena, 'the content,' that they represent for users' edification or enjoyment" (2006, 6). Orphic media complicate this dynamic because *their content is designed to negate itself as content*, creating a perceptual absence rather than attention-grabbing presence for edification or enjoyment. Studying the widespread use of media without content shifts our attention to *the ability to shift attention itself*—the abilities to see or not see, feel or not feel, and hear or not hear that media afford, moving the site of our analysis from the phenomena of media representations to the phenomenological and ontological affordances of media technologies and protocols.

Ultimately, orphic media are useful to consumers—and, I argue, to scholars—because they are, in certain senses, "empty." First, as just indicated, they show us that while media may often function as "container technologies" (Sterne 2006), they don't always carry the representational content we assume. Second, and more fundamentally, orphic media point us away from the everyday perspective, in which media content is shared, used, and manipulated by pregiven individuals. Instead, they point us instead toward an "emptiness" in the Buddhist sense, a perspective in which the world is "without body or form," not made of pregiven subjects, objects, and spaces (Uchiyama 2004, 11). In this empty perspective, the world is a haphazard *process* in which subjects, objects, and spaces arise—and media are a means of grappling with this process of presence- and absence-making, a way of managing the material and attentional unfolding of world and self.

Orphic Media

Orpheus was more than an adventurer who fought the Sirens' sound with sound: Greeks and Romans knew the young Thracian king and shaman as the first poet, the first musician, the inventor of the gods' names, and the first teller of their tales (Wroe 2011, 35). In these rituals and arts, Orpheus used sound not only as a mode of mastery, but also as a medium of divine interconnection that brought people together with one another and the nature of creation (figure 1.8). An unlikely hero, Orpheus wielded only poetry, a lyre, and a melodious voice. His sole prowess was an ability to perturb the air, yet there was great power in those perturbations. Orpheus's sonic ability to figuratively and literally move animals, rocks, rivers, and humans with his songs speaks to the way that sound, as vibration, mediates lived space, fostering social, physical, spatial, and sensory entanglements that can vitalize bodies or threaten to shake them apart. For this reason, Orpheus personifies media's ability to pacify, fortify, and transform both spaces and the selves that inhabit them. In this section, I define orphic media and the sonic "modes" and "potentials" through which they operate.

In defining orphic media, we might think in terms of three concentric circles. In the smallest circle are the tinnitus maskers, white noise machines, LPs, apps, headphones, and hearables in the case studies that follow—technologies designed for the sonic control of one's affective state and environment, usually deployed in utilitarian practices that privilege sleep, concentration, and the freedom to remain unaffected. As stated above, this collection of devices is useful because they provide insights into contemporary media use and the problem of sensitive listening, while also helping us isolate affective potentials and practices in other media. These core technologies are a subset of the second circle, which contains audio media technologies more broadly, all of which modulate affectivity through orphic modes and potentials. Music and film sound, for example, work to construct, energize, unify, pacify, dominate, or terrorize spaces and the subjects that fill them. The third and widest circle contains *all* media, since film, radio, television, and digital media all orphically channel affective desires and modulate our sensory and attentional engagement with our environment and one another. To offer just one example, the safe space that orphic mediation provides is the reason my grandmother slept in the living room, in front of the television, for the rest of her life after my grandfather died. The television's light, sound, and human presences did not serve to entertain or inform in those moments, but rather to soothe, comfort, diffuse attention, and fill the darkness.

ORPHEUS - *1. Orpheus bezweert de wilde dieren.*
LIEBIG PRODUCTEN: kracht en smaak van 't vleesch.

Figure I.8 Orpheus personifies media's ability to pacify, fortify, and transform both spaces and the selves that inhabit them.

Media do this kind of work by altering the "modes" through which we affect and are affected by our environment. As Eric Jenkins describes them, modes are "how one body plugs into or interfaces with another to produce affections. As such, modes are the flip-side of affects, the orientations or manners necessary for certain perceptions to flow forth and thus for certain affects to be sparked" (2014, 15–16). We can think of modes, then, as a snapshot of all the virtual possibilities of affectivity in a given moment—they emerge from the preceding actions of bodies upon one another and they condition the actions to follow. "Media thus shape modes by enabling or disabling certain capacities," reshaping the virtual possibilities of encounters between our perceiving bodies and other "bodies" writ large (17). Media are able to sonically remediate modes only because our perceptions, relations, and subjectivity are already affectively mediated. The subjective experience of environmental sound connects a vibrating object (such as the speaker in a radio), a molecular field of transmission (such as the air), the ear, the brain's neuronal networks (not just the auditory system, but also systems of filtration, memory, and emotion), and an entire discursive and experiential history embodied in the listener. Each of the elements in this resonant relationship—from the electronic to the organic to the cultural—functions as a medium for sound, affecting how all of the other elements affect one another in a web of *biomediation* (Hagood 2017; Thacker 2004).[7]

In essence, people use orphic media to sonically *remediate* uninhabitable relations that emerge between these heterogeneous elements—noxious combinations of material and immaterial bodies that leave subjects feeling "poisoned" or unable to act (Deleuze 1978). For example, a complex combination of economic pressures, poor acoustic design, individual hearing acuity and attentional abilities, a garrulous coworker, and so forth may leave an office worker feeling stressed, diminished in her ability to act, and ready to purchase noise-canceling headphones. From the worker's perspective, she may simply be blocking out the voice of an annoying coworker, but from our analytic perspective, she is using one element in a complex affective space to remediate the modes of relation between all the others. The orphic remediation of this kind of affective "poisoning" can be *intramodal* (fighting sound with sound by *suppressing, masking, canceling,* or simply *shifting aural attention*), and it can also be *cross-modal* (using silence or sound to alter the experience of other sensory modalities, affective states, or the passage of time). The orphic industries and practices I describe in the chapters ahead leverage both intramodal and cross-modal remediation, fighting sound with sound *and* using sound to fight affectivity transmitted through other sensory modes.

In their sensory and attentional focus, intramodal and cross-modal remediation describe orphic processes from the *human* side of the subject–environment relationship. However, we can also describe what orphic media do in terms of the construction, fortification, and demolition of sonic-affective *spaces*. On this side of the equation, I draw on a tripartite schema by Barry Truax (1984) to propose three *sonic potentials*, or ways that sound mediates—and is mediated by—the environment. First, sound can be understood through the *energy transfer model*, which depicts sound as a physical wave carried in a medium such as the air. If the acoustical energy is sufficient and the air is in contact with another resonant medium—say a window pane—the wave motion is transferred from the first to the second medium. As David Cecchetto points out, because a sound is literally nothing but change (in the pressure of a medium), it confounds us as an immaterial phenomenon with very tangible effects, a seemingly consistent object of perception and knowledge that is, in reality, "nothing but difference" (2013, 3). The mediating potential of energy transfer inheres in the fact that it embodies both repetition and difference, as diverse bodies (organic and inorganic) are activated as media, resonating (or not) according to their unique energetic potentials and passing along the energy, expressing a "single" impulse as multiple collisions between bodily differences.[8]

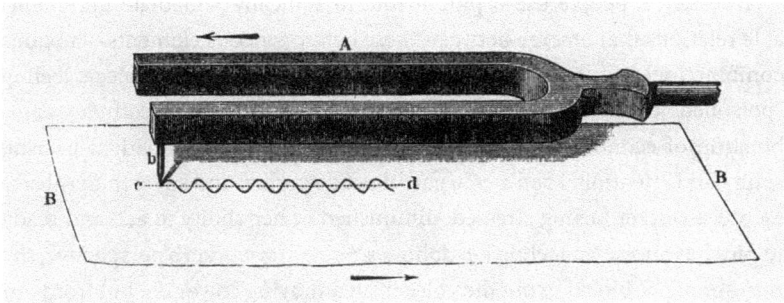

Figure I.9 Hermann Helmholtz's inscription of the sound wave.

In reality, a vibrating object propagates a *three-dimensional* molecular pattern of expansion and compression in a medium, but as a cultural construct, the energy transfer model represents sound as a linear, sender–receiver process—a two-dimensional waveform that transfers its energy along a horizontal axis, as seen in Hermann Helmholtz's nineteenth-century book *On the Sensations of Tone* (1954). "To render the law of such motions more comprehensible to the eye," Helmholtz suggests affixing a stylus to a tuning fork and moving a sheet of paper horizontally beneath it (21; see figure I.9). This abstracted "sound wave" facilitated new technical understandings and practices around harmonics, noise, and the capacities of the human auditory system; it also eventually came to resonate in public consciousness as much as it did on the screens of oscilloscopes, ascribing a false sense of fixity to sound's "nothing but difference." For the purpose of studying orphic media, we can be alert to this cultural history of the energy transfer model and its epistemological distortions, while still also taking advantage of this paradigm's affordances for understanding sound's affective potential. After all, the essence of the energy transfer model is the ability of sound and medium to affect and be affected by one another.

A second and closely related sonic potential is *signal processing*, which, in its classic form, involves the transduction of acoustical energy into an electrical signal by a microphone; the signal's storage, manipulation, and transmission via the "black boxes" of audio media technologies; and, finally, the signal's subsequent transduction back into acoustical energy via a speaker.[9] From an orphic perspective, the purpose of transduction and signal processing is to increase sound's ability to affect and be affected: electroacoustic media extend sound's mutability, reach, and impact, *both as sign and signal at once*, making it a second, human-crafted machine of sonic affectivity. Combined with the epistemological shift of the energy transfer model, the material practice of transduction rendered sound as material, "an object to be contemplated, reconstructed, and manipulated, something that can be fragmented, industrialized, and bought and sold" (Sterne 2003, 9). Usually, these twin revolutions in sound are understood as affording the circulation of sonic messages, representations, and/or reproductions through the phonograph, radio, telephone, and other audio media. However, they also facilitated an unsung revolution in affect management, generating new modalities for the circulation and control of sonic intensities and their perceptual effects. These two models transduce the messy, everchanging, nonlinear sonic environment into more directable, durable, and controllable chains of cause and effect.

In the third potential of sonic mediation, sound is not the thing mediated, but rather the medium itself.[10] From this perspective, sound is "a space of transformation" (Serres 2007, 70), a *mediatic* dimension of connection and disconnection between subjects and between subjects and environment, as indicated in Steve Goodman's term "vibrational ontology" (2010). Sound is a resonance that *requires* a distance but also *bridges* that distance, calling forth the hearer and the heard by awakening the space between them—thus functioning as a medium in the Aristotelian sense (*metaxu*), a resonating gap that both separates and unites the sensed and sensing (Kearney 2015, 108).

The sense humans make in this connective gap is meaningful. Because Spinozan and Deleuzian sound theorists treat sound as material resonance and sonic affects as preconscious impacts, they have sometimes been criticized for minimizing the role of meaning and auditory culture in hearing (Kane 2015, 16). However, for Spinoza, affects include not only enlivening and diminishing relations between bodies, but also the *ideas* that arise *about* those relations—ideas that feed back into and alter the capacities of listening bodies. In other words, a vibrational ontology must remember the microscale vibrations of brain waves and account for sound in its remembered, imagined, phantom, and linguistic forms. As David Novak and Matt Sakakeeny write, "Metaphors for sound construct perceptual conditions of hearing and shape the territories and boundaries of sound in social life. Sound resides in this feedback loop of materiality and metaphor" (2015, 1). Rather than treating affect as "prior" to culture, an affect-minded scholar might, in Brian Kane's words, "demonstrate the successions and relays between cognition and affect" through which "the capacities of the body are cultivated at the same time that cultures become embodied" (2015, 8). The third sonic potential, then, conceives of sound as a communicative space of meaningful material resonance.

To review, modes of orphic mediation are underwritten by the interplay of three different sonic potentials: (1) sound is mediated as mechanical waves in an environmental medium, such as the air; (2) sound can also be mediated and altered as a signal through electroacoustic and digital processes of transduction and signal processing; and (3) sound is also mediatic in itself, a sensory-spatial process of interaction though which subjects and objects emerge in modes of affective relation. Through the first potential, subjects and objects make sound. Through the third potential, sound makes subjects and objects. Using technologies we call electronic media, subjects leverage the second potential of signal processing as they attempt to control the modes of affectivity enacted through the first and third potentials.

Returning to the Beats headphone commercial this introduction opened with, we can see the emergent interaction of the wave, signal, and mediatic potentials of sound. Understood through the first potential, the jeering haters in the Beats Electronics ad are sounding bodies that enact the molecular medium of the shared space they inhabit as mechanical waves to be received by Kaepernick's body. Leveraging the second potential, Kaepernick's noise-canceling headphones intramodally remediate these sound waves into a cancelable electronic signal, while cross-modally dampening the haters' visual and haptic presence. Considered through the third potential, it is Kaepernick, the haters, the headphones, and the space they inhabit that are all mediated by sound, sonically called forth into their actual states by their meaningful relations of resonance, dissonance, and cancellation. The quarterback, the crowd, and the space they share come into being, moment by moment, though sensory experience—enacted in the affective dynamics of jeering, hearing, and electronic remediation.

An orphic reading of "Hear What You Want" presents media use as the amplification, transformation, and tamping down of intensities and sensory perceptions—the mediations through which selves and worlds arise. While Seneca claimed that a quiet mind could maintain its distance from any sonic surroundings, his eventual retreat from sound—like Kaepernick's—speaks to the way that the sensed and the sensing are born in the resonating gap that both separates and unites them. Most orphic media use is motivated by the fear of how easily this empty gap transforms us. Manufacturers readily market the impossible dream of rising above the affective processes that make us what we are. In the next chapter, I examine the electronic remediation of tinnitus to understand how this dream of sonic freedom can ironically catalyze painful sensitivities to sound—even to sounds that, in some respects, can be said not to exist at all.

Part I. Suppression

———————

It was difficult for me so much as to tell what was happening. The noises were neutralizing each other, and it seemed exactly as though my ears were being struck by recurrent waves of frozen silence and meaningless roaring.

—**Yukio Mishima,** *Confessions of a Mask*

Tinnitus and Its Aural Remedies

In the ruins of tragedy, I wish to tune out my own static.

—**Michel Serres**, *The Five Senses: A Philosophy of Mingled Bodies*

When I woke up from the ear surgery there was a low-level humming or elec-tricity in the air. Some kind of crackling or something. It seemed strange to me—I thought, "What the heck is that?" I'd never heard anything like that before. I asked my wife, "Can you hear that?" and she said, "No, I can't hear that." When I went back to the doctor for a post-surgical checkup I asked about it and that's the first time I heard the term "tinnitus." We didn't have a long dis-cussion and I had the impression it would go away. But then I kept going back to the doctor and saying, "It's not going away," and then that's when I heard that sometimes it doesn't go away.

And that was pretty scary. I had been married for about two years and we had a new baby, so I was involved with that. So, I had a lot of things to take my mind off of it, but there were times that I would sit and I would just cry. And I would tell my wife, "I don't know if I can live with this forever."

Terry[1] was thirty-eight when his unsuccessful ear surgery left him with a reduction in hearing acuity accompanied by tinnitus; he was sixty-three when I met him at a Midwestern tinnitus support group meeting. During the intervening twenty-five years, he had been haunted by phantom sounds. There was a sound "like gas escaping from a cylinder" and "a hard insect-type sound like clicking or cicadas." Eventually, he started hearing his own pulse in his ears. Sometimes the pulse would go away, but the hissing was always there.

Tinnitus changed the way Terry listened to his world and navigated his days. In an interview we did some weeks after we first met, he told me that he had come to realize "we live in a loud society" where "people take hearing for granted." His world had become a patchwork of what he called "loud environments" to avoid or pass through as quickly as possible, in fear that loud sounds would make his tinnitus worse. Terry used to be a microbiologist, but now he works in information technology because the laboratory fans were too loud. He used to enjoy going to the movies, but there are so many explosions in them. He would love to go ballroom dancing with his wife, but the music is so loud. He tried going out to bars with his college-age daughter, but he just can't any more.

Sometimes, he won't realize a place is too loud until he leaves and his ears are screaming. "I'm an emotional guy and I get depressed and very anxious," he told me. "I can't be outgoing and go places with other couples." Terry pays someone else to mow his lawn now.

On the other hand, sometimes the world is not too loud, but instead all too quiet. Terry is not a fan of libraries, for example: "It's not easy to sit in a quiet chair and read." Quiet spaces are where the phantom sounds materialize most viscerally and haunt Terry most fearsomely. Quiet spaces like his office: "I've broken down crying at work when I have to think and I can't."

Then there are all the other, non-sonic aspects of Terry's environment that become charged with potential danger because of his tinnitus. Sleep had always been a refuge from the noise, he told me, but twice in the last two years, his tinnitus was "so loud it invaded my dreams." Since this had never happened before, he tried to identify the cause: "Did I eat something too salty? I cut caffeine out entirely already. Sometimes I think vitamins make my tinnitus worse. I tried antidepressants a couple of months ago and that seemed to make it worse. Problems at work when IT systems aren't talking to each other can be stressful—that can make the tinnitus worse too."

Often, people don't understand his condition and the ways it affects his life. Terry says his sister asks him why he doesn't just put some cotton in his ears. But he also told me that people were what had gotten him through twenty-five years of tinnitus—people, as both a support and a responsibility.

Terry has his marriage, church community, tinnitus support groups, and empathetic others who exchange their stories on the internet. "People talk about suicide, but am I going to leave my wife and daughter? So I go to meetings and online and I see how other people deal with it."

The other thing that helps Terry is the same thing that torments him, *sound*: "I like being near pools, running water, wind, birds . . . we like vacationing in tropical places. I like these quiet background sounds. I use a space heater in the office with a blower and it's soothing." Terry also uses the sound of the TV or radio to keep the tinnitus from dominating his attention. And most importantly, since he turned forty-five, he has used hearing aids to compensate for his declining hearing ability. Besides amplifying the speech of others, he says, the hearing aids have the added benefit of turning up the volume on the "normal" sounds around him, giving the tinnitus some competition. In fact, Terry now dreads the times when he has to return the hearing aids to his audiologist for repair.

Interestingly, while Terry's hearing loss is significant enough to make communication challenging at times, he seems unconcerned by this in comparison to his distress around tinnitus. When he says, toward the end of a phone conversation, "I feel a little bit like I'm living with a handicap," he is referring to having *tinnitus*, not to being hard of hearing.

Fear and Phantom Sound

Brian Massumi describes affective intensity in terms of sound and vibration: an echo within the sensory walls of the body, "resonation and feedback that momentarily suspend the linear progress of the narrative present from past to future" (2002, 26). As Terry's story indicates, tinnitus is a type of perceptual and affective feedback that sometimes suspends the *lives* of those who experience it. "Tinnitus," derived from the Latin *tinnītus* (jingling or ringing), is the term used to describe the experience of sounds in the head or ears that have no external physical source. While it is the most common of auditory disorders, affecting some forty million people in the United States alone, tinnitus is also the most enigmatic and elusive—in fact, neuroscientists refer to it as a "phantom auditory perception" (Jastreboff 1990).

Epidemiological and clinical research indicates that, as in Terry's case, sounds that issue from subjects' own auditory systems are most often signs of damage to the hair cells of the cochlea and/or nerve cells in the auditory neural pathways—damage that results in hearing loss (Hoffman and Reed

2004). Tinnitus is thus "comparable to phantom pain felt in an amputated limb," as "in both cases, the firing of central neurons in the brain continues to convey perceptual experiences, even though the corresponding sensory receptor cells have been destroyed" (Rauschecker, Leaver, and Mühlau 2010). But while this relatively new neurological conception has dispelled some of the mystery around tinnitus, it has yet to lead to any established medical treatment for the condition.

This lack of proven medical interventions has made tinnitus sufferers among the most dedicated users of orphic media.[2] While noise has often been considered the bane of modern health care and convalescence (Schwartz 2012), tinnitus sufferers like Terry desire *more* noise to suppress and/or to draw their own attention away from tinnitus. Many people with tinnitus use white noise and nature sound machines and apps as a kind of media folk remedy. Others are prescribed the use of these or other, more specialized sound devices by their audiologists, often as part of a "sound therapy" program designed to change their emotional and physiological reaction to tinnital sound. In both cases, these orphic practices are reflexive moments in which people *listen to their hearing* and then use media to remediate the body and its ability to hear what it wants. And because the sound being masked is perceived to be attached to the very self that needs saving from it, the emotional, social, and even financial stakes of this orphic mediation become very high.

From one angle, the fact that people resort to media as treatment seems to support tinnitus sufferers' claims that the medical community has been slow to take tinnitus seriously. For the people I've met when visiting Midwestern U.S. audiology clinics, attending tinnitus support groups, participating in online message boards, and answering a tinnitus telephone support line, tinnitus *is* serious. Some of them, like Terry, trace the buzzing, ringing, whooshing, or other phantom sounds they hear to a specific source—an illness, medical intervention, or acoustic trauma, such as a gunshot. Others simply noticed the sound of tinnitus one day and were left to wonder what it was, why it came, and whether it would ever go away. Many of my interlocutors, like Terry, describe it to me as a disability. For those seeking help, the phenomenon is a profound and life-altering crisis. Yet often, medical doctors shrug it off as harmless and tell patients to "learn to live with it," leaving tinnitus sufferers literally to their own devices.

From another angle, however, the use of orphic media as medicine has much to tell us about the relationship between media, the body, and experiences of disability. Because of tinnitus's contested, phantom position as both "harmless" and (in Terry's words) "a handicap," and because it is treated less with medication than with media technologies, it provides a unique auditory opportunity to explore ideologies and enactments of ability and disability—and media's roles in these dynamics. Recent years have seen the emergence of the field of "disability media studies" (Ellcessor and Kirkpatrick 2017), including important research occurring at the intersection of disability studies, media studies, and studies of technology (Ellcessor and Kirkpatrick 2017; Ellis and Kent 2010; Goggin and Newell 2005; Mills 2011a, b). This research needs to be done not only to illuminate underrepresented and underserved aspects of disabled people's media use—though this would be reason enough—but also because scholars have so much to learn about media from studying disability. Historically, scientific and social standards of "normal" bodily and sensory function have coevolved with the technologies we use to explore, represent, alter, and extend the body's sensory-functional capacities—an interplay between media and lived embodiment I refer to as "biomediation" (Hagood 2017). As the ethnographic study of tinnitus in this chapter will show, media technologies are often implicated in the emergence of bodies as "able" or "disabled" in a given moment.

Orphic technologies remediate tinnitus by leveraging the fact that the human auditory system operates affectively, altering its activity in homeostatic relation to its environment. As sound that cannot be heard by others—one that doesn't ride on pressure waves of molecules in shared physical space—tinnitus might seem to be as unmediated as human experience ever gets. But in fact, nothing could be farther from the truth: tinnitus becomes louder in quiet spaces and quieter in loud ones, a fact that allows for the affective *suppression* of tinnitus by orphic media. More generally, tinnitus is a profoundly relational phenomenon, the specificities of which emerge in and through sonic, spatial, social, and technological mediation.

There are several questions about tinnitus that I believe open a path to a better understanding of the processes and mechanisms that constitute aurality, affect, and dis/ability in our era of electronic media: Why does tinnital sound like Terry's emerge in one sonic space and not another? Why is tinnitus a harmless apparition to one listener and a terrorizing phantom to another? How do clinicians objectify a subjective sound found only in their patient's head? Under what circumstances is tinnitus experienced as a disability—or denied that status by those who cannot hear it? And how are electronic media implicated in each of the foregoing questions? Answering these questions will shed light on current debates over the instantaneity of affect and the influence of ideology, revealing the neurological mechanisms through which a homeostatic and enculturated body begins to listen in terror.

To answer these questions, I have done what Stefan Helmreich calls "transductive ethnography," identifying and tracing moments and processes of transduction, in which sound is converted from one materiality into another, to produce an ethnography "animated by an auditorily inspired attention to the modulating relations that produce insides and outsides, subjects and objects, sensation and sense data" (Helmreich 2007, 622). Selves, as Helmreich asserts, emerge at sensory boundaries where materiality is transduced into sensed meaning. Sites and technologies of transduction, therefore, present opportunities to study what gets listened to, what gets ignored, what can't be ignored, and what kinds of selves emerge in these mediated listening practices.

To trace the transductive practices and experiences through which tinnitus emerges and is remediated, I conducted fieldwork at American audiology clinics and conferences, at the research facilities of audiological device manufacturers, and in online and face-to-face tinnitus support groups over the course of two years, 2011–13. Additionally, since 2013, I have served as the support liaison for the American Tinnitus Association in a midsized Midwestern city, in which capacity I occasionally talk to distressed tinnitus sufferers, usually for about an hour. More than anything else, it was my experiences of listening to people with tinnitus—and listening to my own tinnitus, which has been a source of suffering for me at times—that led to the conceptions of orphic media and biomediation laid out in this book.

I believe tinnitus catalyzed these insights because of the clarifying power of *fear*. Fear not only heightens the stakes of tinnitus sufferers' orphic media use; it also deepens their attention to their own hearing and practices of listening. Indeed, as I will discuss shortly, my own fear of tinnitus played an agentive role in the production of this chapter. This fear was so agentive, in fact, that I hesitate to call it "my own"—instead, it functioned as an autonomous affect (Massumi 1995), making its own contributions in the field whether I wanted them or not. My transductive ethnography will therefore account for fear's affective role in the experience of tinnital suffering, as well as its role in my own ethnographic efforts to transduce the sound and effects of that suffering into these words before you.

Although I opened this chapter with the story of Terry's fearful listening, I could have selected practically any tinnitus sufferer I interviewed or tried to help on the support line. While the specific circumstances surrounding the onset of each individual's tinnitus are unique, I learned in these conversations that certain dynamics emerge in every case, making a tinnitus *sufferer* out of someone like Terry, as opposed to someone who merely *experiences* tinnitus. At some point in these cases, an affect of fear emerges and attaches to the phantom sound. Once this happens, the tinnitus sufferer's audible world becomes akin to "an ecology of fear" (Goodman 2010). Tinnitus sufferers realize they inhabit and navigate a vibrational matrix of loud presences (which threaten to trigger future tinnitus) and quiet absences (which reveal phantom sounds lurking in the background, waiting to make themselves heard). As Hasana Sharp writes, summarizing Spinoza's concept of fearful affects, "Nature suddenly appears to be seething with signification. Everything and anything can seem to have a message, of either hope or doom, for the fearful" (2005, 599). To Terry, quotidian objects such as a cup of coffee or a vitamin become potential sonic threats, while a heater fan, birdsong, or hearing aid can offer the hope of a tinnital respite. Similarly, Terry's social world is reconfigured by the fear of tinnitus and its effects on his own performance, as he tries to live up to his responsibilities to others while haunted by a sound that none of them can hear.

In the remainder of this chapter, I will present several case studies and interviews to show how tinnitus emerges and is remediated, not only through material relations but also through subjects' beliefs about the location, nature, and causality of the unwanted sound. First, I will discuss the condition's vexed position as a "phantom disability," of uncertain social and ontological status, invisible and inaudible to all but the sufferer. What disability theorists call an "ideology of ability"—a fear of nonconforming bodies and minds—is implicated both in subjects' tinnital suffering *and* in the skepticism and aversion it can inspire in those around them. However, the stubborn presence of tinnitus cannot be reduced to ideology alone, so I will also draw on the neurophysiological model of tinnitus to transductively trace its emergence, providing insights into the nature of affective cognition and the biomediation of all listening bodies.

Next, I will explore the culturally influenced habits of listening that perpetuate tinnital fear and suffering in a North American context of neoliberal individualism and personal responsibility. This context necessitates the use of *clinical media* technologies such as the audiometer. Ironically, as a communication-focused diagnostic technology, the audiometer and its attendant practices at first helped obscure tinnitus as an auditory impairment, since tinnitus did not in itself hinder speech communication. However, today the audiometer is used to help isolate and externalize the phantom sound of tinnitus as "real" object. Using an ethnographic method of "praxiology"—the study of how disease is made "visible, audible, tangible, knowable" in the clinic (Mol 2002, 33)—I will show how media make tinnitus amenable to treatment, worthy of empathy from those who cannot hear it, and objective enough to possibly mitigate the responsibilities of those who do. Finally, I will conclude by discussing how orphic media are used in the *treatment* of tinnitus, the success of which is less dependent on technological specificities than it is upon subjects' abilities to weaken the affect of fear through changed habits of listening.

Hearing the Ideology of Ability

I first met Lara three weeks after the morning she awoke to the sounds of "whooshing and jingle bells." For a couple of weeks she had been noticing these sounds intermittently, but by the time she walked into a tinnitus support group meeting in a suburb of a large Midwestern city, they were a nearly constant presence. She had spent the past week in a state of anxiety, asking questions familiar to all of us who had gathered that day in a public library meeting room: "Why is this happening to me? Will I be like this forever?" These questions had led her to the support group, but she already had some tentative answers in mind. Lara told us she knew what tinnitus was because she was once a patient care coordinator for Miracle Ear, calling the hearing aid company's patients, reminding them about appointments, and answering their questions over the phone. During training she had learned that tinnitus often accompanies hearing loss. Lara associated the condition with old age and hearing damage, and she knew there was no medical cure. "I never thought that I would be one of those people," she told the group. Earlier in the week, she had visited an audiologist, who found that Lara did exhibit hearing loss and told her that hearing aids would help with the tinnitus, partially suppressing it by amplifying environmental sound. "I ordered hearing aids in my color—brown," the Jamaica-born fifty-five-year-old told the otherwise all-white group, laughing.

But while Lara attributed the tinnitus to her body "falling apart" with age, she sometimes referred to a different cause as well, one she succinctly described to me as "the music, man!" She first raised the issue of loud music during the support group meeting: "I was the one at the concert standing next to the speaker. We didn't know we were harming ourselves." During a phone conversation we had a couple of weeks after the meeting, Lara worked at untangling thoughts and feelings in which—at least to my ears—tinnitus, mediated sound, personal responsibility, and disability all seemed knotted together. Like most of the tinnitus sufferers I have met, she was highly self-reflexive and sensitive to her own experience. Yet for someone newly experiencing anxiety over tinnitus, Lara also had an admirable ability to revel in life's joyous and humorous moments. She started talking about music because of a party she had recently attended:

> Last night I went to a party and, of course, the music was *blaring*. And I didn't remember I had tinnitus until I got home. Which was kind of cool, you know? I didn't focus on it. I didn't think about it. I was just having a good time. The power of the mind is awesome if we use it to the capacity that God allows us. My daughter asks me this all the time, "Why do you worry so much?" Well, it's a part of me, it's a part of my makeup, it's what I do. But if you take life as it comes and don't focus on it so much—stay busy and do other things to divert your attention—then it's not so bad at all. So this is how I've been dealing with it. I say to the tinnitus, "You're not going to run my life. You're not going to defeat me." Focus on living and not focus so much on, "Okay, I have a disability." 'Cause I think it's a disability. Do you?

I was uncertain of how to respond to Lara's question. It was early in my fieldwork and this was the first time anyone had raised the term "disability," yet the word rang true for me—in more ways than one.

Weirdly enough, just a few months earlier, a bicycle tire burst only inches from my left ear when I overfilled it with air at a gas station. The gunshot-like sound was loud enough that I saw people turn their heads two blocks away—and my own head was ringing with a volume I had never experienced before. As a rock musician who had been careless about hearing protection, I already had a certain level of tinnitus, but now I felt dizzy, faint, and sonically detached from my world. These feelings subsided over the next few hours, but the ringing persisted, at a somewhat reduced volume, as I began my already-planned fieldwork on tinnitus. I felt afraid of the sound and its potential impact on my life, angry over how stupid I had been, and regretful about the damage I believed I had done to myself—in other words, I was *suffering* from tinnitus. And now my fieldwork was going to force me to dwell on the sound, to confront it as an object of study. It was as if the phantom perception of tinnitus wanted to make sure I achieved real anthropological "immersion." Fearful of being perceived as neurotic, I decided not to tell people about my current suffering. When I went to support group meetings and did interviews, I described my tinnitus only as the lingering but manageable effects of my earlier days in music.

Now, on hearing Lara's question about disability, I was torn between the human desire for an open conversation between two people battling noises in their heads and the ethnographic desire to hear more of her opinion before introducing my own. It also dawned on me that I had never considered disability in connection with tinnitus—and in fact, I had no working definition of "disability" at all. (I correctly foresaw a lot of additional reading in my future.) "You know, I guess . . . ," I stumbled, "I haven't thought about it like that. But I guess if it disables you from doing certain things, then I guess it would be a disability?"

Lara responded:

> It's a disability because it's occurring to us, happening to us. I would say it's a disability because a disability comes in where . . . you're not yourself because this thing is happening to you. It's not the norm. It's not the usual occurrence for everyone, every day. It's something that was thrust upon us because, um . . . you know, we didn't take care of our hearing. [Here we both laughed.] You have a similar story to mine—*the music, man!* I'm a music person. I've always been. You talk to a hundred or a thousand people [with tinnitus] and I bet they'll tell you the same thing—that it was the music.

Later, listening back to the digital file of our conversation, I heard in Lara's words two strands of belief in personal responsibility, both ambivalently tangled up with media use.

The first strand is the belief that individuals are responsible for protecting their own hearing from the effects of mediated sound. Lara both takes on and disavows this responsibility. She believes that "we didn't take care of our hearing," but also that, as she said at the meeting, "we didn't know we were harming ourselves." The second strand of personal responsibility involves "divert[ing] your attention" from "worry"—in other words, managing one's own attention and affect, and in so doing, managing one's own life and resisting emotional "defeat" by tinnitus. Here, media use comes into play as a useful tool: the blaring recorded music at the party helped Lara realize the power of her mind to ignore the sound of tinnitus and the worry it had been causing her. But again, Lara is ambivalent about this responsibility as well. Tinnitus might instead be a "disability" thrust upon her, one that has made her something other than herself. And if she is no longer herself, can she still be held responsible for her reaction to the sound that has changed her?

As I began reading the literature in the humanistic field of disability studies, I quickly realized that Lara and I held implicit definitions of disability that were in opposition to those of disability theorists. Like most people, we conceived of disability as a bodily or mental flaw that "disables you from doing certain things" (my words to Lara) or something "not the norm" that makes you "not yourself" (Lara's to me). Disability theory, on the other hand, considers disability to be "not a physical or mental defect, but a cultural and minority identity" (Siebers 2008: 4); it takes as a given the diversity of human bodies and abilities and it interrogates the ways that bodies are enabled and disabled by ideology, structures of power, and sociomaterial spaces and practices. Furthermore, disability theory acknowledges that—unless we die young, "perfect," and suddenly—all of us will be disabled at some point in our lives. This is the unacceptable truth that we try to ignore: disability is normal, inevitable even. Tobin Siebers describes this aversion to reality as an "ideology of ability," or preference for able-bodiedness, one that sets social standards for body, mind, and even human status itself. The fear embedded in this ideology both powers and obscures a central contradiction in Western understandings and practices of the body: the conflict between our Cartesian belief that the body is an unimportant housing for the mind and our cultural obsession with perfecting the body at all costs. "Disability identity stands in uneasy relationship to the ideology of ability," Siebers writes, "presenting a critical framework that disturbs and critiques it" (2008, 9).

As seen in both my and Lara's reactions to tinnitus, the usual response to the disabled body is aversion and fear. "The ideology of ability stands ready to attack any desire to know and to accept the disabled body in its current state," Siebers writes. "The more likely response to disability is to try to erase any signs of change, to wish to return the body magically to a past era of supposed perfection, to insist that the body has no value as human variation if it is not flawless" (26). This reaction is evident in my unhappiness that my research would force me to dwell on my tinnitus. It is also present in Lara's contradictory beliefs that (1) she should ignore her body's phantom sounds like a good Cartesian subject and that (2) she is no longer herself, *no longer the same subject*, because of her tinnitus. Lara's refusal to accept the new state of her body spurred her immediate visit to an audiologist and her purchase of hearing aids—prosthetically designed "in [her] own color." She hoped to magically restore her body to an imagined former state of perfection, just as I was secretly grieving over my own imagined loss of perfection.

Here we find fear—the fear of loss, even the fear of one's own impaired body. Drawing on John Protevi's formulation of "affective cognition" or "the directed action of a living being in its world" (2013, 74), we can sense a process in which both an affect of fear and a way of listening to tinnitus are being activated in a collision between bodies, ideology, and phantom sound. Protevi points out that "sense" has three meanings: sensibility, signification, and (archaic in English but still present in French) directionality. All life, from single-celled organisms to human beings, senses its world in all three of these senses, biologically engaging its environment according to its body's abilities, "making sense" of the encounter as good or bad, and directing itself toward or away from the experience (2009, 16–17). From the perspective of affective cognition, humans' elaborate forms of signification are different in complexity *but not in kind* from the sense-making of the bacterium. The pervasive presence of the ideology of ability in our social environment influenced not only the conscious sense Lara and I made of tinnitus, but also the sensation itself, as well as our orientation or *stance* toward tinnitus, the way a person "actively grappl[es] with an entity that is independent from her and bring[s] that entity into experience" (Berger 2009, 16). In a very real sense, when Lara and I listened to our tinnitus as a fearsome signal of loss, we were hearing the ideology of ability.

And yet others could not hear our tinnitus at all. The phantom nature of tinnitus puts tinnitus sufferers in a vexed position with regard to the social acknowledgment and validation of their experience. This is the flip side of the ideology of ability—the way it influences how we perceive the bodies of others. While many disabled people struggle with social prejudice against their visibly nonconforming bodies, tinnitus sufferers struggle with the social prejudices and ignorance that can surround what Ellen Samuels calls "invisible disability" (2003). Elaine Scarry's aphorism, "To have pain is to have certainty; to hear about pain is to have doubt" (1985, 13) is equally applicable to tinnitus: the condition's very reality is always in doubt because no one else can hear it.[3] The tinnitus sufferer is potentially perceived as mentally or morally weak, a malingerer.

Doubt has suffused even the nomenclature of tinnitus since the early days of Western modernity, when the doctor Jean Marc Gaspard Itard (who treated Jean-Jacques Rousseau for the condition) drew a distinction between "objective" and "false" tinnitus. "Objective tinnitus," often called "somatosound" today, refers to otological sound audible to the physician; this relatively rare form of tinnitus is frequently due to vascular or muscular issues and is often "pulsatile," or in sync with the patient's heartbeat. Itard's "false tinnitus" was actually the predominant form—tinnitus with no acoustic basis, often called "subjective tinnitus" today (Andersson et al. 2005, 3).[4]

The fact that many people have tinnitus and are unbothered by it further exacerbates the doubt and suspicion around those who do. Subjective experiences of ringing, buzzing, humming, and other sounds seem to be common across cultures and throughout recorded history. And yet, while prevalence studies of tinnitus suggest that it is experienced by 10–15 percent of First World populations, only 0.5–3 percent experience it as a significant problem (Andersson et al. 2005, 23). As Lara's daughter's question, *Why do you worry so much?* indicates, family, friends, and employers frequently blame tinnitus sufferers, subtly or overtly, for their suffering. But why do some suffer from the sound of tinnitus while others do not?

Here we must enter into the liminal and phantom space between ideology and materiality, body and mind, thought and synaptic impulse, physiology and technology. To trace the conversions between these domains, I will take a transductive approach. Throughout this book, I conceive of human aurality as biomediated—an interplay between molecular waves, physical spaces, the cilia of the cochlea, neuronal webs, cultural technopractice and discourse, and individual ideation. Because hearing subjects are already biomediated in this way, they can use audio media to reflexively *remediate* their experience of tinnitus. It is in the specificities of these transductive practices of listening and remediation that different tinnituses emerge—or don't.

Tinnital Affectivity and the Biomediated Body

The phenomenon of suffering from tinnitus cannot be reduced simply to the ideology of ability. Indeed, to claim as much would be to reinvent the most simplistic dismissal of tinnital suffering: "It's just in your head!" (Of course it is!) Portraying tinnitus as a form of ideological and auditory "false consciousness" would impose on tinnitus sufferers the aforementioned Cartesian responsibility for mental mastery over the body, ironically reinforcing the ideology of ability. Therefore, understanding tinnitus and the roles that mediation plays in its experience requires attention to its phenomenology and physiology as well as to its ideological dimensions. We must enter the head of the tinnitus sufferer in more ways than one.

Phantom sound is, paradoxically, also a material phenomenon. Tinnitus exists in a liminal space between our epistemological distinctions of body and mind, real and imaginary, subject and object. When I suffer from tinnitus, I other its sound as an intrusive presence—*and yet*, this sound is actually of myself. Physiologically, tinnitus is the sound of my own body-mind—*and yet*, phenomenologically, it waxes and wanes in relation to the sounds in the air around me, almost as if it too is in the air and not "merely" in my head. In fact, when I lie in bed with the windows open on an early spring night, I am never certain whether the crickets I hear are within me or without me (a soothing uncertainty, actually). As phantom sound, tinnitus haunts the edges of auditory imagination—*and yet*, for the sufferer, it is incredibly, oppressively real.

Over the past decade and a half, a number of researchers have made significant advances into the etiology and treatment of this enigma, perhaps none more important than Pawel Jastreboff, a Polish-born scientist who applied insights from his training in neurophysiology and behavioral conditioning to tinnitus. While studying at the Nencki Institute of Experimental Biology in Warsaw, Jastreboff was the last doctoral student of Jerzy Konorski (1903–73), whose work "Conditioned Reflexes and Neuron Organization" (1948) helped establish contemporary neuroscience (Zieliński 2006, 75). Both student and rival to the father of classical conditioning, Ivan Pavlov, Konorski not only improved upon Pavlov's model of conditioned reflexes, but also began the work of linking these observable behaviors to sites and processes hidden in the brain. This latter work stands in contrast to that of the American B. F. Skinner (1904–90), whose behaviorist psychology— which popularized Pavlov's work in the West—treated the brain as a "black box" and limited itself to the study of observable behavior. Konorski's path-breaking work was initially disregarded by American behaviorists and many neurophysiologists, but this did not prevent the Polish scientist from indoctrinating his graduate students in his neurophysiology of conditioned reflexes. "I hated conditioned reflexes, but I had to learn it whether I liked it or not," Pavel Jastreboff told me when I interviewed him at the annual meeting of the American Academy of Audiology in 2012.

Nevertheless, it was precisely Jastreboff's training in classical conditioning that came into play when, in 1983, Clarence Sasaki, a Yale physician with a National Institutes of Health grant for tinnitus research, asked him for help. Sasaki wanted to create an animal model of tinnitus, verifiably inducing the condition in lab rats for study and for the development of potential therapies and cures. This was a task many thought impossible—after all, if one could not know for sure whether a fellow human had tinnitus, who could discern the presence of phantom sounds in a rat's head? Jastreboff knew little of tinnitus, but he immediately saw that he could improve the current methods of research, cleverly leveraging the fact that sound had been used to create conditioned responses ever since Pavlov himself used a buzzer, harmonium, or metronome (though never, it turns out, a bell) to make dogs salivate without the presence of food (Todes 2014, 1).

Jastreboff's approach to the problem was an ingenious application of classical conditioning (Jastreboff et al. 1988). At his new lab at Yale, his research team raised rats in the presence of a constant background noise, training them to expect an electrical shock whenever the noise was removed. The rats were kept thirsty until experimental observations, during which they would be provided with water to drink. When relaxed, the rats would drink enthusiastically, but when the background sound was removed, the rats would instantly stop drinking, revealing that their startle reflex from the electric shock had been conditionally paired to the stimulus of silence. Next, the team injected one group of rats with sodium salicylate, which is known to cause temporary tinnitus in humans. Finally, the background sound was removed again, and the injected group of rats happily continued drinking their water, demonstrating that they now perceived tinnitus. This technique and its many subsequent variations would become the gold standard for testing tinnitus therapies on animals.

During this same period, Jastreboff began applying his knowledge of neurophysiology to the problem of tinnitus in humans. However, he told me, the theory he developed was in such radical contradiction to then-current tinnitus science that he "put it away" for several years. In Jastreboff's neurophysiological model of tinnitus, he hypothesized that tinnitus was not, as generally thought, a problem generated in the auditory system per se, but was rather a "phantom perception" associated with a network of activity linking the *auditory system*, the body-regulating *autonomic nervous system*, and the *limbic system*—the subcortical network associated with instinct, drives, and affect. Having never worked with human tinnitus sufferers, Jastreboff was hesitant to circulate his model. It was only after he visited the London tinnitus clinic of physician Jonathan Hazell and audiologist Jacqueline Sheldrake in 1988 and realized that their observations of patients accorded with the implications of his theory, that he decided to pursue his model, publishing his paper "Phantom Auditory Perception (Tinnitus): Mechanisms of Generation and Perception" in the journal *Neuroscience Research* in 1990. It would be eight years before PET scan research provided evidence of "aberrant links between the limbic and auditory systems" (Lockwood et al. 1998), the first of many studies that would confirm and refine the model.

One of the fundamental axioms of the neurophysiological model is that the auditory system is homeostatic, regulating itself in relation to the sonic environment. "The auditory system needs sound like the body needs food," Jastreboff told me: when it is deprived of sound, hearing becomes more acute. Animal experiments in the 1990s indeed showed that auditory neurons become more sensitive in quiet environments (Boettcher and Salvi 1993; Gerken 1996), connecting a physiological mechanism to the long-observed fact that a ticking clock sounds much louder in a quiet room. Known as "automatic gain control" (AGC), this compensatory sensitivity in the auditory system creates a strong association between reduced auditory input and tinnitus, as sound-deprived individuals are more likely to experience the normal, random neuronal firing of auditory neurons (which might be thought of as "a code for silence") as sound (Jastreboff and Hazell 2004, 23). Tinnitus, then, is a phenomenon comparable to a sound engineer turning up the volume on a weak signal and thus amplifying the amplifier's inherent noise—the aforementioned random firing of synapses.

AGC is an audible manifestation of the cybernetic insight that the human sensorium is always self-regulating in relation to the fluctuations of its changing environment. As Jastreboff and Hazell write, "Our hearing and vision are adjusting all the time to the average level of sound or light around us, illustrating the principle of automatic gain control. For instance, a small candle will appear to be very bright in a darkened room but is hardly visible in broad daylight" (2004, 23). AGC neatly explains the results of a classic 1953 study in which 94 percent of people with "normal hearing" experienced tinnitus when placed in the dead silence of an anechoic chamber (Heller and Bergman 1953). AGC is also an important reason that a tinnitus sufferer like Terry enjoys relaxing in sonic surroundings of running water, wind, and the like—these sounds "raise the noise floor" and so allow his auditory system to "turn down the volume." Thus, while the word *masking* is generally used to describe orphic media's effect on tinnitus, the more accurate word is "suppression." Tinnitus sufferers "are reacting not to the absolute strength of the [tinnitus] stimulus but rather to its relative strength compared with the background" (Jastreboff and Hazell 2004, 23).

This emergence and suppression of tinnitus in relation to the sonic environment provide a clear example of affectivity, a relation of "bodies" in the broad Spinozan sense. Take an experience familiar to many: at a loud concert, your auditory system is affected by the powerful sonic force of the PA system, causing "temporary threshold shift," an immediate reduction in hearing acuity (Ward, Glorig, and Sklar 1959). After you leave the concert, AGC attempts to compensate for the auditory system's reduced ability to perceive its environment, producing that familiar ringing in your ears. In a Spinozan sense, tinnitus is an affective result of the body's reduced capacity to act. And yet, this tinnitus—which will likely disappear in time—may not bother you at all. In fact, you might even joke or brag about it, taking it as a sign of a night well spent.

Why, then, does it bother some so terribly? This is where the combined insights of neurophysiology and classical conditioning come into play. Jastreboff's model treats tinnitus as a *stimulus* and suffering as a *conditioned reflex*, enacted through neural networking. This aspect of the model relies upon a simple taxonomy of sound. Sounds can be classified in three general categories: neutral (not significant), having some positive (pleasant) meaning, and having a negative (unpleasant) association or meaning. During this process, with every new sound, the limbic and the autonomic nervous systems are activated to some extent (figure 1.1). This results in an orientation reaction in which the head may be turned in the direction of a sound to learn more about it. Meanwhile, our autonomic nervous system is preparing our body for an appropriate reaction should it be needed (Jastreboff and Hazell 2004, 35).

In the case of the happy concertgoer, leaving the venue with friends after a euphoric evening, the new sound of tinnitus is likely to be perceived as insignificant—or it might even take on a positive meaning. In this case, connections between the activity in the auditory periphery and the limbic and autonomic nervous systems quickly weaken and the auditory subconscious filters out the sound. This filtering is called a *habituation of perception*, and it allows us to ignore most of the sounds that we experience in everyday life so that we can concentrate on what we perceive to be important.

In the case of the tinnitus sufferer, however, a negative association attaches to tinnital sound, networking with the limbic system, creating a sense of fear or annoyance and reflexively activating a "fight-or-flight" response in the autonomic nervous system. The sound perception is immediately shuttled to consciousness for evaluation, at which point thoughts come into play. Often these are fearful thoughts—*This may never go away! What if I go crazy?*—that further increase limbic and autonomic reactivity. Once made, these neural connections have a tendency to strengthen in a vicious circle, as the perception that tinnitus is an aural threat encourages auditory pathways to "turn up the volume," further increasing the perceived presence and volume of

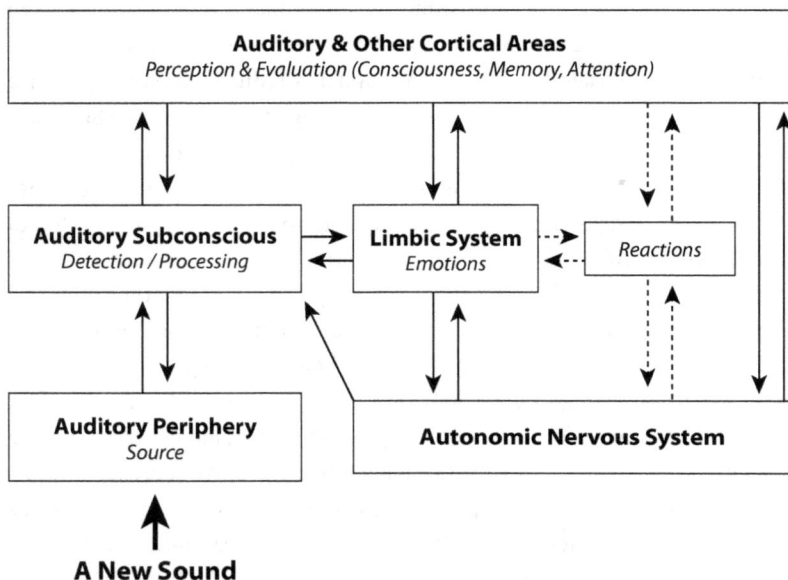

```
┌─────────────────────────────────────────────────────────────────┐
│              Auditory & Other Cortical Areas                     │
│    Perception & Evaluation (Consciousness, Memory, Attention)    │
└─────────────────────────────────────────────────────────────────┘

┌──────────────────────┐   ┌──────────────────┐   ┌──────────────┐
│ Auditory Subconscious │──▶│   Limbic System  │--▶│   Reactions  │
│  Detection / Processing│◀──│     Emotions     │◀--│              │
└──────────────────────┘   └──────────────────┘   └──────────────┘

┌──────────────────────┐   ┌──────────────────────────────────────┐
│   Auditory Periphery  │   │       Autonomic Nervous System       │
│        Source         │   │                                      │
└──────────────────────┘   └──────────────────────────────────────┘

                    ▲
                    │
                A New Sound
```

Figure 1.1 The network of interactions through which a sound goes unnoticed—or becomes impossible to ignore (Jastreboff and Hazell 2004).

tinnitus. This feedback loop of suffering is a conditioned reflex: "Once we associate a stimulus with something negative, or we are simply annoyed by it, we are unable to remove this association easily because it has become part of a conditioned reflex. An example would be trying to hold a conversation in the presence of an untethered wild animal. Our attention would be drawn to the animal, and it would be very difficult, or just impossible, to carry on a conversation. Conscious attempts to control this monitoring process will be unsuccessful, as we have no means of directly controlling or altering these reflex-based reactions" (Jastreboff and Hazell 2004, 38).

However distasteful all this talk of conditioning may be to some humanities scholars, the science behind it is well established. This embodied and reflexive reaction to sound is the reason we cannot simply reduce tinnital suffering to the ideology of ability—critique is no cure for conditioned reflex. To address the problem in its totality, we need to acknowledge and account for the ways that ideology articulates with the instantaneous affectivity through which a homeostatic body begins to listen in terror.

The existence of conditioned reflexes, in fact, indicates the mutually supportive and reliant roles of medical science on the one hand and the humanities and qualitative social sciences on the other (Varela, Thompson, and Rosch 1991, 150). Science assumes the existence of subjectively "pleasant," "unpleasant," and "neutral" sounds without an adequate theory for how those categorizations are enacted in sociocultural discourse and practice, while the humanities and social sciences lack adequate knowledge of the bodies that enact this discourse and practice. A synthesis between affect theory in the humanities and the neurophysiological model may better account for all the dimensions of biomediation that enact tinnital suffering, from the molecular to the discursive.

From an American perspective, it may seem odd to integrate a behavioristic model with affect theory since American behaviorism attempted to rid psychology of the messiness of affectivity: "The 'emotions' are excellent examples of the fictional causes to which we commonly attribute behavior," B. F. Skinner once wrote (1953, 160). However, this was not true of the man who *inspired* American behaviorism, Pavlov, who was preoccupied with subjective experience and dreamed of identifying the physiological bases of "our consciousness and its torments" (Todes 2014, 2). As intellectual descendants of Pavlov, Konorski and Jastreboff set their sights on identifying what we might call the neurological modalities of affective emergence. As a recent neuroscientific article explains, both tinnitus and chronic pain are "sensory-perceptual disorders associated with negative affect and high impact on well-being and behavior," involving both "higher cognitive and affective brain systems" (Rauschecker et al. 2015). Taking an affective humanities approach to the neurophysiological emergence of tinnital suffering, it is possible to speak of ideology at the level of conditioned reflex.

So how exactly does ideology articulate with the instantaneous affectivity of neurophysiology? Ruth Leys's critique of the turn to affect in the humanities centers on just this question; she writes that affect theorists and neuroscientists believe "that cognition or thinking comes 'too late' for reasons, beliefs, intentions, and meanings to play the role in action and behavior usually accorded to them" (2011, 443). In a move apropos to the present discussion, Leys turns to the common claim that music has physical effects that are not the same as its meanings—a claim similar to this chapter's assertion that tinnitus is a form of affectivity without an inherently negative or positive meaning. In Leys's view, such claims result from an impoverished, "rationalist concept of meaning and an unexamined assumption that everything that is not 'meaning' in this limited sense belongs to the body" (458). In fact, affect theory affords us a more sophisticated model of the interplay of meaning and embodiment than Leys acknowledges. In Spinoza's and Deleuze's accounts of affectivity, a subject's subsequent *ideas about* a reduction or increase in the capacity to act contribute to the network of affects that continually produce the actual out of the virtual. In John Protevi's synthesis of systems theory and affect theory, materially and culturally embodied subjects attempt to maintain their structural coherence in their interactions with their environments, acquiring learned "behavioral modules" over time through these interactions. While affect operates almost instantaneously, it also unfolds *slowly* through individual and social history. And while embodied subjects' behavioral modules help them maintain their autonomy as living systems, that does not mean that these behaviors are beneficial to the embodied subject: "In other words, many people incorporate behavioral modules that hurt them" (Protevi 2013, 31).

In the case of tinnitus, before one even knows it, one's affective cognition might emerge as a jolt of panic (*What is happening to me?*) or a ripple of laughter (*What a concert!*). In such a contingent moment, affective cognition reinforces itself to *change the sound of the tinnitus*, potentially changing volume, pitch, or timbre—or extinguishing the sound, as nearly instantaneous feedback between the auditory subconscious, limbic system, autonomic nervous system, and memory feed into the prefrontal cortex's conscious (im)perception and evaluation of the phantom sound. This is not an entirely individual phenomenon: just as the emergence of phantom sound depends in part on the subject's current sonic environment, the entire body-mind has also been primed by a slow history of cultural ideologies, technologies, and practices. It is also through subjective emergence within this larger apparatus that tinnital suffering actualizes in its specificity—or doesn't. Therefore, tinnitus is not a singular, but a multiple phenomenon. It is produced in different moments of experience, under different sonic, spatial, social, and technological conditions. As I will show in the next section, in both individual histories and world history, we find different practices of listening, ways of thinking, and material conditions that produce not only different understandings of tinnitus, but profoundly different sonic phenomenologies—*different tinnituses, different experiences of disability, different fears*. If most tinnituses are sonic afterimages of acoustic traumas, however mild—the ghosts of hearing past—they are also the lingering effects of a lifetime of learning and conditioning—habits of haunted listening. Therefore, we must investigate differing cultures of tinnitus.

Freedom of Choice as Habitus of Listening

Elaine, a forty-nine-year-old schoolteacher, told me she developed tinnitus during panic attacks caused by withdrawal from a sleeping medication she had been prescribed. When I met her at a support group meeting, she had already spent two years listening to her tinnitus—which had reduced her to working part-time at a preschool—and trying to make the right choices to get rid of it. "I'm very careful about diet and I have food sensitivities, but I can't figure out anything that corresponds to my tinnitus," she told me. "I haven't had [an alcoholic] drink in a long time, because that seemed to make it worse." Like other tinnitus sufferers, she has tried many types of therapies: vitamins, Chinese medicine, acupuncture, and chiropractic medicine. Media devices and mediated sound figure prominently into Elaine's arena of choice, as she uses radio, TV, an iPod, a Sharper Image sound machine, and mp3s of natural sounds on her computer to manage her awareness of the teakettle she hears whistling in her head. When I met Elaine, she had already been to an audiologist, who told her that her hearing was normal, but she was about to make an appointment with a second audiologist to ask about purchasing a wearable sound generator to mask her tinnitus.

Applying Jastreboff's model to Elaine's case, we might surmise that the trauma of the panic attack caused her to listen fearfully, either problematizing a little-noticed tinnitus that was already there or perceiving her synapses' random firing as phantom sound for the first time. In either case, a self-reinforcing network between her limbic system, autonomic nervous system, prefrontal cortex, and auditory system was producing tinnitus as a powerfully fearsome phenomenological experience. "The most frightening thought for someone who suddenly starts to hear a strange sound inside the ear is that it never will disappear," writes a research scientist who has worked with tinnitus patients for decades (Tyler 2008, 51). But we should be cautious in using a medical model of disability to portray this particular fear as the "natural" result of a flawed brain. Instead, it is important to consider the reciprocal economy between social representation and the body (Siebers 2008, 25).

Over the two years I studied Americans with tinnitus, I increasingly came to understand the fear of tinnitus and the struggle to end it as a knotty problem of sound, selfhood, mediation, and responsibility. As sound not chosen by the subjects who hear it—and, in fact, attached to the subjects who hear it—tinnitus is an affront to historically Western, liberal notions of selfhood as an ability and obligation to enact one's life in terms of choice. Such a self-concept emerges within political, economic, and social frameworks in which roles and identities are dictated not by tradition but rather by a series of open-ended personal, professional, and consumer choices. Tinnitus sufferers use electronic media such as iPods, sound machines, and hearing aids as technologies of the self, shoring up the self in order to restore freedom of choice and control of their own subjectivity.

Tinnitus interferes with the Western notion of the person, which Clifford Geertz characterizes as "a bounded, unique, more or less integrated motivational and cognitive universe, a dynamic center of awareness, emotion, judgment, and action organized into a distinctive whole and set contrastively both against other such wholes and against its social and natural background" (1983, 59). Tinnitus is understood to be an interaction between a self and a sound, but upon close inspection, the boundaries between these entities become indistinct. A self so ephemeral as to be interfered with by a "nonexistent" sound must be a fragile construct indeed.

Threatened and driven to distraction by the porous, aurally mediated nature of their subjectivity, tinnitus sufferers use orphic technologies such as digital sound machines, hearing aids, white noise apps, or Neuromonics units (a Walkman-like sound therapy device) to help them cope with the inescapable sound in their heads, providing a means of self-control through sound control. I have met many people who use these sound devices in what they perceive as a high-stakes war. Their battles with tinnitus have resulted in their going months with little sleep, quitting jobs, selling off businesses, taking anxiety medication, being institutionalized, and even attempting suicide. Those who suffer from tinnitus express to me a profound grief over the loss of silence, as well as an associated grief and guilt over a perceived loss of self, as in Lara's feeling that "you're not yourself because this thing is happening to you."

Listening to tinnitus and hearing it as a loss of silence, a loss of choice, and finally, as a loss of self, is central to the suffering of people like Lara. It involves constantly monitoring oneself, listening to one's own hearing and framing the sound of tinnitus in terms of choices in consumption. When their tinnitus gets louder, tinnitus sufferers ask themselves what choices they recently made to cause the change—was it food, drink, medication, exercise, a loud movie? When their tinnitus gets quieter, they try to discern what choices might have caused *that* change. Tinnital suffering is a fearful affective relation to a world seething with sonic significance. People who suffer from tinnitus spend a lot of time monitoring its sound and their choices, always with an ear toward the future, trying to decide what choices they should make so that their tinnitus will get better, not worse.

From a modern, Western perspective, it is natural to hear head noise as an aberrant threat to one's sanity and identity, and to set its sound in the key of personal choice. In other places and times, however, other assessments of tinnitus have prevailed—a bewitched ear (ancient Egypt), a hungry but harmless spirit asking for food (Inuit tradition), or an internal omen (in Western antiquity) (Connor 2010). The sixteenth-century Saint Teresa of Avila tried to understand why she experienced her painful head noises in the same part of the head where she felt the entering and exiting of the Holy Spirit (Schwartz 2011, 339). The point is not merely that cultural *explanations* vary, but that there is cultural variance between individuals' *habitus of listening*, which ethnomusicologist Judith Becker conceives as

> an inclination, a disposition to listen with a particular kind of focus, to expect to experience particular kinds of emotion . . . and to interpret the meaning of the sounds and one's emotional responses . . . in somewhat (never totally) predictable ways. The stance of the listener is not a given, not natural, but necessarily influenced by place, time, the shared context of culture, and the intricate and irreproducible details of one's personal biography. (2004, 71)

Becker deploys habitus to better understand the differences between *musical* listening practices, such as those between the motionless and autonomous Western classical music audience member and the trancing Javanese gamelan participant. While the latter "must necessarily surrender personal will and accept the penetration of her bodily boundaries" by spirits, the former—as a bounded, "rational," singular, Cartesian self—is unwilling and unable to trance in this way (11). The scholar who takes the Western listening self as a universal given, explains Becker, will never understand the dynamics of Javanese trancing.

Turning Becker's habitus of listening to tinnitus, one can make a similar claim about Western subjects resisting phantom sounds perceived to violate bodily boundaries. "I'm pissed. [Tinnitus is] trying to ruin my life," Lara told me. "I'm retired, I should have no problems," said one man at a support group meeting. "I used to like to sit quietly in a 'nothing' state," Elaine told me, but tinnitus had taken that from her. My interlocutors with problematic tinnitus inhabit a way of listening informed by the idea that a natural self has the option of complete silence, unencumbered by sound. It feels unnatural to them that one should surrender one's personal will to penetration by an intruding signal. To experience tinnitus with such a habitus of listening is "to listen with a particular kind of focus, to expect to experience particular kinds of emotion . . . and to interpret the meaning of the sounds" in terms of losing the self and making the right choices in order to restore it.

Ironically, however, the behavioral module of monitoring tinnitus and trying to form meaningful connections between its fluctuations and one's personal choices actually *perpetuates* tinnitus awareness, anxiety, and volume, making tinnitus ever more present, ever more real (cf. McKenna and Andersson 2008). This form of listening *is* suffering. Again, though prevalence studies of tinnitus suggest that it is experienced by 10–15 percent of people, only about 0.5–3 percent of this group experiences it as a significant problem. One might assume that people who suffer are experiencing a much louder or more piercing than average tinnitus, but when audiologists work to objectify and compare different people's tinnitus (using techniques examined later in this chapter), this does not appear to be the case (Henry and Meikle 2000). As Jill Meltzer, the doctor of audiology whom Elaine went to see about a sound generator, told Elaine at their first meeting, "The loudness of a person's tinnitus does not necessarily equate with how disturbing it is. You could be driven crazy by tinnitus that's two decibels and the person whose tinnitus is nine or twelve decibels might say, 'Eh, it hardly bothers me.' I like to compare it to a pebble in your shoe. It doesn't have to be the biggest stone. It can be the smallest rock and it can bug the crap out of you."

Though there has been some controversy around this point (Tyler 2005, 2), today clinicians mostly agree on treating tinnital suffering as a problem in which cognition profoundly affects psychoacoustics. In short, researchers consider problematic tinnitus to be more a problem of *listening* than a problem of hearing, conceiving in terms of emergent networks between the brain's "fear center" and auditory system. Similar linkages are found in the conditions of hyperacusis (extreme sound sensitivity) and misophonia (in which everyday sounds induce feelings of rage or panic), both of which are frequently comorbid with tinnitus (Jastreboff and Hazell 2004, 11–14). In each of these three conditions, the listener engages her sonic environment in ways that are homeostatic yet not beneficial: these ways of listening are oriented around maintaining autonomy, yet they are behavioral modules that literally hurt the listener.

At this point, I should make explicitly clear that I am not blaming individuals who suffer from tinnitus for inhabiting this form of listening. Indeed, to do so would be to fall prey to the illusion of individual autonomy that I deploy tinnitus to dispel in this chapter. I am also not suggesting that only Western, modern subjects suffer from the sound of tinnitus. But tinnitus is not a transhistorical phenomenological experience that is merely *interpreted* differently in different milieux. Instead, following Annemarie Mol's actor–network–inspired studies of diseases such as anemia and arteriosclerosis, in which "'disease' becomes a part of what is done in practice" (2002, 13), I suggest that the meaning, suffering, treatment, and even the *sound* of tinnitus are *enacted* differently in different practices of listening and mediation.[5]

The enacted, performed nature of tinnitus is evident, for example, in the way that its sound intensifies and diminishes as subjects move between quiet and loud spaces. Even its pitch, timbre, and position in the head or ears can change with one's movements, emotional state, or attentional focus. Tinnitus is a multiple, not a singular condition. It is indicative of Mol's larger point that all objects, subjects, and bodies are multiple, emerging in different moments through different sets of contingent events and relations.

However, when confronted with the multiplicity of tinnitus, medical doctors, friends, and family members do not generally become suspicious of their own tacit understandings of bodies and disease; rather, their suspicions often tend to fall on tinnitus and the person who claims to suffer from it. Elaine, for example, told me of a dismissive ear, nose, and throat doctor who told her everything was fine and had little else to say, as well as a neurologist who did an MRI, said her tinnitus was "ideopathic," and concluded there was nothing to be done. When individuals are implicitly understood as being obliged to be singular, free, and in control of their own subjectivity, a person incapacitated by an inaudible sound is more likely to be understood as not living up to their responsibilities to family and society.

Individuals are also blamed or feel responsible for getting tinnitus as a result of making bad media choices. Audiologists warn that, as tinnitus is so often associated with some degree of hearing loss, it frequently turns up in musicians, DJs, habitual iPod users, and others exposed to highly amplified music. When such events are repeated, permanent shifts of hearing thresholds are more and more likely to occur. At the two annual meetings of the American Academy of Audiology that I attended, I saw many panels, posters, and organization booths focused on the need to educate the public concerning amplified sound (particularly iPods) and hearing loss and tinnitus.

To some extent, the message seems to have gotten out already. The cultural notion of tinnitus as the aftermath of excessive musical pleasure can be seen in the name of the popular mp3 blog GIMME TINNITUS (www

.gimmetinnitus.com), as well as references to the condition in a number of popular songs. While I observed testing at a hearing aid manufacturer, one tinnitus patient looked at the "notches" of hearing loss in his audiogram and said, "Half of that was probably [the alternative rock band] Jane's Addiction, 2007. I thought I'd never recover." Now that he had tinnitus, this patient was regretful about his past concertgoing and careful to avoid high-amplitude mediated environments for fear of exacerbating his condition. As my conversation with Lara also indicates, the sound of tinnitus is frequently tied up with feelings of regret over past choices in media use.

"Bad" media use is one dimension of a plethora of relations in which tinnital experience emerges, relations that transcend scale and typology—a spatially distributed network of causality that forms the unstable object of tinnitus. These networks biomediate both what is understood as the bounded, unique person and the tinnital sounds that sabotage that person. However, these networks can also be further mediated to reinforce the apparent boundaries of that self by controlling its sonic experience. Electronic media are deployed transductively to alter these networks, first to objectify tinnitus as a treatable condition in the audiologist's office and then to fragment these networks, weakening tinnitus as an ontological presence.

Chasing Phantoms, Objectifying Disability

"All right, for the next part, this is where we're going to chase your tinnitus. My ultimate goal is to have you *not* focusing on your tinnitus, but this is the part where I stick you in the booth and say 'I want you to look for your tinnitus.'" "The booth" is a small, soundproofed room where Elaine sits in a chair, wearing headphones. Dr. Jill Meltzer, her audiologist, is speaking to her through a microphone and looking at her through the double pane of glass that separates them. Like many other local tinnitus sufferers, Elaine heard about Meltzer's services at the tinnitus support group where we first met. Meltzer has allowed me to attend tinnitus screenings and consultations at her office in a suburb of a large Midwestern city.

I came to the audiologist's office to listen and observe and to better understand how and why orphic media are prescribed for tinnitus. However, during visits like these, I quickly became fascinated with the technological practices involved in audiology writ large—practices that involve recognizable media technologies such as microphones, headphones, mixers, and computers. I soon found myself doing a transductive version of what Annemarie

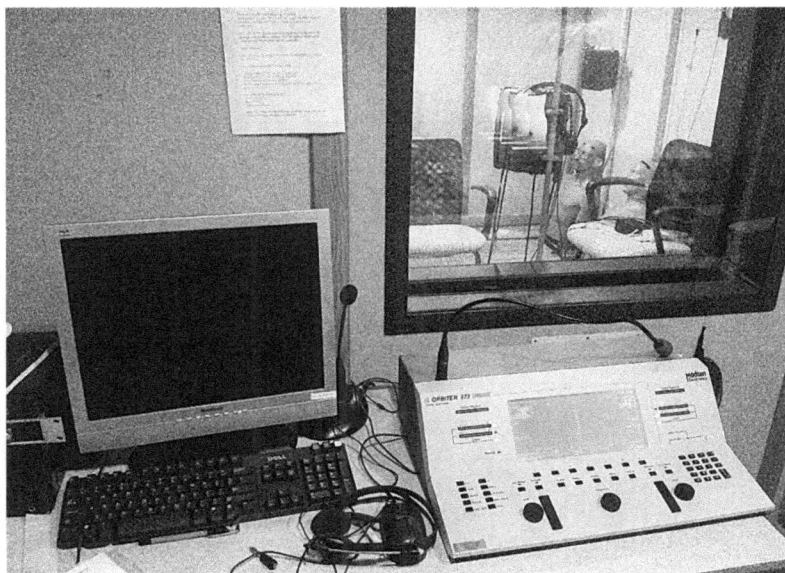

Figure 1.2 An audiometer and, beyond the glass, an audiometric testing booth, part of the research facilities of a hearing aid manufacturer. Photo by author.

Mol calls "praxiology," the ethnographic investigation of the clinical practices through which a disease or medical condition emerges as an object. "An ethnographer/praxiographer out to investigate diseases never isolates these from the practices in which they are, what one might call, enacted," Mol writes. "She stubbornly takes notice of the techniques that make things visible, audible, tangible, knowable. She may talk bodies—but she never forgets about microscopes" (2002: 33).

There is no microscope in Dr. Meltzer's clinic. Rather, she sits behind a diagnostic audiometer, which looks similar to an audio engineer's digital mixing board. Like a studio mixer, the audiometer allows her to route and transduce different audio signals, directing them to either one or both channels of Elaine's headphones. As a lapsed musician, I felt a moment of recognition when I first entered one of these spaces. The entire setup—the control room and sound booth with the double pane of glass between them—looks very much like a digital recording studio (figure 1.2). The audiologist's job, however, is not to record sound, but to record *hearing itself*, although Meltzer's audiological specialty makes her practice a bit different: she and her client are about to transduce and record phantom sound.

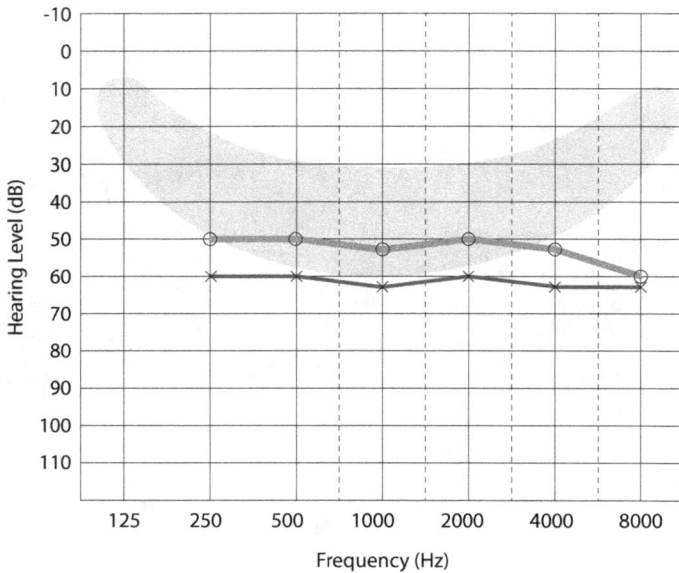

Figure 1.3 An audiogram. The horizontal axis represents frequency (pitch), while the vertical axis represents decibel level (loudness), with 0 dB representing the quietest sound audible to the "normal" ear. The subject's left ear response is charted with xs, while the right ear response is charted with os. The lower a line is plotted, the less hearing acuity. Note the "speech banana" shadow, which represents the typical frequency and volume range of human speech.

"So, we're going to look for the pitch of the tinnitus, or at least a *component* of your tinnitus. It may not be the exact sound, but if I get to a pitch that's fairly close to what you usually hear, press the button," Meltzer says, indicating the subject-response hand switch Elaine holds. Meltzer uses the audiometer to generate tones in the headphones as they pursue the teakettle sound Elaine hears in her right ear. Meltzer is choosing her starting pitch based on a graph displayed on the screen in front of her, a visual representation of Elaine's hearing thresholds across different frequencies, shown in relation to average thresholds. Meltzer and Elaine just finished creating this representation with the help of the audiometer: Meltzer played tones of different pitches and loudness levels through the headphones, Elaine pressed her button if she heard them, and the audiometer generated the graph on the screen to represent the limits of Elaine's hearing across a frequency spectrum—her audiogram (figure 1.3).

Meltzer has objectified Elaine's hearing through the media of the head-phones, subject-response hand switch, audiometer, and screen—an important first step in chasing the phantom of her tinnitus. Creating the audiogram makes it easier to externalize the tinnitus, transducing it into a visible and audible object, because Elaine's tinnitus pitch is likely to reside in the vicinity of any hearing loss she has. Even though Elaine's hearing falls within the "normal" range, some of the hair cells of her cochlea have been damaged over time by the loud sounds of everyday life. As is the case for most of us, it is the hair cells responsible for transducing higher frequencies that have taken the brunt of the damage. This is because these hairs are located closest to the ear canal—"It's the carpet by the front door that wears out first," Meltzer tells me later. Due to compensatory neural activity, Meltzer believes, Elaine's tinnitus will likely correspond to the high frequencies her cochlea once converted and transmitted with greater gusto.

But while the audiometer and its attendant practices help Meltzer identify and isolate tinnitus today, they may also in some ways have helped obscure tinnitus and its connection to hearing loss in the past. The development of audiometry was intertwined with the desire to standardize human hearing for the development of efficient telecommunications technologies, part of a longer history of conceiving hearing as *hearing speech*. Mara Mills writes, "In the absence of amplification devices and precise audiometric measurements, 'deaf-mute' or 'deaf and dumb' referred to those who—from an early age—could not hear the frequency range of the human voice" (2015, 46). Telephone technologies, whose invention enabled the subsequent development of the audiometer and whose own refinement would depend upon the audiometer's ability to standardize human hearing, ensured that this vococentric and communicative model of hearing subjects would be built into audiometric technologies and practices. This communicative model and diagnostic technology are suitable for identifying hearing loss only in the specific range of amplitudes and frequencies in which phonemes—the sounds of human speech—are audible, approximately 125 Hz–8k Hz (see the shaded area in figure 1.3). Even today, audiometers are typically calibrated for sounds within this so-called speech banana, failing to test the much wider range of possible human hearing (approximately 20 Hz–20 kHz). Similarly, audiology's main tool on the treatment side, the hearing aid, is fitted and tuned with intelligible speech in mind. Due to this history, audiology is generally less concerned with identifying and treating the most common form of hearing loss—the erosion of high frequencies that most of us experience over time.

While tinnitus most often occurs in an individual's "lost" frequencies, many people's tinnitus will fall outside the range of traditional audiological testing and amplification. I have found no large-scale meta-studies identifying the most commonly perceived tinnitus frequencies over the past decades of tinnitus research. One study of 195 participants found that seventy-five of them had tinnitus at or above the highest frequency of standard audiometry, 8 kHz, but failed to identify a clear relationship between tinnitus pitch and hearing loss frequencies (Pan et al. 2009). The maker of one online tool for self-administered tinnitus frequency identification found its users reported a normal distribution or "bell curve" of frequencies centering at roughly 8 kHz, meaning that roughly half of these tinnitus cases would be unidentifiable by standard audiometry (Phua 2015). Jastreboff thinks the problem is worse than that: "If you are only testing to 8 kilohertz, you don't know what's happening in the frequency range where tinnitus and misophonia originate," he told me. "The technology today is available, but it's a matter of tradition and inertia. Testing higher frequencies takes more time and requires better audiometers and headphones, so some people are sticking to audiological standards and not bothering to go higher than 8 kilohertz."

Since Jill Meltzer specializes in the treatment of tinnitus, hyperacusis, and misophonia, she has invested in equipment that engages the higher frequencies these phenomena often haunt. With the audiogram as a guide, she begins using the audiometer to play sounds through Elaine's headphones. "I'm guessing I'm low?" Meltzer asks. I see Elaine's lips move through the glass pane, but I can't hear her response, which is routed through Meltzer's own headset. "Is it more tonal or is it more of a hiss, like this?" Jill plays another sound I can't hear in Elaine's ears. The tones are indeed too low in frequency at first. The test continues, and it's slow going. Sometimes Elaine feels that her own sound might be changing as it interacts with the sound from the audiometer—a common experience. "Pesky little tinnitus," Meltzer murmurs.

In using the audiometer to pursue the tinnitus, Meltzer is following in the footsteps of E. M. Josephson, a medical doctor who noted in the 1930s that tinnitus did not interact with other sounds as a sound in the air would do. When playing a tone similar to that of a subject's tinnitus near the ear, "a masking of the superimposed note by the tinnitus is found, instead of a summation of intensities; one would not expect this result if the mechanism of tinnitus and of hearing of sound from the outer world were similar," he wrote (1931, 282). This observation allowed Josephson, using a frequency oscillator and amplifier to generate tones and a vacuum tube voltmeter to measure intensities, to identify the pitch and intensity of sound necessary for "drowning out" the tinnitus.

It is far from being a surefire technique. The first problem is that tinnitus is often experienced as a cluster of sounds, and it can be hard or impossible for a patient to identify individual pitches. (Anecdotally, musicians seem to be better at this—a guitarist I know can tune his instrument using the G he hears in his head since experiencing a bomb blast in Kandahar, Afghanistan.) Even more confounding is the fact that tinnitus can interact with external sounds in a number of ways that Josephson did not observe, spontaneously changing in volume, pitch, or timbre as the auditory system attempts to maintain homeostasis in the presence of new environmental sounds. In a real worst-case scenario of the observer effect, tinnitus can *worsen* or be temporarily *suppressed* by the audiometric testing that pursues it. In fact, so flighty is this phantom sound that often the tinnitus in one ear will change in reaction to an audiometric tone being played in the other.

Despite these challenges, Meltzer and Elaine are finally closing in on their phantom. "I'll present two sounds; tell me which is closer, the first or the second," says Meltzer. Perhaps for my benefit, she switches on the speaker attached to the audiometer. Now I can hear Elaine's response: "I'm not sure, it's like being at the eye doctor." Eventually, they settle on 6 kHz, a pitch higher than the highest note on an eighty-eight-key piano, located within what we might call the "teakettle range." Meltzer plays the tone for me through the speaker on the board. I'm listening to something like Elaine's tinnitus, now externalized and objectified.

Meltzer moves on to volume matching. Placing the 6-kHz tone in Elaine's left ear, she raises the volume in 2-dB steps to see what loudness matches the perceived intensity of her right ear's tinnitus. When the tone from the audiometer reaches a match with the subjective sound in her head, Elaine clicks the subject-response button. A kind of cybernetic, sensory homeostasis is achieved, a balance between two sounds. The first haunts the right ear, an absence of input transduced by neurons into auditory experience—a ghost in Elaine's perceptual machinery. The second stimulates the left ear—an electronic sound, generated by an oscillator in the audiometer and transduced into molecular ripples by the headphone diaphragm. Due to the painstaking pitch and volume matching, these two sounds now blend together at the limens of internal and external, body and mind, real and imaginary, subject and object. "I think that's it," says Elaine. "*Now I'm not sure what's me and what's you.*"

Thinking transductively about the feat that Meltzer and Elaine just accomplished brings us back to biomediation: their work was possible because the experience of problematic tinnitus is already transductively mediated, a network of relations in need of *remediation*. The first type of remediation tinnitus requires—the one just witnessed—is objectification or realization, the transduction of phantom sound into a form that accords with the representational and practical logics of a given culture. Elaine's twenty-first-century, North American tinnitus is realized as a dip on an audiometric graph or an electronic sound for others to hear. This objectification is a small victory for what Leigh Eric Schmidt calls "an Enlightenment acoustics of demystification," the imperative to, through techniques and technologies of rational listening, silence irrational, imaginary, or mystical sounds and voices (2000, 1). Even if, at this point, clinician and patient have yet to silence the tinnitus, they have at least, through rational listening, objectified it.

Such objectifying media technologies are central to Western medicine. From stethoscopes to X-ray machines to ultrasound to the *Diagnostic and Statistical Manual of Mental Disorders* to WebMD, media technologies are used in "biomediating practices that produce bodies of knowledge and known bodies, locating the latter in matrices of ability and responsibility" (Hagood 2017). Taking a biomedial approach to hearing, we can examine the roles of technological remediation in the production of aural experiences, norms, practices, identities, and publics. When tinnitus is biomediated through audiometry, it is strengthened as an object, which in turn lends credibility to its sufferer. Fleshing out the phantom on paper grants Itard's "false" tinnitus objective status.

Some patients find substantial relief simply through the validation that tinnitus pitch and loudness matching provides. Michael Piskosz, global audiologist for the hearing aid manufacturer ReSound, presented to me the following scenario:

> Let's say you've got a dad who has lost his job and he's been stressed out and he's got this tinnitus thing going on. And his family is sick of hearing about it because they can't hear it. And they're coming down on him and the tinnitus is getting worse. Finally he comes in to see a clinician, who does pitch matching and loudness matching. What I think that information does is provide a graph. It gives the family a picture of what that looks like in the real world. It quantifies it. You can show them, "this is what he's hearing all the time," and hopefully they sympathize with him. If you have the support of the people you love, it always makes things easier.

A graphic representation—and better yet, a sonic reproduction like the teakettle sound Jill Meltzer played for me in her clinic—takes on special resonance within a culture focused on autonomy and the responsibility to choose. However out of fashion it may be in some sectors of the academy, a Cartesian substance dualism holds sway in everyday American life. Tinnitus is suspect because it is literally "all in the head." When the mind is implicitly thought of as separate from—and the pilot of—the body, mental disability takes on stigmas of moral laxity and incompetence. Through remediation, the father in Piskosz's scenario may find a reprieve from suspicions of malingering or neurosis. By objectifying tinnitus, the audiometer, audiologist, and patient may validate the patient's subjectivity and help restore his role as a responsible actor. This is particularly important in cases of suspected malingering and workman's compensation (Hain 2014). With this process of externalization complete, Meltzer and Elaine will now begin to discuss a second remediating practice, in which orphic media are used to disassemble the behavioral module of listening-as-suffering.

Remedial Media

The audiologist's second form of tinnital biomediation is *re*medial, both in the sense that it is intended as a remedy and in the sense that it is intended to provide training in a problem area. The remedial use of orphic media electronically leverages tinnitus's homeostatic emergence and diminishment in relation to changing levels of environmental sound. Lara first noticed her tinnitus in the quiet of her bed, but she completely forgot about it at the loud party, despite the acute anxiety she had been feeling about it that week. Once back in the quiet of her home at night, however, she became conscious of her tinnitus again. Lara's hearing aids remediate this homeostatic relation, taking on the function of amplification in Lara's stead, allowing her auditory system, which is overcompensating for a lack of input in the frequencies of her hearing loss, to turn down its own volume. Before going to see audiologist Jill Meltzer, Elaine did what many do: she intuitively remediated her tinnitus through television, radio, an iPod, a sound machine, and what we might call the "streaming media" of the shower (a vibrational force in which she finds her greatest relief from the teakettle).

While cultural scholars have analyzed the utility of radio, Walkman, and iPod music in managing the rhythms and emotions of everyday life (Bull 2007; DeNora 1999), the remediation of tinnitus is a rather pointed example of a different sort of widespread media practice that deserves greater attention in media studies—namely, that people use media to care for themselves. When one is responsible for cultivating one's affect through choice, an mp3 player or a digital machine that makes a waterfall sound is no mere entertainment or novelty gadget. For a person suffering from tinnitus, an orphic device of this sort is a technological choice with the potential to restore one's lost place as an authentic, responsible self. Some tinnitus sufferers find a way to a happier aural equilibrium through these improvised media practices.

However, as seen in Elaine's case, this sort of self-treatment is sometimes not enough for the tinnitus sufferer to find adequate relief, in which case, she may turn to an audiologist, who deploys the same (or similar but more specialized) technologies, using them as what Mara Mills calls "prescription media" (2012). Once it is established that a patient's tinnitus is not a symptom of pathology, the goal of a clinician like Jill Meltzer is to help her patient habituate to the sound so that it is no longer an impediment to daily life.

In this final section of this chapter, I will use two case studies to explore the remedial role of orphic media practices in the struggle for habituation. In each case, Jill Meltzer prescribed a wearable audiological device to remediate her patient's tinnitus and alter a tormented habitus of listening. In each case, the patient entered Meltzer's office thinking that *the technology itself* would be the total remedy, when in fact Meltzer intended the technology to help facilitate *a change in listening*. Similar to the ethnographer who wants to understand tinnitus, the patient would have to learn to understand and enact certain practices of listening. The first patient I will discuss, Joel, learned through Meltzer's counseling to use an orphic device called Neuromonics Oasis to help change his listening practices, eventually finding a great deal of relief for his tinnitus and hyperacusis. The second patient, Elaine, purchased a wearable sound generator from Meltzer but did not participate in a program to change her habitus of listening. While she derives some relief from the sound generator, she still suffers a great deal from her tinnitus.

Joel

Joel Styzens is currently the leader of the tinnitus support group in his city. The fact that he initiated and leads such a group is indicative of the almost friendly relationship he has established with his tinnitus. As a musician, Joel has used his tinnitus as an inspiration for composition, even going so far as to name his record label A Sharp Records, after its pitch. Things weren't nearly so easy at first, however. Like Lara, he first noticed tinnitus in the quiet of his bed. Joel awoke one morning to a sound he describes as like "an old tube TV, a very high-pitched, steady, constant tone." He got up and went to the bathroom to wash his face. When he turned on the water, Styzens experienced a painful crackling in his left ear "like a speaker being overdriven." A drummer and music teacher then in his twenties, Joel was already what Judith Becker would call a "deep listener," someone who trains their aural attention into a highly developed state (2004). Now his refined sense of listening had become a form of torment. For the next month, Styzens barely left his apartment due to this sudden onset of tinnitus and its close relative hyperacusis, a sound sensitivity he came to attribute to his history of loud concerts and childhood ear surgeries. He was now painfully aware of what a chaotically resonant environment his city was, full of rumbling commuter trains, hissing bus air brakes, honking car horns, and loud music and voices in restaurants and bars. The space of the city became a sonic minefield that Joel had no power to clear. When he did venture out, he was in a constant state of anxiety, anticipating the next random sonic assault. He began wearing earplugs everywhere.

Like Terry, Joel found himself suddenly acutely sensitive to his situation in the complex topography of vibration that we all inhabit, "the materiality of sensation . . . the operations of power that distribute vibration and produce sonic affects" (Goodman 2010, 199). If ever there was a condition that revealed a vibrational ecology and its fearsome affective potential, it is hyperacusis. Although there may be representational aspects to the media that audiologists deploy to remediate tinnitus, their core utility involves the remediation of neural networks and the control of vibrational force, not representation. The vibrations and impulses that mediated Joel Styzens's tinnitus and hyperacusis transcended distinctions of scale, interiority and exteriority, and subject and object as they connected the sounds of the street or the silence of his bedroom with the mechanisms of his ears and the neurons of his higher auditory system. Ironically, Joel's use of earplugs only made his hyperacusis and tinnitus worse, as AGC "turned up the volume" in reaction to the reduced stimulus. But his tinnitus and hyperacusis could potentially be *re*mediated through technological practices involving white noise generators, music, or other sound enrichment. These practices rework these networks and allow for a gradual increased tolerance to vibrational force (in the case of hyperacusis) or its lack (in the case of tinnitus).

Such contemporary audiological approaches to tinnitus and hyperacusis are often directly or indirectly based on neuroscientist Jastreboff's neurophysiological model. In my interviews with Jastreboff and several audiologists, they repeatedly told me that clinicians essentially have two tools for helping people habituate: counseling and sound. The counseling assures patients that tinnitus is manageable and not a threat. It also gives patients the skills to use media to master their experience of tinnitus, lowering its perceived volume and giving themselves a sense of control by partially masking its sound. One well-known and effective program of habituation is Jastreboff and Hazell's tinnitus retraining therapy (TRT), which uses practical training and wearable broadband sound (noise) generators to "weaken the tinnitus signal at both the perceptual and subconscious levels" (2004, 16). Other programs and approaches use digital music or nonrepeating, fractal-based tone sequences instead of noise, but the combination of sound and counseling generally prevails. Renowned tinnitus researcher Robert Sweetow summarized the state of the art in a talk at the 2012 meeting of the American Academy of Audiology. There are three aspects of tinnitus that must be addressed, he said: the auditory, attentional, and emotional. The combination of counseling and sound enrichment treats all three, reducing the auditory contrast of the tinnitus to the environment, fostering a diminished level of attention to tinnitus, a less emotional response (what Jastreboff and Hazell call "habituation of reaction"), and, if possible, an eventual diminishment of actual perception ("habituation of perception") even when the sound enrichment device is removed (Jastreboff and Hazell 2004, 16; Sweetow 2012). TRT, progressive tinnitus management (PTM), Neuromonics, and similar kinds of remediating tinnitus all work roughly in this manner. Optimally, the person becomes habituated to the tinnitus, seldom noticing it or paying it any mind, no longer using media to manage the phantom sound.

In Joel Styzens's case, he contacted Meltzer because he was interested in Neuromonics, which he had read about on the internet. The Neuromonics program deploys counseling and an iPod-like device that combines soothing music with a masking noise tuned to the results of the patient's tinnitus pitch and volume test (figure 1.4). For months patients use the device for two to four hours a day, developing a relaxation response to the music and lowered perception of tinnitus. Eventually, the masking sound is removed, allowing the tinnitus sound to come through the music more clearly. In this stage, it is hoped that the relaxation response that the user has developed will occur even though the tinnitus is now clearly audible. The use of the device is a form of practice in which Joel would learn to retrain his attention and emotional response, letting go of the habitus of listening in which one monitors one's tinnitus for changes and retroactively evaluates one's personal choices in terms of the fluctuation of its sound.

Figure 1.4 The Neuro-monics Oasis.

Like other tinnitus sufferers inhabiting a mode of listening centered on choice, however, Joel was focused on the technology—in this case, the Neuromonics Oasis device—itself. "Neuromonics was $5,000. I didn't have the money, but I had a credit card and I slowly paid it off. At first, I was like, 'Wow, this new tech is a miracle device. I'll throw it on a card and fix my ears.' I had no idea it would be a drawn-out process." To some extent, the Australia-based Neuromonics company encourages this kind of thinking in its marketing by framing the device in terms of its rewiring of neural pathways: "A small, lightweight Oasis™ device with headphones delivers precisely designed music embedded with a pleasant acoustic neural stimulus. These sounds, customized for each user's audiological profile, stimulate the auditory pathway to promote neural plastic changes. Over time, these new connections help the brain filter out tinnitus disturbance, providing long-term relief from symptoms."[6]

Without the careful guidance of a skillful counseling audiologist, however, the patient is unlikely to develop these neurological changes. Regular meetings with Meltzer were included in the price Joel paid for Neuromonics and were as important as the device itself. These meetings framed the use of the device and encouraged a changed mode of listening in which Joel was not constantly "visiting the tinnitus," as Meltzer puts it. Meltzer also repeatedly used tests that objectified Styzens's suffering of tinnitus and hyperacusis. These included the written Tinnitus Handicap Inventory and the loudness tolerance test, in which Meltzer measures the loudest sound that a person with hyperacusis can tolerate. Although Joel originally expected the device itself to solve his problems, he was open to Meltzer's suggestions and faithfully came to their monthly meetings. He found it helpful to see external evidence of progress, even after months during which he thought he had floundered.

Through the Neuromonics program, Joel developed a sense of control and relaxation, allowing him to venture outside for the first time in two months. "What I found great about that was that it offered some relief and blocked out the ringing, so I could focus on other sounds," Styzens told me. "It became a comfort for me. I was able to get out of my house and deal with the sounds of the city environment. I would walk throughout the city for at least two hours every day with this device. I got used to the environmental sounds. I slowly started doing activities I did before." Despite the improvement, Styzens's progress was much slower than the eight months that Neuromonics claims is typical. It was more than a year before Joel was comfortable with Meltzer removing the white noise sound from Joel's Oasis. It was more than another year before Styzens had developed a comfortable enough listening relationship with his surroundings to stop using the device altogether. The entire process took two and a half years.

It was the combination of sound technology and techniques of listening that remediated Joel Styzens's cognitive-affective response to the sounds of his tinnitus and the city streets, helping him achieve a healthier equilibrium within himself and with his vibrational environment. As his fear diminished, he gradually stopped evaluating his choices in moving through the city and life in terms of their potential effects on his ears. Though he still has some trouble with hyperacusis, he has returned to his work as a music teacher and musician (albeit as an acoustic guitarist rather than a drummer). He has also taken on tinnitus and hyperacusis as a cause, starting a local support group and composing music inspired by his experience.

Joel's story shows the utility of orphic technologies in remediating a problematic network of relations, short-circuiting Styzens's tinnitus and hyperacusis. However, these changes were not mechanically deterministic. Instead, they facilitated—and were facilitated by—a reflexive change in Joel's stance on his aural experience. He had to do more than use the technology; he had to reflect upon a painful, vigilant form of listening that seemed completely natural, and let it go.

Elaine

Like Joel, Elaine went to Jill Meltzer's office with a particular technology in mind, a wearable sound generator. As a clinician, Meltzer is rather agnostic about the kind of technology her patients choose. In addition to Neuromonics, she is trained in a number of approaches to tinnitus. She has studied, for example, with Pawel Jastreboff, and frequently prescribes sound generators as part of Jastreboff's tinnitus reduction therapy, TRT. "If you would like to work with me, it isn't predicated on you buying any kind of device. I'm the tour guide. I'll help you build a tool kit," she told Elaine.

The audiologist stressed that the point of the technological options was to facilitate "making friends with your tinnitus." "Don't treat it as an enemy," she said to Elaine. "I think a lot about what happened to me and I get angry," Elaine responded. "I feel like my tinnitus can be healed. I've driven myself crazy trying to find cures. I exercise as much as I can, but that's hard for me." She recited all the techniques she had tried to get rid of her tinnitus. Nothing worked. "Don't try to outthink it," Meltzer responded. "The problem isn't that you have tinnitus, it's that it *bothers* you. You are constantly bombarded with bodily sensations all day, like the feeling of your rear in the chair right now. You don't pay special attention to it. That's how we want you to treat your tinnitus."

Jill Meltzer was stressing that changing Elaine's listening practices was the goal, while the type of media used to help facilitate this change was secondary. Her patient, however, seemed more interested in the tour of technological choices; she tried out several potential tools for her tool kit that day and heard about many more. The audiologist provided a dizzying array of options that ranged from free to thousands of dollars: fans, bubblers, mp3 downloads of white noise and nature sounds on iTunes and Amazon, smartphone apps such as Tinnitus Masker, a fractal tone–generating hearing aid called Widex Clear 440, relaxing music on Pandora or Grooveshark, and on and on. Elaine enthusiastically tried the Neuromonics Oasis unit, the Widex hearing aid, and a General Hearing Instruments Tranquil Simplicity OTE (Over the Ear) sound generator. When Meltzer discussed changing Elaine's cognitive approach to her tinnitus, however, Elaine seemed less engaged. She would quickly agree with the audiologist's words in a way that seemed preemptive, affirmatively responding before Meltzer had finished a sentence, as if to say, "Yes, I've heard all this before." This made me wonder if she was really taking in the practice suggestions the doctor was making. After her appointment, I asked Elaine what she found helpful or what she learned from the nearly three-hour evaluation and consultation. She said she had not learned much but she appreciated being able to try all of the technological options.

At a subsequent appointment, Elaine bought the Tranquil Simplicity sound generator she had tried at the first meeting, now tuned to the loudness of her tinnitus. A consumer pamphlet for hearing aid and sound generator manufacturer ReSound explains the role of the sound generator with the oft-used candle analogy. In a dark room, the candle seems to burn bright, dominating one's vision, but in a well-lit restaurant full of people, the same candle may hardly be noticed. Similarly, the steady-state noise of the wearable sound generator (figure 1.5) makes tinnitus less noticeable. Jastreboff stresses that the loudness of the sound generator should be set so that the tinnitus signal is still apparent—completely masking the signal will not allow for habituation. Rather, the idea is that when a person "visits their tinnitus" to check for potential fluctuations, the sound is indistinct and less worthy of attention and emotional response. In effect, the resolution of the tinnitus is lowered as part of a program designed to take the limbic and autonomic nervous systems out of the listening loop. Just as with Joel, Meltzer recommended a program of returning to her office for counseling and checking external measures such as the Tinnitus Handicap Inventory.

When I checked in with Elaine a year later, however, she had not been meeting with the audiologist to work on her listening practices or to check her THI. She did use the sound generator every day, finding it helpful, but not as helpful as she had hoped. "It depends on the day," she told me. "The tinnitus level fluctuates. On bad days, the sound generator doesn't help, but on good days it does." Elaine said she had also been using Chinese herbs and acupuncture, which, along with the sound generator, had changed the quality of her tinnitus. What used to be a teakettle sound now fluctuated into buzzing and other kinds of sounds. She was still listening carefully to it.

Clearly, I have set up a contrast in which Joel "got it," engaging in media practices that eventually changed his habitus of listening and restored his freedom and mobility; Elaine, on the other hand, remained stuck in a habit of listening that perpetuated her suffering. My interest, however, is not to laud the former and blame or psychologize the latter. Unlike some psychologists and at least one tinnitus self-help book (Hogan and Battaglino 2010, 25), I do not speculate about "secondary gains" (indirect benefits of illness) in tinnitus. As seen in the counseling aspect of tinnitus audiology, a psychological understanding of tinnitus can be a useful technology in helping subjects accept or withstand its sound. Psychology does not, however, provide

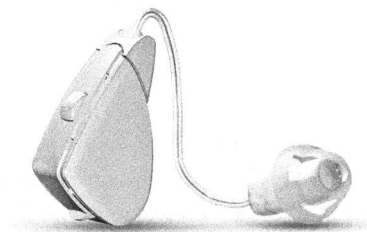

Figure 1.5 A ReSound wearable sound generator, which looks like a hearing aid but actually suppresses the sound of tinnitus with noise.

an elevated vantage point from which to scan all the networks that mediate the experience of these two individuals and make them more or less amenable to the remediations Jill Meltzer had to offer.

Moreover, if we chalked the difference in Joel and Elaine's stories up to "gumption," "willpower," or some other moral force, we would then have to ask how one person came to have this mysterious quality and the other did not. It is impossible to fully retrace the lines of causality that allowed Joel, Meltzer, the audiometer, and the Neuromonics Oasis to short the neuronal circuit that had developed between his auditory pathways and limbic and autonomic nervous systems—lines extend far beyond Joel himself. The same can be said of the plethora of factors that caused Elaine to listen to her tinnitus, but not to Meltzer's practical suggestions. As I wrote at the outset of this chapter, different practices of listening, ways of thinking, and material conditions produce different tinnituses and different suffering.

....

There are some ironies involved in the foregoing story of tinnital techniques and technologies. Perhaps the greatest irony is that, in order to restore the patient's perceived agency as a free, unencumbered self, the audiologist and her digital allies must help the patient give up on being free from, and unencumbered by, tinnitus. In order to make the patient free once again, they must enable the patient to let go of freedom of choice as a habitus of listening.

The orphic techniques used in this effort present a second irony: In Meltzer's clinical practice, orphic media are used make tinnitus easier to ignore by weakening its presence as an object, but in order to do this, Meltzer first *strengthens* tinnitus as an object, materializing its "false" sound in the objective measures and reproductions of audiometry. This allows her to tune devices such as the Neuromonics Oasis and check for progress in the future (though it should be noted that Jastreboff and Hazell's TRT does not require audiometric tinnitus matching, since it uses broadband noise that can accommodate any tinnitus pitch and volume).

A third irony: Orphic technologies are helpful only insofar as they help patients stop fixating on how free they are to choose what they hear, yet audiology presents itself to patients as a marketplace of choices. The practice of audiology has historically centered on the sale of hearing aids, sound generators, and other devices—and every year there are more choices on the market competing for attention. The entire structure of audiology as a capitalist enterprise is built around the research, development, and sale of these media devices. The large, elaborate display booths erected by hearing aid manufacturers at the annual conference of the American Academy of Audiology would not look out of place at International CES (formerly known as the Consumer Electronics Show). An audiologist like Meltzer, who tries to decenter devices in favor of technique, is working against the grain of both audiological history and consumer expectations, as I saw when her patient Elaine got lost in the supermarket of remedial media. Ontologically, the experience of tinnitus is a fluctuating set of relations, but in terms of everyday empiricism, tinnitus is a thing and a self is a self. When people with tinnitus walk through Meltzer's door, they want to buy something to defeat it, so they can feel like themselves again.

Part II. Masking

The room was very quiet. I walked over to the TV set
and turned it on to a dead channel—white noise at maximum
decibels, a fine sound for sleeping, a powerful continuous
hiss to drown out everything strange.

—**Hunter S. Thompson,** *Fear and Loathing in Las Vegas*

2

Sleep-Mates and Sound Screens

Sound, Speed, and Circulation in Postwar America

> Thus considered, what a strange chaos is this wide atmosphere
> we breathe!
> —**Charles Babbage**, in *Making Noise: From Babel to
> the Big Bang and Beyond*, by Hillel Schwartz

Like any good creation tale, the genesis story of the electromechanical
sound conditioner is both beloved and contested among those whose lives it
has most changed. If one were to weigh equally the versions told by owners,
family members, and employees of the Marpac Corporation, past and present, it would be impossible to stage a definitive reenactment of the sound
conditioner's conception, though it would be possible to assemble a telling
collection of sounds, spaces, objects, and people. The setting is a room in a
nameless roadside motel, somewhere in America, circa 1960—that much
and that little seems agreed upon. The protagonist is a lone traveling salesman . . . *or a young married couple on vacation*. The main set element is a
broken window-mounted air conditioner of the sort still seen in some

motels today . . . *or was it a broken circular fan?* The conflict: the rumble and roar of trucks on the adjacent highway—*or was it an all-night poker game in the next room?*—kept the would-be sleeper(s) tossing and turning all night. Then a moment of sleep-deprived inspiration: "If I only had the sound of that broken A/C (*fan*) to block out that noise," said the salesman('s *wife*), "I'd be sound asleep right now. Certainly I (*you*) could design something to make that sound, couldn't I (*you*)?" Whatever the details, it was in such a moment, in such a transient space penetrated by the uncontrolled sounds of strangers, that a sleepless self conceived a new technology of sonic mediation.

The man in that noisy motel room, James K. Buckwalter, was both a personable salesman and an inveterate tinkerer. While he excelled on the business side, eventually rising to the position of vice president of sales at the Wooster Rubber Company (now known as Rubbermaid), he was also the inventor of patented Wooster products such as the rubberized dishwasher rack and rubber auto floor mats. Those closest to the origin story, Buckwalter's spouse, Gertrude "Trudy" Buckwalter, and his protégée and eventual successor as Marpac president, Dave Theissen, affirm that Mrs. Buckwalter was there that sleepless night as well. Despite her absence from the official narrative on the Marpac website, it was she, they told me, who had the idea of what they would come to call *sound conditioning*.

When the couple returned home, "Buck" began experimenting with a few household items: a plywood-and-carpet-padding base he cut into a circle, the electrical supply and motor from a record turntable, fan blades he cut from a coffee can lid, and a housing made from a tin saucepan (*or dog dish, according to the company website*). Buckwalter plugged his device into an electrical outlet and listened—the blades inside the pan (*dish*) whirred, circulating air in the housing and creating a muted whooshing sound. Using a "church key" can opener, Buckwalter made some openings in the housing, which increased both the volume and the frequency spectrum of the device. That night the Buckwalters slept with the device on their nightstand, just as they did the next night, and the one after that (figure 2.1). The device was the basis a new patent—this one in Buckwalter's own name—and a new company, founded in 1962. Briefly called Buck Manufacturing, then renamed Tru-Buck (a combination of the couple's nicknames), the company has been known since 1968 as Marpac. Today, the original sound conditioner sits encased in the lobby of the company's unassuming offices and production facility in Rocky Point, North Carolina. It still works if you plug it in.

The media scholar reading this story may be tempted at this point to thank the author for an amusing anecdote and be on her way. Perhaps this

Figure 2.1 The original sound conditioner, housed in a tin saucepan. Photo by author.

invention rates a footnote in a history of home technologies,[1] but it hardly seems germane to a book on media. This is, after all, the story of a fan that doesn't blow air and a turntable that doesn't play music—it's practically an artifact of technological *de*volution, not a media technology. Nevertheless, I would argue that this whooshing saucepan *is* a media device. In its orphic ability to sonically reconfigure the spatial and affective relations between subjects and objects in its environment, this whooshing saucepan crystalizes one of the mediating capacities also found in the phonograph, radio, mp3 player, and other media technologies.

Returning to the three sonic potentials described in the introduction, the sound conditioner differs from electronic and electroacoustic media in that it is an electromechanical device rather than a transductive device. That is, like Orpheus's lyre, it remediates the ambient medium of sound by directly generating mechanical waves—not by transducing and manipulating sound waves as raw material for subsequent playback through a speaker or earphone. In the academic tradition of media studies, this distinction makes all the difference in the world, but in terms of the "empty" media practices that I study, it is a distinction without a difference. In fact, understanding this most basic of electrical devices will help to isolate the orphic properties and uses of electronic media with greater specificity.

Clearly, treating "a fan in a pan" as a media device is a bit of a provocation. If we let this object into the media studies tent, wouldn't we have to admit just about anything? The truthful answer is, "maybe so." Admittedly, things get a bit messy in the shift from thinking about media as a prespecified group of technologies to thinking about them as objects and processes associated with mediating practices. However, this messiness is needed if we are to understand the full range of spatial and temporal relations involved in orphic mediation. As Jody Berland has noted, media users

> are not simply listeners to sound, or watchers of images, but occupants of spaces for listening and watching who, by being there, help to produce definite meanings and effects. These "spaces for listening" proliferate and fragment continuously with the development of new audio technologies. Technological and social changes combine to make them more diverse, more mobile, and more omnipresent. Such changes represent complex negotiations between corporations, consumers, producers, desires, and everyday life. (2009, 132)

For example, as sound scholar Tim Anderson has shown, during the same postwar period in which the sound conditioner emerged, American producers of hi-fi music had to figure out how to represent space in the new medium, while consumers had to figure out how to integrate this sonic medium into the space of the home (2006). By bracketing the textuality of media technology use, the study of orphic media focuses attention on the material and sensory nature of these spatial proliferations and fragmentations; moreover, it highlights how media create not just spaces for listening, but spaces for *not* listening. If we take the fan in a pan seriously, an alternate history of sound media emerges, one less about media "making sense" than about media remaking *sensation*. In this history, the sound conditioner marks a shift when the passive noise attenuation of architectural fixes and earplugs was joined by new electric means of altering the sonic shape of lived space.

Performatively, the fan in the pan functioned in the Buckwalters' bedroom as a mediator, something that can "transform, translate, distort, and modify" relations of meaning and/or material elements, reshaping how subjects and objects come into being through their associations with one another (Latour 2005, 39). When the window air conditioner failed to function, the resulting assemblage of sounds, spaces, objects, and people in that motel room included the sleepless Buckwalters, who were inspired to invent a simple device with the power to remediate such complex sonic assemblages.

In this chapter, I study the history, production, patent, and marketing of the sound conditioner to learn about the technological assemblage of subjective-spatial relations in the American home. Drawing on Don Ihde's schema of sensory technics, I argue that sound conditioners became a sensible way of "domesticating noise"—putting it to work in the home—precisely because the home and the spaces around it had already become penetrated and destabilized by new flows of technological circulation, flows driven by the military and economic exigencies of World War II and postwar America. Nevertheless, it took discursive work to integrate sound conditioners into millions of American homes—in particular, Marpac's mechanical noise needed to be patented, naturalized, feminized, and brought into the home-making practices of American women through *metaculture*, discourse that facilitates the circulation of cultural objects (Urban 2001). This metaculture has changed over the decades, as the noise generator has been increasingly accepted as a normal—even "natural"—domestic appliance.

Microperception in the Soundscape of Modernity

For a time after Buck invented the sound conditioner in 1960 or 1961, the fan in the pan simply did its job on the Buckwalters' own nightstand, raising the noise floor of their bedroom in the Elkhart, Indiana, home they shared with their three children.[2] Eventually, however, family and friends got wind of the device and began requesting their own, inspiring Buckwalter to re-design the unit for commercial production. According to both Dave Theissen and the Buckwalters' daughter Janet Zimmerman, it was actually during this early production period that Buckwalter moved from the original tin saucepan to using plastic dog dishes for the housing. Buckwalter cut multiple holes into the sides of the dishes and fitted them one inside the other to create a rotatable outer sleeve; by twisting the sleeve, the user could change the alignment of the holes in the inner and outer sleeves, altering the volume and frequency characteristics of the circulating air. The result was a more modern-looking, user-controllable sound machine. Soon, the entire Buckwalter family was working in a basement assembly line installing c-frame motors (typically used in bathroom exhaust fans) and fan blades in the dog-dish housing. By this time, Buckwalter had been working as a marketing consultant for other inventors and had managed to land a few products in the Sears Roebuck catalog. Encouraged by these successes and the enthusiasm others expressed for his machine, Buckwalter began seeking investors and designed an even sleeker, mass-producible version of the device, which he pitched to Sears Roebuck.

On February 11, 1964, James K. Buckwalter of Elkhart, Indiana, and 10 percent stakeholder William F. Lahey of Wooster, Ohio, were awarded the patent for their "Sleep-Inducing Sound-Producing Device." Lahey purchased his share with $5,000, which enabled Buckwalter to buy injection molds for custom plastic housings, creating a more polished-looking product that took less time to produce than the dog-dish sleeves (figures 2.2 and 2.3). Production speed was now of the essence, as Sears Roebuck had decided to carry the product in their *Big Book* catalog (figure 2.4). Buck rented an oversized, dual-bay garage that had been used to paint mobile homes, converting one bay into an office and assembly area and the other side into a shipping and receiving warehouse. The Buckwalter children worked after school assembling the units. Trudy was both assembly line worker and receptionist, directing calls to the company's purchasing agent, president, and others, all of whom had different names, but all of whom were in reality Jim Buckwalter. Through this assemblage of family, friends, fictional entities, salesmanship, ingenuity, rental property, mechanical parts, catalog circulation, and patent law, "sleep-inducing sound-producing devices" began to find their way into bedrooms around the country. The Buckwalters named their new product the "Sleep-Mate."

Robert Carlyle's soundproofed study and Hugo Gernsback's Isolator were—pardon the joke—isolated cases, respectively expensive and ridiculous failures to control modes of sonic affect in the nineteenth and early twentieth centuries. In contrast, by 1966, the Sleep-Mate made its way into the catalog that practically defined the standard contents of the American home. Today, the Sleep-Mate and its offspring are used daily (or at least nightly) in millions of American homes. Dave Theissen estimates Marpac had sold at least two million electromechanical devices by the time he sold the company in 2010, while the new owners, Jimmy Sloan and Gordon Wallace, report strongly increasing sales. Buckwalter and Theissen would also invent analog and digital nightstand machines that emulated the Sleep-Mate's "white noise" and added sounds such as ocean surf. While the electromechanical device has never been successfully imitated, competing electronic sound machines have proliferated, eclipsing the mechanical version in sales. Combined, these devices represent a significant chunk of what one market research firm calls "personal therapy sensory devices," a market that exceeded $1 billion in 2006.[3]

Figures 2.2 and 2.3 An early model of Buckwalter's sound conditioner. Photos by author.

What technological and sensory changes between Carlyle's time and our own have made orphic practices more possible, useful, and necessary? Answers are present in the collection of sounds, spaces, objects, and people assembled in the sound conditioner's creation tale: the roadside motel, the trucks on the road, the air conditioner, the sleepless listeners themselves. Both the problem and the solution in the tale were shaped by what Emily Thompson calls "the soundscape of modernity," a set of sensory-spatial conditions that arose with the turn of the twentieth century, changing both sound and listening over its first few decades. Sound changed, in part, because of "technological mediation," a catchphrase that Thompson uses to refer not only to the phonograph, radio, and the like, but also to architectural forms and materials used to control the behavior of sound in space. Listening was changing as well, as people conceived, deployed, and evaluated the results of new forms of sonic mediation and control (2002, 2).

This coevolution of technology and sensory engagement is the central theme of Don Ihde's *postphenomenology*—which I will briefly describe and position with regard to the study of media before using it as a frame for the changing sonic-spatial relations in postwar America. In books such as

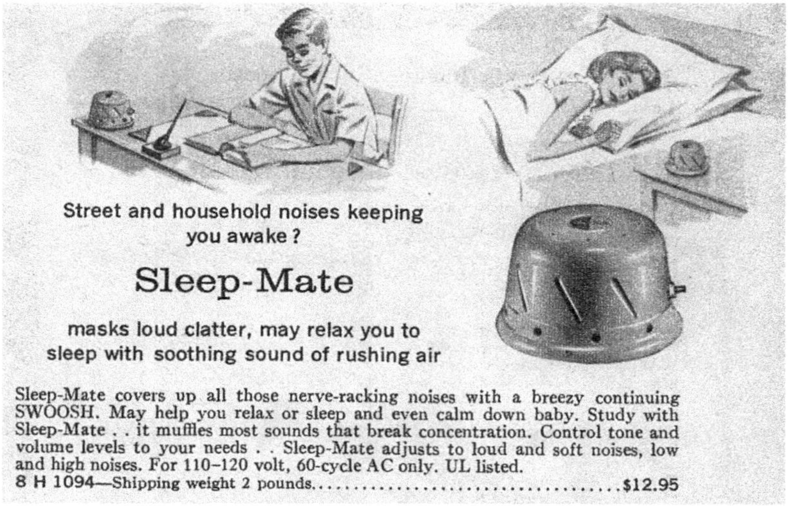

Street and household noises keeping
you awake ?

Sleep-Mate

masks loud clatter, may relax you to
sleep with soothing sound of rushing air

Sleep-Mate covers up all those nerve-racking noises with a breezy continuing SWOOSH. May help you relax or sleep and even calm down baby. Study with Sleep-Mate . . it muffles most sounds that break concentration. Control tone and volume levels to your needs . . Sleep-Mate adjusts to loud and soft noises, low and high noises. For 110–120 volt, 60-cycle AC only. UL listed.
8 H 1094—Shipping weight 2 pounds...$12.95

Figure 2.4 The Sleep-Mate in Sears Roebuck's fall/winter 1966–67 catalog. Image courtesy of the Browne Popular Culture Library, Bowling Green State University.

Technology and the Lifeworld (1990) and *Postphenomenology* (1993), Ihde examines the human–technology relationship as both embodied and cultural, informed by the "microperceptions" of bodies in motion (associated with the phenomenology of Edmund Husserl and Maurice Merleau-Ponty) and the "macroperceptual" influence of history and cultural context (associated with the hermeneutics of Martin Heidegger and Michel Foucault). Postphenomenology may at first seem a poor fit for an affective approach to media. Deleuze criticized phenomenology for assuming the existence of an already formed subject whose consciousness is always directed toward something else—what Husserl called the essential "intentionality" of consciousness (Smith and McIntyre 1982). "To the phenomenologists 'consciousness is always *of* something' (cognitive prefit)," Massumi writes, "Deleuze responds 'consciousness always *is* something' (ontological emergence)" (1998, emphasis his). Then again, this difference arises precisely from the fact that Deleuze was influenced by—and sought to transform—the work of phenomenologists such as Jean-Paul Sartre, Heidegger, and Merleau-Ponty (Guenzel 2014). Like Deleuze, Ihde moves away from "traditional" phenomenology to examine the interplay between bodies writ large. For Ihde, not only subjects, but also technologies have intentionalities—and it is in the material interplay between subjects and technological objects that experiences of "lifeworlds" emerge. Yet we could just as easily describe Ihde's lifeworlds as the emergence of subjects and objects themselves, as phenomenology and ontology codependently arise.[4]

Ihde divides technological mediation into four major types of human–technology relationships or *technics*—small-scale practices through which subjects' perception of their lifeworld (their experience of reality) emerges. The first of these is *embodiment relations*, which expresses the sort of symbiosis that can occur between a human body and an appropriately functioning artifact such as a hammer, telescope, or hearing aid—all of which extend an embodied potential or ability of the user. To use the classic example from Heidegger, a hammer becomes "ready-to-hand," in use, withdrawing from perception as an object separate from its user, and becoming instead a seamless means of perceiving and affecting the world (1962, 101). Ihde deploys an audio media metaphor to explain the ways these technologies mediate users' microperceptual relationship to the environment, describing an amplification/reduction structure in which "with every amplification, there is a simultaneous and necessary reduction" (1979, 21). For example, the telephone spatially extends hearing while also reducing hearing's acuity in terms of signal-to-noise ratio and range of frequency response. Users seldom notice, let alone mind, these trade-offs, Ihde claims, as "fascination attaches to magnification, amplification, enhancement," while "what is concealed may be forgotten" (1990, 78). For the media scholar concerned with affect, these embodiment relations are an essential site for investigating modes of affectivity. In what ways do specific media amplify and reduce affective intensities? What modes of embodiment relations do they afford?

Traditional media scholarship, however, tends to focus on the second of Ihde's technics, *hermeneutic relations*, which entail the reading or interpretation of the technological artifact, as seen in print, technical gauges, film, and computer code. Whereas embodiment relations rely upon an isomorphism between human and artifact, in hermeneutic relations the subject profits not from an *amplification* of human sensory modalities but from the *differences* in perception that textual inscription, translation, manipulation, and interpretation afford. For example, the reading on a thermometer gives access to a different manifestation of heat or cold than does the skin. Nevertheless, it is important to note the continuities between hermeneutic relations and embodiment relations. Just as a text has a relation to a real or imagined world, a human body must inhabit a material relation to the textual artifact in order to "see through it" and access or cultivate the world of the text. Just as a telescope is meant to transparently recede as an object to reveal a world beyond, so do signifiers become transparent to reveal their referential worlds.

Some new media scholarship implicitly focuses on Ihde's third technics, *alterity relations*. In this mode, the dynamic of transparency/opacity changes: the artifact retains its "objectness" to become the terminus of attention itself, something approaching an "other," as seen in examples such as sacred objects, mechanical automata, video games, or artificial intelligence (AI).[5] The famed Turing test, in which true AI is said to be achieved if it fools us into believing it is human, could be understood as a test of alterity relations—does the computer succeed in achieving full alterity from the subject's perspective? But in fact, from an affective perspective, alterity relations raise a more important question than does the Turing test: not "Does the AI fool me?" but "Do I affectively engage with it *as human*, even if I know it isn't?" (We might think of our relationships with Siri or Alexa, for example.) Focusing on alterity relations can counterbalance information discourse, which tends to erase alterity by understanding both human and AI as self-organized information: the notion of alterity retains the humanistic orientation derived from its phenomenological roots.

To understand a specific medium *materially*, one can attempt to situate it within this suite of embodiment, hermeneutic, and alterity technics and place it in its spatial contexts of architectural, mechanical, electric, and electronic technology. The soundscape of modernity was paradoxical in that it consisted of a proliferation of human and technological intentionalities: the circulation of sound had never been so controllable nor provided such a variety of pleasures, but it also sounded out of any individual's control—a sonic context in which fighting sound with sound would increasingly come to make sense. And yet, though the sound conditioner makes intuitive sense, it is little discussed or paid attention to in comparison to the radio, Spotify, or other sonic media we engage with in everyday life. Perhaps fittingly, the privatization and individualization of domestic environments that orphic media provide seem to be intuited as private and individual phenomena, not as a widespread response to our similar neurophysiological, historical, and spatial conditions.

To understand this obscured aspect of orphic mediation, we turn to Ihde's fourth and final major technics, *background relations*, which are the least considered relations with regard to media technologies and the type that I aim to foreground in this book. Examples of background technologies include shelters such as caves or houses, as well as lighting, refrigeration, heating, and air conditioning. Unlike the technologies mentioned earlier, these do not function along a transparency/opacity continuum; rather, they take on "a background or field position" in experience, a "present absence" that envelops the subject and provides much of the lived world's "techno-logical texturing" (1990, 108–9). Sound plays a large role in Ihde's description of these background relations: "In the electric home, there is virtually a constant hum of one sort or the other, which is part of the technological texture. Ordinarily, this 'white noise' may go unnoticed, although I am always reassured that it remains part of fringe awareness, as when guests visit my mountain home in Vermont. The inevitable comment is about the silence of the woods. At once, the absence of background hum becomes noticeable" (109).

Just as the hammer's opaque, independent materiality is noticed when it breaks and is no longer transparently ready to hand, the "absent presence" of background "white noise" is foregrounded when it is missing—when the power goes out or the refrigerator dies. In moments of breakdown such as these, we get a sense of technologies' intentionalities, their praxis-shaping presence in our interactions with the world:

> Different technologies texture environments differently. They exhibit unique forms of non-neutrality through the different ways in which they are interlinked with the human lifeworld. Background technologies, no less than focal ones, transform the gestalts of human experience and, pre-cisely because they are absent presences, may exert more subtle indirect effects upon the way a world is experienced. There are also involvements both with wider circles of connection and amplification/reduction selec-tivities that may be discovered in the roles of background relations. (112)

The Sleep-Mate reflects and repurposes this technological texture of every-day life. The whooshing saucepan entered into and remediated a set of background technological mediations already present in the Buckwalters' home, each of which embodied its own preexisting technological inten-tionality: the thick walls and physical separation of their suburban house, the drone of their refrigerator, and the atmospheric control of their HVAC system. These mediations create what Ihde calls the "technological cocoon" of the modern home, the specific site within which people seek to engage others and their world through media technologies such as radio, television, telephone, and internet.[6]

In the interactions of these technological intentionalities and desires, different presences and absences, transparencies and opacities, emerge: for example, subjects may disappear the presence of their own bodies and that of the television as they engage a fictional otherness through the se-miotic and technological transparency of TV—only to run aground on the stubbornly opaque presence of an interrupted satellite signal or the seldom-ready-to-hand complexity of a "universal" remote control. They may enjoy the pleasures of the automotive cocoon (Bijsterveld et al. 2013) while also contributing to the noise that keeps would-be sleepers awake in a road-side motel, thus inspiring the invention of a new noise-making technology. Michel Serres' (2007) insight that the noise of communicative interruptions is itself productive of new forms of order applies here, as new problems generate new technological presences with their own intentionalities, pleasures, and problems to control—the proliferation and fragmentation of mediated spaces that Berland describes. In the technologically textured home, so often centered on a praxis of control and a panoply of choices that delight and disrupt, it makes sense that *the background itself* would come to the fore as a new kind of mediating technology—not merely an absent presence, but an absent presence intended to *facilitate the absence of unwanted presences.*

Speed, Circulation, and Macroperception

James Buckwalter gained intimate knowledge of the soporific background hum and whoosh of motorized, circulating blades long before he designed the Sleep-Mate. As a World War II U.S. Navy pilot, he flew a Consolidated Aircraft PBY Catalina off the coast of Belem, Brazil. A long-range "flying boat" capable of sea takeoff and landing, the PBY's twin propellers were located above and slightly behind the cockpit, where they were free from aquatic immersion, but quite near the head and body of the pilot (figure 2.5). For the pilot, a propeller airplane is both a bodily extension (embodiment relation) that enables flight and a "technological cocoon" (background relation) that houses and protects the airborne body while enveloping it in drone and vibration. Marpac's vice president of production, Mac McCoy, told me about the tranquilizing influence the PBY had on Marpac's founder during submarine reconnaissance missions. McCoy began at the company in 1981, the year after "Mr. B" retired from day-to-day operations, but he knew Buckwalter and gives the PBY its own role in company's creation story: "On some of these flights . . . he remembered he'd get that *woom-woom-woom* of the engine and he said it would just about knock [him] out. He'd get settled back [in the plane] and the drone of that engine would just about put [him] out." McCoy believes that this wartime memory made Buck more amenable to Trudy Buckwalter's idea that sleepless night in the motel: "They say necessity

Figure 2.5 The Consolidated Aircraft PBY Catalina, a soporific wartime flying machine.

is the mother of invention and Mrs. B came up with a comment and Mr. B came up with a line [of products]."

Materially, fossil fuel–powered mechanical and electrical technologies caused the blades of both the PBY and the Sleep-Mate to whirl, spinning out the vibrational cocoon of aircraft and bedroom alike. But what else animated those circulating blades? In this section I will turn to Ihde's concept of macroperception to argue that the World War II era's accelerated and militarized practices of circulation strongly reshaped relations to sound and space in the United States.

In Ihde's formulation, microperception takes its form only within the context of macroperception, or cultural hermeneutics. Inspired by Foucault's *episteme*, the epistemological conditions that structure what is knowable in a given era (2002), macroperception denotes evolving and historically situated discourses or frameworks of practice and interpretation. Ihde emphasizes the essential "interrelationality" between the micro and macro: "[T]here is no bare or isolated microperception except in its field of hermeneutic or macroperceptual surrounding; nor may macroperception have any focus without its fulfillment in microperceptual (bodily-sensory) experience" (1993, 77). Just as perceiving subjects and perceived objects emerge through one another in mediating practices, so do technological and cultural intentionalities mediate one another. This interplay makes technologies "multistable," meaning "not only that artifacts can have different meanings in different contexts, but also that specific goals can be technologically realized in different ways by a range of artifacts" (Verbeek 2005, 136). The soundscape of modernity, then, emerged in the interplay between individual moments of technological mediation and the longer histories of belief, practice, and power that structured those moments.

As a microperceptual practice, orphic media use arises in the context of modern material spaces rationalized and abstracted to accelerate the circulation of subjects, objects, and information. As Marxist geographers and critics have indicated, an evolving spatial macroperception informed Enlightenment efforts to rationalize space, culminating in the eventual proliferation of transportation and communication technologies that profoundly changed humans' spatiotemporal relations to their environment, perceptually shrinking and fragmenting the world at once (Harvey 2003, 254–59). The spaces modernity produces are often contradictory, providing a certain mastery and control of the world at the macro level while also undermining the sense of self-mastery and control at the level of microperception. Quite often, we uneasily inhabit these spaces of circulation. The roadside motel where the Buckwalters spent that sleepless night was meant to provide motorists with fast and easy access to accommodation and relaxation, yet the noise of circulating highway traffic left them unable to sleep. Conversely, the circulating blades of Buckwalter's PBY were intended to give him mastery over space on submarine reconnaissance missions, yet the vibrational noise of those blades could degrade his attentional duty of surveillance.

Both the motel and the PBY were built in service of *speed*, which is of the essence in warfare and the guiding logic of capitalist spatial practices. In warfare, personnel, weapons, and supplies must be deployed as quickly as possible; in peacetime, commercial logistics becomes an organizing principle of modern life. In both settings, speed does violence to landscapes, social cohesion, the political power of the *demos*, and our modes of sensory perception and experience. Surprisingly, Paul Virilio's critique *Speed and Politics* (1986) pays little attention to the *sonic* dimensions of speed and warfare. In the case of pilot Jim Buckwalter's PBY, for example, increasing speed by doubling the velocity of the propeller's rotation would have created a sixty-four-fold increase in sound pressure (Fehr and Wells 1955), indicating an exponential relationship between circulatory speed and acoustic noise. Such aircraft noise can be heard as evidence for Virilio's claims that speed is a form of assault and that "violence can be reduced to nothing but movement," especially since aeronautical innovation is so often the brain-child of the military-industrial complex (1986, 38). Aerodynamic noise is an unavoidable by-product of the movement of goods and bodies at high speeds, which causes air molecules to compress and expand, generating a sound that reminds us of our physical embodiedness and the resistances of gravity and air. Prolonged exposure to high aerodynamic and machine noise levels affects human health, elevating levels of stress and antisocial behavior (Kryter 1994), suggesting that the human body has sonic-affective limits that human–machine movement can transgress.

To illustrate how World War II and the economic boom that followed it would necessitate new forms of noise control in response to the spatial-affective results of speed, we can briefly examine the career of Buckwalter's better-known noise-taming contemporary, acoustician Leo Beranek. As Jonathan Sterne (2012) has shown, by the time of Buckwalter's patent application in 1963, the "domestication" of noise—that is, its conversion from an unwanted industrial by-product into a useful resource—was well under way in the research labs of psychologists, acousticians, and telecommunications engineers, particularly at Harvard, MIT, and Bell Laboratories. While Sterne emphasizes the communications industry's role in the domestication of noise, military aviation played at least as important a role. Beranek, the father of American noise control and architectural acoustics, began his noise research with a commission from the U.S. Air Force and the National Defense Research Committee (NRDC) in 1940. In those early days of World War II, American pilots flying B-17s with British markings on long bombing raids over Germany reported high fatigue and communications difficulty due to propeller noise, which Beranek combated with sound-absorptive materials (developed using Corning's new fiberglass) and improved headphones and microphones (Beranek 1989). During the war, Beranek led Harvard's Electro-Acoustic Laboratory, where, among other things, he developed the anechoic chamber now standard in acoustical and audiological research, initially used to test experimental high-intensity acoustic weaponry intended for the battlefield (Lang and Maling 2014). Combined with colleague J. C. R. Licklider's physiological and psychological research at Harvard's Psycho-Acoustic Laboratory (Alperin et al. 2001), Beranek's wartime research laid the groundwork for subsequent innovations in sound absorption, speaker and microphone design, architectural acoustics, and other areas (Beranek 1949).

Like Buckwalter, Beranek would follow his wartime experience with propeller noise by experimenting with the sound of circulating air indoors. In

1946, he left Harvard to become an associate professor at MIT and technical director of MIT's Acoustics Laboratory under director Richard Bolt, where he created a dedicated fan noise lab. In 1948, Beranek and Bolt would join with Bolt's former student Robert Newman to create the renowned acoustical consulting firm BBN, which would go on to design the acoustics of the United Nations Assembly Hall; implement the military's internet forerunner, ARPANET (thanks to Licklider, who was hired in 1957); help pass and implement the U.S. Noise Control Act of 1972; and lead the way in using noise to fight noise in American open-plan offices. Unaware of one another but working within the same wartime and postwar culture of macroperception, both Beranek and Buckwalter would come to isolate noise as a problem and deploy it as a solution—one working scientifically at the heart of the military-industrial-academic complex, the other working intuitively at its periphery.

The noise of war may have had an additional influence on Buckwalter's mechanical mediation of sound and subjectivity. The close proximity of the engines to the PBY's poorly insulated fuselage (Creed 1985, 37), combined with long and frequent periods of flight time, would likely have induced noise-related hearing loss. As one former pilot states, "Noise in the PBY didn't seem to be an issue with the U.S. Navy until we were all near deaf from sitting between those very loud radial engines."[7] Tinnitus frequently results from such noise exposure. Due to the noise of munitions and logistics in World War II, military hearing loss and tinnitus were widespread and severe enough to catalyze the birth of audiology as a profession in the United States, as researchers and clinicians designed and fitted returning veterans with another unsung media device, the hearing aid (Katz 2002). As already discussed, tinnitus sufferers have been among the most avid users of devices such as the Sleep-Mate, in part because tinnitus tends to become more apparent at night in the relative quiet of the bedroom. When I asked Trudy Buckwalter whether her late husband had tinnitus, she replied, "I think he did. Not to the extreme, [but] he would turn up the sound machine a little more than I did." If Buckwalter did have tinnitus, it would be just one more signal that the aural history of noise generation and control, like the histories of the tape recorder and the vocoder (Tompkins 2010), is inseparable from that of World War II and its circulatory sonic excesses.

In the wake of this wartime noise, came new, economically motivated increases and innovations in the speed and spread of circulation, which spun off new forms of postwar *quiet*. Two economically motivated forms of circulation—the interstate highway system and air conditioning—spread through the United States in the postwar era, encouraging families to move into the suburbs and the Sun Belt. "Nuclear families," thicker walls and windows, larger housing plots, separate commercial and residential zones, and suburban cul-de-sacs reconditioned middle-class Americans' listening in the second half of the twentieth century. These factors tuned American ears for the "separation, division, and clarity" that "form the spatial expressions found within the suburb" (LaBelle 2010, 57). Moreover, as Buckwalter's preferred marketing term, *sound conditioner*, indicates, the cooling *whoosh* of air conditioning also contributed to a growing sense that one's atmosphere could and should be controlled and privatized.[8]

Blackboxing Noise: Patents as Metaculture

In order for a technology of microperceptual control to become a useful medium, it must be made meaningful within its macroperceptual cultural context. In the second half of this chapter, I examine two kinds of discourse—the patent and advertising—through which Marpac has integrated its device into the cultural meanings and practices of the American home. A cultural object does not circulate on its own—it needs additional, discursive cultural productions to help it do so. Greg Urban calls such productions *metaculture*, discourse that focuses consciousness onto cultural objects in order to ensure their movement through space-time. In capitalist, novelty-seeking modernity, metacultural discourse promotes or evaluates new objects in terms of their uniqueness. Advertising touts the uniqueness of a product, for example, while a film review evaluates how skillfully a film combines and innovates upon preexisting elements of film history. Metaculture, then, is discourse that allows objects to compete for attention, create consumer interest, and reshape social space. But of course, for metacultural texts to be useful, they must make sense within—and appeal to—prevailing ideologies (Urban 2001).

Methodologically, studying the metaculture around the sound conditioner allows us to combine attention to the material, affective dimensions of media technologies with close readings of texts to form a mutually supportive strategy. Metacultural analysis helps us better discern the affective understandings of sound, space, self, and sociality built into the sound conditioner by its makers when it was new and map the changing meanings of the device across time. Moreover, the device's patent citations provide access to a history of earlier sonic-affective technologies.

Like all patents, Jim Buckwalter's "Sleep-Inducing Sound-Producing Device" (1964) is inscribed as a reflexive moment in its culture of production, a moment in which the Sleep-Mate's creator stepped back to describe it, situating it within social and industrial contexts in order to show that it was both new and useful. For the cultural scholar, then, a patent does more than illuminate the inventor's conception of the invention—it also sheds light on her conception of its users and their environment. Both the reflexivity of patents and the intent behind them—facilitating the production and circulation of new technologies—make them examples of metaculture. However, unlike Urban's examples of film and advertising, patents are not written for consumers but rather for regulators, who impose their own editorial influence on the final text.

Once granted by the patent agent, Marpac's patent staked out conceptual, spatial, and temporal turf to ensure the Sleep-Mate's proprietary circulation. However, in order to be successful, the patent application had to situate its object's novelty within the already done, making reference to prior patents in such a way as to legitimize the new object within preexisting traditions of utility. In this regard, patents are an important aspect of "science in action," efforts that turn claims into *facts* or new technologies into taken-for-granted *black boxes* (Latour 1987). The truth or utility of scientific statements and technologies are always determined by future use—they become facts or black boxes only when they are accepted and incorporated into subsequent research and technologies. Successful patents are similar to successful academic research, citing earlier patents to highlight difference and (perhaps) subsequently receiving citation by later patents. But patents' metacultural utility also makes them important to the creation of black boxes, as they leverage the imprimatur of government to facilitate the profitable circulation of technology.[9]

There is one important difference with academic citations, however: academic citations are generally the work of the paper's author. Patent citations, on the other hand, may be *suggested* by the applicant, but are actually determined the patent examiner, who reviews the application and decides which citations are salient, based on whether these prior works in any way limit the claims made by the applicant (Leydesdorff 2007). This dynamic has led some economists to judge the technological significance and market value of technologies by the number of patent citations they have accumulated over the years (Hall, Jaffe, and Trajtenberg 2006; Trajtenberg 1990).

Looking at the citations made in the Buckwalter patent, we find five patents referenced—two sirens and three "sleep-inducing" devices. Both cited siren designs generate sound by circulating air through a dome-like housing, thus utilizing a similar design principle for a (drastically) different effect (Lyman 1951; Millard 1945; figures 2.6 and 2.7). Conversely, the other three designs aspire to outcomes similar to those of the Buckwalter design, but utilize different technologies to generate sleep-inducing sound. The first uses electrical power to vibrate a metal plate housed in a resonant box constructed of metal, wood, or plastic and fitted with an intensity control "for the attainment of a pleasing and harmonious sound" (Wiesman 1953; figure 2.8). A second device operates on a similar principle (Horton 1960; figure 2.9). It is a small dome-shaped object containing a battery and a small motor that functions as a "vibratory and audible device for soothing infants" when placed in a crib. Like Buckwalter's design, each of these devices deploys the vibrational by-products of embodiment technics—the sounds of production and circulation usually characterized as noise—for the purposes of peaceful sleep. The third device instrumentalizes a different kind of audible industrial by-product—a hum. It consists of a simple electrical circuit design connected to a speaker that transduces and projects as hum the sinusoidal waves of household alternating current (AC) electrical power (Beazley 1953; figure 2.10). Whereas electrical hum is usually carefully filtered out in audio engineering, the "Slumberbug" deploys the sound of circulating current as allegedly soporific sound. In approving the patent with these citations as precedent, the patent examiner positions the new and useful nature of Buckwalter's invention as residing in its combination of preexisting schematics and pragmatics. Buckwalter's device combines the circulation of air associated with a siren with the soporific qualities associated with these now-forgotten vibrational devices. This is precisely the sort of novelty-seeking hybridity that Urban characterizes as the metaculture of modernity—combining the old to create something new.

There is a problem with this sort of metacultural analysis, however, and that is the unlikelihood that the Buckwalters were aware of any of these other, commercially unsuccessful sleep machines on that night of inspiration in the motel room. Where Urban's model presents us with a linear and infocentric picture of cultural transmission between senders and receivers, the Buckwalters' moment of inspiration occurred within a cultural space of ambient, macroperceptual influence and a physical space shaped by metastable technologies. Such moments do not result from the clearly linear, informatic transmission of culture. This assertion is borne out repeatedly by "multiple discoveries," in which scientific breakthroughs are achieved at roughly the same time in different places (Merton 1963) and by the longer history of orphic technologies, in which new players reinvent ambient sound conditioning as an isolating helmet, a recording, an analog machine, an app—most of them unaware of their inventive predecessors, as if the very idea of ambient sound control was itself ambient.

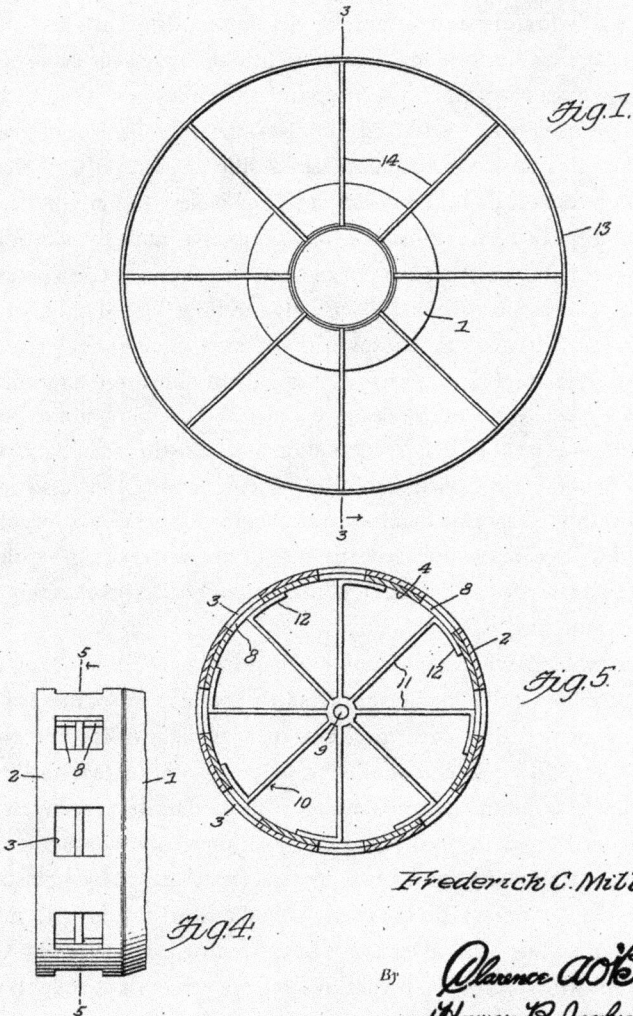

Figure 2.6 Air-generated siren (Millard) cited in Buckwalter's patent.

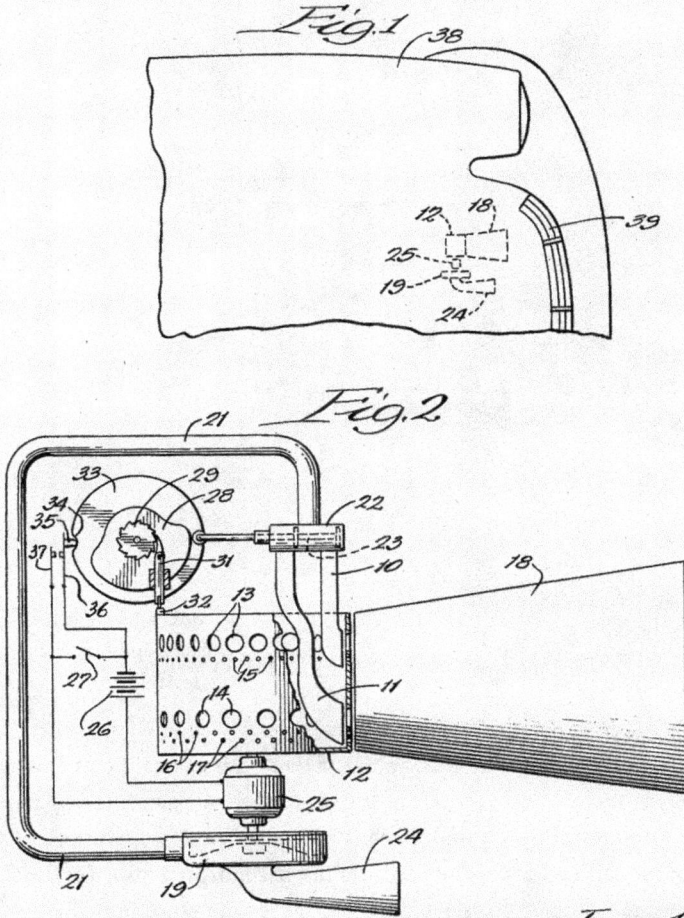

Aug. 21, 1951   K. E. LYMAN   2,564,984

WARNING SIGNAL FOR VEHICLES

Filed Jan. 21, 1948

Fig.1

Fig.2

Inventor:
Kenneth E. Lyman,

By Dawson, Ooms, Portheus & Spangenberg,
Attorneys.

Figure 2.7 Warning signal (Lyman) cited in Buckwalter's patent.

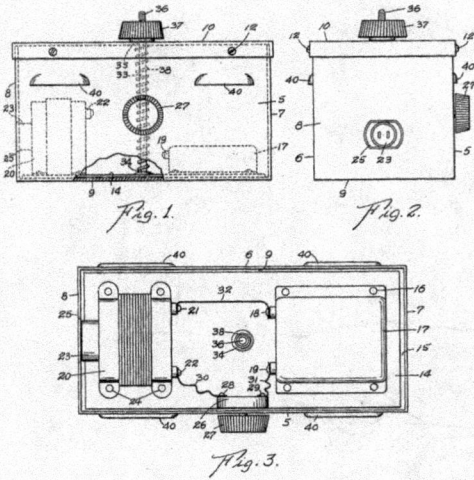

Nov. 10, 1953   F. H. WIESMAN   2,659,073
DEVICE FOR INDUCING SLEEP AND REST
Filed Feb. 26, 1952

Fig. 1.   *Fig. 2.*

Fig. 3.

INVENTOR.
FRANK H. WIESMAN
BY Joseph I. Zugelter
Atty.

Figure 2.8 Wiesman's sleep and rest-inducing device.

In short, the case of the Buckwalter patent both substantiates and complicates the metacultural model, as the orphic history presented by patents contains interesting gaps and elisions of influence and discourse. While three of the earlier devices cited did attempt to repurpose noise (in the sense of "unwanted sound") for sleep, they did not create noise in the acoustical sense of aperiodic broadband sound. In fact, all of the cited devices generate "tonal" sound of particular frequency or frequencies—the 120 cycles per second of alternating current, the specific resonance of mechanical vibration, or the rise and fall of a siren. The sound coming from these devices could be characterized as a humming, buzzing, or wailing, but not the kind of masking sound Buckwalter's device generates—the sound popularly conceived as "white noise" today. This gap undermines the patent's retroactive narrative that the sound conditioner drew its utility from one set of technologies and its mechanism from another. Instead, both problem and solution presented

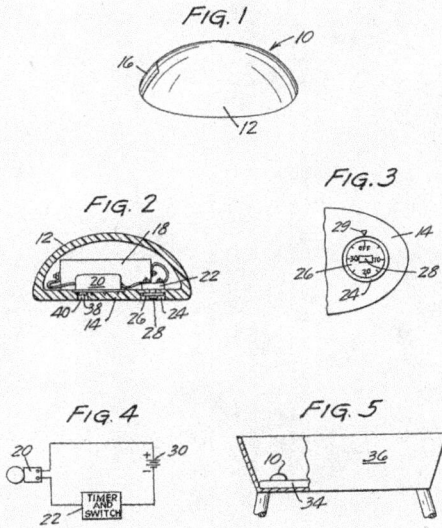

April 12, 1960   R. R. HORTON   2,932,821

INFANT PACIFYING DEVICE

Filed July 22, 1958

FIG. 1

FIG. 2

FIG. 3

FIG. 4

FIG. 5

INVENTOR

ROBERT R. HORTON

BY

Donald M. Sell

ATTORNEY

Figure 2.9 Horton's infant pacifying device.

themselves to the Buckwalters through their orphic engagement with their sociomaterial environment.

A second metacultural gap exists in the patent, in that the Buckwalter patent does not reflect the research of Beranek and others who *were* working with acoustical noise as a means of affective control—nor do subsequent white noise masking patents credit the Buckwalter device. Beranek's wartime research led to the publication of the noise criterion (NC), which quantified acceptable levels of noise in public buildings in the 1950s. By 1971, Beranek had domesticated noise by developing systems and standards for its use in open offices (1971). Beranek did not, however, use circulating air for this purpose, having discovered that the amount of airflow necessary to control sound in an office setting would cause thermal discomfort for office workers. Instead, BBN installed noise-producing speakers above the dropped ceiling or plenum of offices, the main technique still used today.

    C. BEAZLEY   2,644,153
ACOUSTIC SLEEP INDUCING APPARATUS
Filed April 12, 1950

Fig. 1.

SLUMBERBUG

Fig. 2.

Fig. 3.

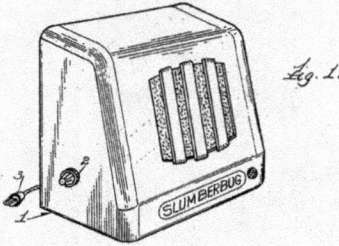

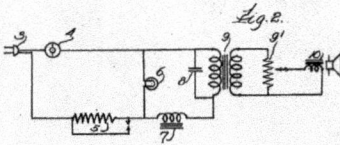

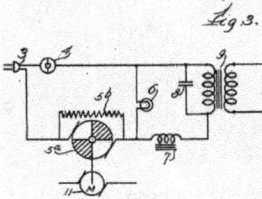

INVENTOR.
Charles Beazley.
BY *H.J. Sanders*
ATTORNEY.

Figure 2.10 Beazley's sleep-inducing device.

As discussed below, Buckwalter's machine would come to be used in office settings as well, though on an individual rather than an institutional scale. Nevertheless, just as Buckwalter was seemingly unaware of Beranek and his research, those who filed the many patents for office noise-masking devices, all of which seem to come *after* Buckwalter's patent was granted in 1964, never cite his sleep-inducing, sound-producing device. This disconnect results in part from the different social worlds that the two noise domesticators, Beranek and Buckwalter, were operating in, but it also results from an epistemological aspect of patents, the U.S. Patent Classification System (USPC), which divides inventions into one or more collections based on subject matter, with each of these divisions consisting of a "class" (delineating one type of technology from another) and a "subclass" (delineating processes, structural features, and functional features). Buckwalter's patent was classified with two USPC codes that would keep his invention out of the metacultural discourse of commercial noise control, filed away from the purview of office-minded patent applicants and examiners. These classifications are:

A61M21/00 — Other devices or methods to cause a change in the state of consciousness; Devices for producing or ending sleep by mechanical, optical, or acoustical means, e.g. for hypnosis

A61M2021/0027 — Other devices or methods to cause a change in the state of consciousness; Devices for producing or ending sleep by mechanical, optical, or acoustical means, e.g. for hypnosis by the use of a particular sense, or stimulus by the hearing sense

In contrast to the professional and industrial domestication of noise studied by Sterne, the Buckwalters' domestication of noise was of and for the domicile. Because he and Trudy conceived the sound conditioner in bed, as a device for sleeping, Jim Buckwalter would write his patent in such a way that their brainchild would never take an official place in the white noise lineage that was its birthright. Buckwalter's work is simply never cited in patents for noise control in offices.

Patented Self-Invention

Moving beyond the citations, the text of the patent "Sleep-Inducing Sound-Producing Device" does more than describe a technological object—it also intimates the macroperceptual conceptions of sound, space, otherness, and self that its technics is designed to mediate on the microperceptual level. The first two pages of the patent are straightforward diagrams of the device itself. Page one (figure 2.11) shows side views of the outer housing and internal components, as well as a top view of the fan, while page two diagrams the adjustable openings on the housing that allow for changes in tone and volume.

The written text that follows these images, however, begins not with a detailed description of the *object*, but rather with an examination of the interior life of the *subject* imagined to use it:

This invention relates to a sleep-inducing sound-producing device.

There are various conditions which lead to or cause sleeplessness on the part of different individuals. Some of these conditions are internal

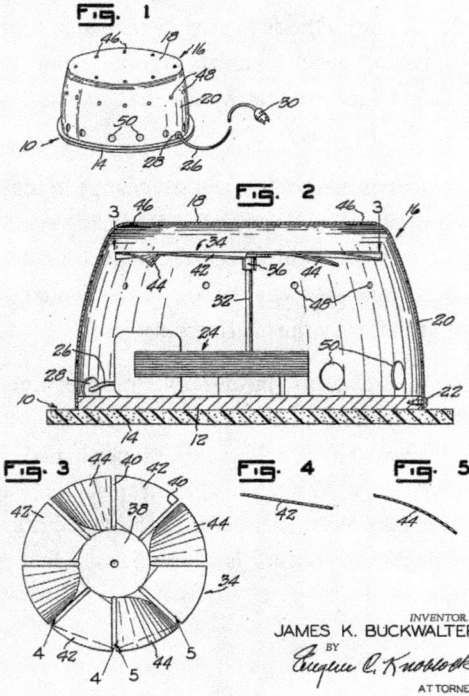

Figure 2.11 Page 1 of the Buckwalter patent, "Sleep-Inducing Sound-Producing Device."

or self-generating, such as nervousness and worry. Other conditions are external, such as sensitivity to strange surroundings and particularly to strange ambient sounds or noises. External conditions are likely to result in termination of sleep before a person has fully rested. Thus some authorities report that it is quite common for sleepers to alternate between deep sleep and light sleep, with the depth of sleep reducing and the periods of light sleep increasing progressively.

Thus a sleeper becomes progressively subject to being wakened by surrounding noise disturbances, and particularly unusual noise disturbances, during the light sleeping parts of his sleep cycle.

It is the primary object of this invention to provide a device for inducing sleep which is effective in cases of sleeplessness for both internal and external causes, which is inexpensive to construct and to operate, and which is readily portable.

A further object is to provide a device of this character capable of producing acoustical privacy by the exclusion of part of ambient sound of disturbing character to render it less noticeable and thereby to aid in the achievement of natural sleep.

A further object is to provide a device of this character which produces a restful sound tending to shut out disturbing ambient noises and thus producing a condition conducive to starting of sleep and continuance of sleep during a normal sleep period.

A further object is to provide a device of this character which blends a variety of sleep promoting sound tones which can be likened to musical tones, and thus produces an environment conducive to restful sleep.

A further object is to provide a device of this character which is light in weight, which is adjustable by the user relative to pitch and volume of emitted sound, and which utilizes the principle of movement of air as a means to produce sound of restful character as a barrier to sound and noises of disturbing character. (Buckwalter 1964)

Although his patent "relates to a sleep-inducing sound-producing device," Buckwalter's first rhetorical invention is a *self* that needs such a device. In order to clarify the intervention that his machine is designed to make, the inventor first presents a theory of the sleepless self, sorting the "various conditions which lead to or cause sleeplessness on the part of different individuals" into two types, internal and external. The central purpose of the machine is "the achievement of natural sleep" through the eradication of sleeplessness due to either "internal or self-generating [causes] such as nervousness and worry" or external causes such as "strange surroundings" and "strange ambient sounds or noises." It is a curious turn of phrase in which "natural sleep" becomes an "achievement," a phrasing that, I believe, carries great significance. Buckwalter is constructing a self that is *already denatured*, a self that will require some artifice of renaturalization. The machine's intervention is to "[produce] an environment conducive to restful sleep," one that acoustically privatizes the outer space of the user's room while it penetrates the inner space of the self to soothe the worried mind.

The self Buckwalter constructs in the patent is thoroughly modern, containing the contradictions of a liberal, capitalist society. This self is highly autonomous, responsible both for its own "self-generating" distress and for finding a patented technological solution. Yet for all its autonomy, this self is also highly sensitive to the strangeness of its environment, requiring "exclusion" of what the patent calls "sound of disturbing character" (one imagines it lurking outside in a trench coat) in order to achieve sleep. Tellingly, this exclusion is achieved through the manipulation of sonic space because the self is not able to regulate its own boundaries alone. Herein lies the modern contradiction: the modern self requires autonomy yet is too porous, and inhabits a space too penetrated by stimuli, to achieve autonomy on its own. It needs Buckwalter's spatially mediating technology of the self to shore up its own boundaries.

The construction and maintenance of self in the Buckwalter patent is suggestive of a sonically spatialized mode of governmentality, in which technologies of power go beyond the presupposition of freedom and actively participate in the construction of free selves. The sound conditioner and its cousins in the marketplace of "personal sensory therapy" function similarly to psychology, psychiatry, and other therapies, which, Nikolas Rose writes, "fabricate subjects—human men, women, and children—capable of bearing the burdens of liberty" in an era of consumer choice and hands-off governance (1999, viii). Buckwalter's patent argues for his sound machine's utility in controlling the self and its interaction with its surrounding spaces. It implicitly characterizes shared space as strange, unnatural, and beyond one's control. The means of regulation is not an appeal to official regulatory authorities, but rather the privatization of a small sphere of that space by way of a wall of sound to keep out disturbing characters.

As Karin Bijsterveld notes in her study of Dutch urban gramophone and radio noise, experts in acoustics and psychoacoustics worried about urban dwellers as essential economic agents who "were already exposed to a multitude of sensory experiences throughout the day [and thus] badly needed their sleep" (Bijsterveld 2008, 187). Yet despite the perceived seriousness of urban noise, governments in the Netherlands and elsewhere found that a number of factors impeded top-down regulation: first, the transient noise of neighbors was difficult for authorities to objectify through measurement; second, scientific research raised awareness of the subjective nature of noise perception, further destabilizing its status as an objective problem; and (consequently) third, noise abatement groups were unsuccessful in arguing that noise was a greater intrusion of privacy than the police enforcement of noise codes. Citing Rose's work on responsibilization, Bijsterveld finds that, although some noise-abating laws were passed, for the most part, individuals were left responsible for limiting the noise they created and expanding the noise they tolerated (191).

Buckwalter's invention and the other orphic technologies I discuss in these pages represent the commercial history of this responsibilization, as individuals seek out personal technologies for bearing the private burden of noise. Understanding the sleep-inducing, noise-producing device as a spatial technology of the self clarifies the pragmatics of Buckwalter's somewhat unusual use of the term *privacy*. On reading Buckwalter's claim that one of his objectives is creating a device "capable of producing acoustical privacy," one would logically expect that he is describing a technology that frees the subject from *being heard*. In fact, his device only frees one from *hearing*. Due to the way that sound travels through space, a sound-emitting device in a room will decrease the spatial range of hearing—or "acoustic horizon"—of a subject inside that room (Blesser and Salter 2007, 22; Truax 1984, 23). Such a device, however, does less to dampen sounds emitted *from* the room, which may still be heard by others, as it does not strongly diminish a given sound's "acoustic arena"—the range in which the sound is audible. This is not to say that such devices cannot be helpful in preventing eavesdropping, but in order to do so, they are placed near the would-be listener, outside the room that requires privacy.

This latter form of acoustic privacy—privacy *from* listening—would eventually come to be a major selling point for the sound conditioner in commercial settings, but that is not the type of acoustical privacy Buckwalter describes in his patent. Rather, the type of privacy that Buckwalter imagines—privatized listening—is the right to be a private self, one whose subjectivity is free from the sonic influence and distraction of shared or public space. In the patent, noise is portrayed as the aural other "of disturbing character." It is a circulating intensity, an affective potential that the subject does not want to be affected by. The sound machine offers a sensory refuge from affectivity by remediating and privatizing the shared vibrational medium of space that we all inhabit. The sleep-inducing, sound-producing device, the patent claims, "utilizes the principle of movement of air as a means to produce sound of restful character as a barrier." It was the cessation of circulating air in the motel room with the broken air conditioner that revealed other types of circulation that penetrated the would-be sleeper, be it the circulation of commodities on the highway or capital over the poker table. In doing so, this cessation of circulation also revealed the fragile, spatial nature of subjective agency and coherence.

Having explored space and circulation in the Buckwalter patent, we can now circle back to Ihde's four kinds of technological mediation to articulate the intentionality of this sleep-inducing, sound-producing device. The sound conditioner inverts Ihde's technics in some interesting ways: Where embodiment relations usually aspire to a transparent extension of sensory faculties, the Buckwalter device aspires to impair audition through opacity. Where hermeneutic relations are designed to open up access to new inputs or knowledge through systems of semiotic difference, this machine is designed to mute the sound of difference, hiding external inputs of "strange" significance behind a wall of sonic sameness. And though the sound conditioner rejects transparency to become a terminus of auditory perception, its sound has no attentional handles to grasp onto—it never approaches something like otherness, as seen in Ihde's alterity relations. Instead, the technics of the sound conditioner most resemble the background relations of its namesake, the air conditioner, yet Buckwalter amplifies this background presence, bringing it to the fore as a resource to dampen other presences.

We might think about the intentionality of orphic media, then, in terms of a spatial process in which circulating fields or entities amplify or dampen aspects of other fields or entities. When the circulation of electrical current is used to power the mechanical circulation of air, it contracts the acoustic horizon of a listening subject, mediating both space and subject, literally changing the physical state of each and their affective relations with one another. When that electromechanical movement ceases, the cessation reveals that both space and subject were already sonically mediated by other spatial planes and flows. This is the message of the song of Orpheus—that subjectivity is distributed, spatial, and sonically mediated. But in a macroperceptual world fragmented for speed and control, Orpheus easily becomes a disturbing character, a threat to the autonomy that we are responsible to live up to. In this context, the technological cocoon is not merely a side effect of modernity—it is a necessity for modern living. Orpheus must be disciplined. Noise must become a domestic servant.

Domesticating and Feminizing Noise

Although Trudy Buckwalter has, at times, been absent from Marpac's history as presented on its website, in the company's early days, she was the face of peaceful sleep in its marketing. In a photograph used in early sound conditioner brochures and catalogs, Mrs. Buckwalter lies in bed, eyes closed, face tilted slightly toward the foregrounded sound conditioner on the nightstand (figure 2.12). It is a simple, tightly cropped image that recurs repeatedly in Marpac's advertising (figures 2.13–2.17).

Thus far, I have examined the spatial relations that prompted the sound conditioner's invention and discussed the spatial transformation of these relations that the machine is designed to effect. But as Rick Altman points out, "media are not fully and self-evidently defined by their components and configurations" (2004, 16). In this section, I examine the *representation*

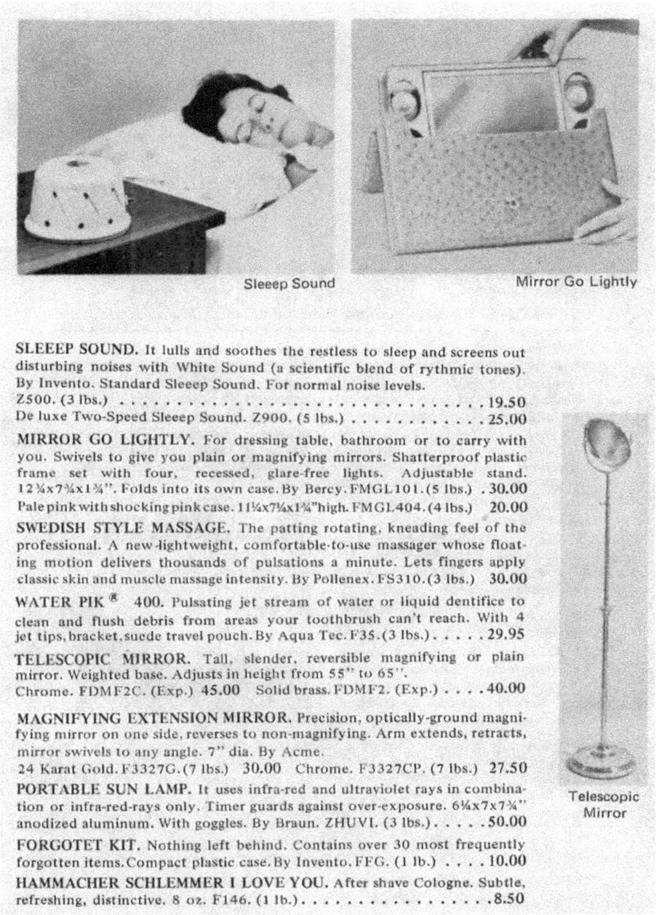

Sleeep Sound   Mirror Go Lightly

SLEEEP SOUND. It lulls and soothes the restless to sleep and screens out disturbing noises with White Sound (a scientific blend of rythmic tones). By Invento. Standard Sleeep Sound. For normal noise levels.
Z500. (3 lbs.) 19.50
De luxe Two-Speed Sleeep Sound. Z900. (5 lbs.) 25.00

MIRROR GO LIGHTLY. For dressing table, bathroom or to carry with you. Swivels to give you plain or magnifying mirrors. Shatterproof plastic frame set with four, recessed, glare-free lights. Adjustable stand. 12¼x7¾x1¾". Folds into its own case. By Bercy. FMGL101. (5 lbs.) . 30.00
Pale pink with shocking pink case. 11¼x7¼x1¾" high. FMGL404. (4 lbs.) 20.00

SWEDISH STYLE MASSAGE. The patting rotating, kneading feel of the professional. A new-lightweight, comfortable-to-use massager whose floating motion delivers thousands of pulsations a minute. Lets fingers apply classic skin and muscle massage intensity. By Pollenex. FS310. (3 lbs.) 30.00

WATER PIK ® 400. Pulsating jet stream of water or liquid dentifrice to clean and flush debris from areas your toothbrush can't reach. With 4 jet tips, bracket, suede travel pouch. By Aqua Tec. F35. (3 lbs.) 29.95

TELESCOPIC MIRROR. Tall, slender, reversible magnifying or plain mirror. Weighted base. Adjusts in height from 55" to 65".
Chrome. FDMF2C. (Exp.) 45.00   Solid brass. FDMF2. (Exp.) 40.00

MAGNIFYING EXTENSION MIRROR. Precision, optically-ground magnifying mirror on one side, reverses to non-magnifying. Arm extends, retracts, mirror swivels to any angle. 7" dia. By Acme.
24 Karat Gold. F3327G. (7 lbs.) 30.00   Chrome. F3327CP. (7 lbs.) 27.50

PORTABLE SUN LAMP. It uses infra-red and ultraviolet rays in combination or infra-red-rays only. Timer guards against over-exposure. 6¼x7x7¾" anodized aluminum. With goggles. By Braun. ZHUVI. (3 lbs.) 50.00

FORGOTET KIT. Nothing left behind. Contains over 30 most frequently forgotten items. Compact plastic case. By Invento. FFG. (1 lb.) 10.00

HAMMACHER SCHLEMMER I LOVE YOU. After shave Cologne. Subtle, refreshing, distinctive. 8 oz. F146. (1 lb.) 8.50

Telescopic
Mirror

Figure 2.12 Marpac's sound conditioner, branded as "Sleeep Sound" in a 1968 Hammacher Schlemmer catalog. Image courtesy of the Browne Popular Culture Library, Bowling Green State University.

of space in Marpac's marketing, showing how the company has worked to domesticate white noise for purposes of sleep and productivity. Trudy Buckwalter's brainchild was largely marketed as a homemaking device. The image of a sleeping woman is suggestive of the peaceful domestic space that a sound machine can help create, but it also represents an effort on the part of Marpac to domesticate the machine itself, making it a natural part of the space of the home. By the late 1960s, the sound conditioner was sold under several different brand names, as specified in contracts with different distributors

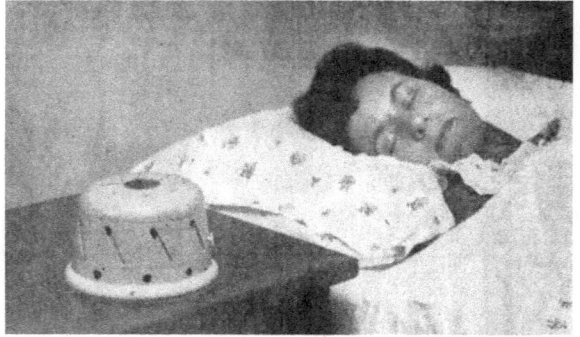

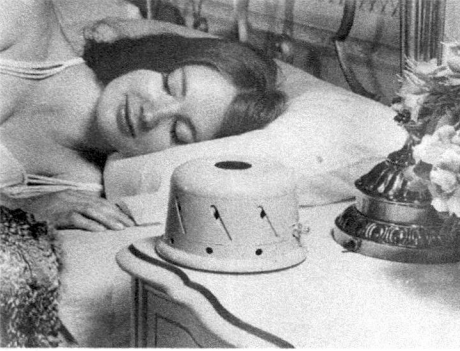

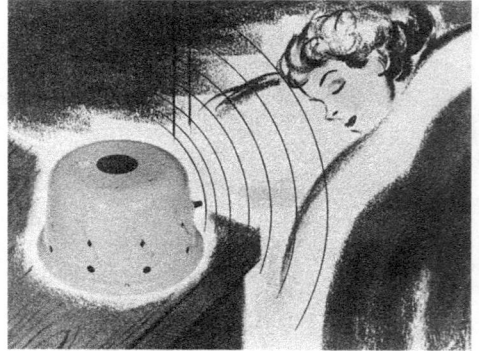

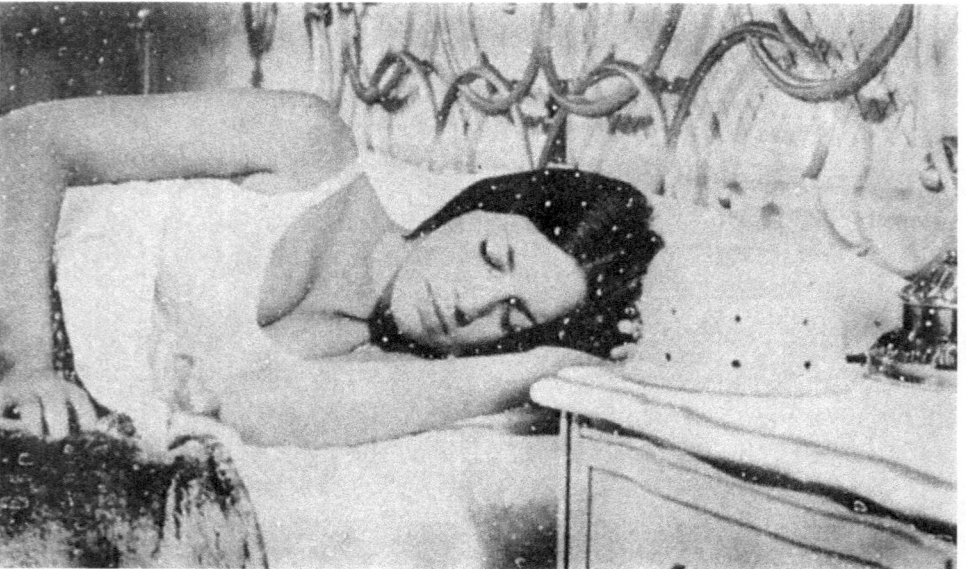

Figures 2.13–2.17 The image of a sleeping woman was a mainstay in Marpac ads for decades. Images courtesy of Marpac Incorporated.

and retailers: the Sound-O-Sleep, the Sleep-Mate, and in the pages of the Hammacher Schlemmer catalog, the Sleeep [sic] Sound. Clearly, sleep was the constant. Unlike its patent, Marpac's marketing tended not to emphasize the intrusive sounds and intrusive thoughts that the machine could whoosh away. Rather, its ads and pamphlets used the image of a woman asleep in bed to suggest a sonically calmed and domesticated space.

Figure 2.12, in which Trudy Buckwalter sleeps with the Sleeep Sound beside her on a nightstand, is taken from a 1968 Hammacher catalog. The description beneath the image reads, "It lulls and soothes the restless to sleep and screens out disturbing noises with White Sound (a scientific blend of rythmic [sic] tones)." The choice of "rythmic" is curious, as there is, in fact, no rhythm to the steady sound produced by the circulation of air through the machine. The appeal to science also catches the eye, particularly because the term *White Sound* is substituted for the conventional term, *white noise*. Just as white light results from a combination of all the wavelengths in the color spectrum, "white noise" usually refers to the randomization of frequencies across the audible spectrum. Because of its broad sound spectrum, white noise is good for masking other sounds, no matter their tonal characteristics. Although the electromechanical sound generator does not technically produce white noise, its broadband sound and functional characteristics are close enough to those of white noise that James Buckwalter wanted to invoke the science behind its utility.

Buckwalter did not, however, want to use the term *noise*. For most of Marpac's history, company marketing has avoided any confusion or negative connotations that might result from admitting its product makes noise. Whether or not the term would have caused confusion in 1968, "white noise" is accepted today—for example, in the popular sound-generating iPhone/Android app White Noise. Market research done by Marpac's new owners more recently showed that white noise is generally understood by contemporary consumers as a potentially soothing sound. In the early years of the sound conditioner, however, its marketers were still trying to find the best language to describe its function. A Hammacher ad from 1973 uses the Buckwalter photo and goes to such pains to avoid "noise" that its ad copy becomes suggestive of suffocation: "Induces sleep and relaxation by lulling you in a vacuum of scientifically blended, soft, non-noisy rythmic [sic] tones."

There is a tonal tension at work in these product descriptions, a soft sell of hard science. Unlike most sound technologies, which have been associated with "male" spaces such as the garage (ham radio) (Haring 2003) and the den or bachelor pad ("hi-fi" systems) (Keightley 1996), the Sleep-Mate was intended for the bedroom, a space marked for control by the female consumer. The association with feminine domestic space is reinforced by product placement in catalogs such as Hammacher Schlemmer and Sears Roebuck. The Hammacher ad in figure 2.16 is situated on a page that features a lighted makeup mirror, a sun lamp, a Water Pik teeth cleaner, an electric "Swedish Style Massage," and other domestic items. In a 1966–67 Sears catalog, the Sleep-Mate is found on a page of "Sears Bed Accessories" and "Hospital-quality Instruments and Aids for home use" (figure 2.18).

The medicinal positioning of sound machines as devices of self-care persisted even after their internal technologies moved more clearly into the terrain of electronics. Marpac's competitor Sound Oasis markets its products as "sound therapy," and its ads present its sound designers in white coats suggestive of a doctor or medical researcher. In general, sound machines continue to be associated with the retail "health and wellness" category and are promoted at the International Home and Housewares Show rather than at International CES (formerly the Consumer Electronics Show).

Jim Buckwalter soon learned, however, that people were finding uses other than sleep for his machine, as customers reported that it aided their concentration at work. Still others found that it provided an acoustical privacy he did not delineate in his patent—not freedom from *hearing*, but freedom from *being heard*. In particular, psychotherapists, counselors, and other professionals found that a sound conditioner placed in the waiting room prevented those waiting from hearing any emoting or sensitive information coming from the office. Buckwalter soon added this work-oriented utility to his advertising, as seen in the aforementioned 1966–67 Sears ad. Beside the image of the sleeping woman, a boy does homework with a Sleep-Mate on his desk. The copy reads, "Study with Sleep-Mate . . [sic] it muffles most sounds that break concentration." The image of a child at work in his bedroom, however, still conforms with the Sleep-Mate's marketing as a device that makes domestic space livable—and it probably would have muddied the narrative of the brand to refer to its use in commercial settings. In any case, Buckwalter had gotten feedback from commercial users that the Sleep-Mate badge on top of the sound conditioner did not project a professional image, a complaint that led to another spin-off brand.

Though the exact chronology of the company's different brand names is uncertain, Dave Theissen says that by the time he joined the company in 1972, Marpac had solved the conceptual problem of working with a Sleep-Mate by adding a second product—the Sound Screen—marketed toward professionals and college students. This version was likely produced in the

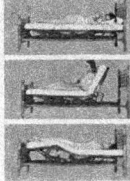

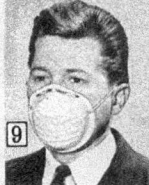
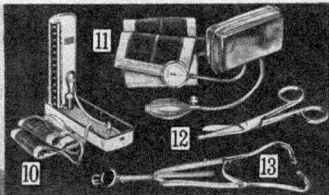

Figure 2.18 The Sleep-Mate was positioned among "bed accessories" and "hospital quality instruments and aids for home use" in Sears Roebuck's fall/winter 1966–67 catalog.

Figures 2.19 and 2.20 Dual branding of the same device solved a marketing problem and established the sleep/concentration binary that would characterize the use of subsequent orphic media.

late 1960s, and two vintage posters found today in Marpac's lobby were created to promote the two units (figures 2.19 and 2.20). The Sleep-Mate is said to create "a blend of soothing sounds" that "helps relax over active minds: Just plug it in, turn it on, then SLEEP without pills!" The Sound Screen is promoted as "a must for any serious student," designed to "improve your study environment" by eliminating "those thought distracting noises beyond your control." The first poster depicts not a woman, but a sleeping young boy, perhaps a toddler, while the second shows a male college student productively at work despite rowdy classmates and a loud record player in a nearby room. These two Marpac products, with their ostensibly diametrically opposed functions—sleep and concentration—are actually one and the same. The Sleep-Mate and Sound Screen were identical with the exception

Improve Your **STUDY ENVIRONMENT**

with *SOUND* **SCREEN**

Yes! Now you can do something about those thought distracting noises beyond your control.

● THE CONSTANT SOUND OF THIS SMALL ELECTRICAL APPLIANCE HELPS MASK OR BLANKET INTERMITTENT NOISES AND HELP IMPROVE YOUR STUDY.

● A MUST FOR EVERY SERIOUS STUDENT

AVAILABLE THROUGH COLLEGE BOOKSTORES

SOUND **SCREEN** $

THE SOUND TO STUDY BY

of the small circular badges on the top of the units, which bore the different brand names.

By the end of the sixties, then, before the commercial advent of orphic nature recordings or electronic sound machines, Marpac had more or less established the scope of utility that would predominate in the use of orphic media in succeeding decades. The machines fabricated private spaces suitable for work, sleep, or relaxation. As seen above, however, discovering this range of uses, explaining it in consumer-friendly language, and branding the devices effectively were neither simple nor linear tasks. The sound conditioner suffered from what Altman would call an "identity crisis" or "multiple identification" of media technology (2004, 19). There were amorphous qualities to the sound conditioner's sonic signature and uses that made marketing a challenge: "White Sound" or "white noise"? Scientific intervention or fixture of a cozy bedroom? Sleep or concentration? The many different names and descriptions affixed over the years to this device speak to the challenges of conceptualizing, representing, and circulating this new technology.

Despite these challenges, Marpac proved to be a successful small business over five decades, creating new designs of analog and digital sound conditioners while tweaking and continuing to sell the Sleep-Mate/Sound Screen. By 1968, the company had outgrown both the Buckwalter basement and the small Elkhart, Indiana, facility. When it was time to find a larger facility, the Buckwalters selected Wilmington, North Carolina, because it was halfway between Buck's family in Pennsylvania and Trudy's family in Florida; later, as the business continued to grow, it moved some fourteen miles north to Rocky Point. While Marpac does not dominate the electronic sleep machine market, it has never been surpassed in the electromechanical sector. By the 2000s, the company was selling its electromechanical devices only on its website and through Hammacher, yet sales grew annually by double digits, mainly by word of mouth. The company sold some one million units in the seven or eight years before its sale in 2010. For Dave Theissen, this period of strong sales produced an opportune time to retire. He sold his majority share of the company to Jimmy Sloan and Gordon Wallace, who had approached him after Sloan looked at the underside of his twenty-year-old Sleep-Mate and noticed that it was built in his own state of North Carolina.

When I visited Marpac in 2013, thirty-five people worked there in a steel building in a sparsely occupied industrial park. Since 2010, the company's new owners have set out to clarify what they see as a certain degree of marketplace confusion around their electromechanical product. They also wanted to grow the company at a greater pace by abandoning Marpac's plain white packaging and word-of-mouth approach. To do this, they have taken a risk, scrapping the Sleep-Mate and Sound Screen brands that had become familiar to the company's most loyal customers. When I first met Sloan and Wallace in Chicago at the 2012 International Home and Housewares Show, they had recently renamed the now-fifty-year-old sound conditioner and were launching a new marketing campaign with a redesigned website, a new consumer video, and other promotional materials. Even retail partners such as Hammacher, which had long sold Marpac sound conditioners under their own label, would now be asked to use the new brand name: Dohm (figure 2.21). The Marpac booth was decked out in the company's new color scheme of blue, silver, and white, reflecting the clean, light, contemporary, minimalist aesthetic typically associated with both tech maker Apple and the marketing of healthy lifestyle products and services such as yoga supplies and classes— an impression reinforced by the "om" sound nested in the name *Dohm*.

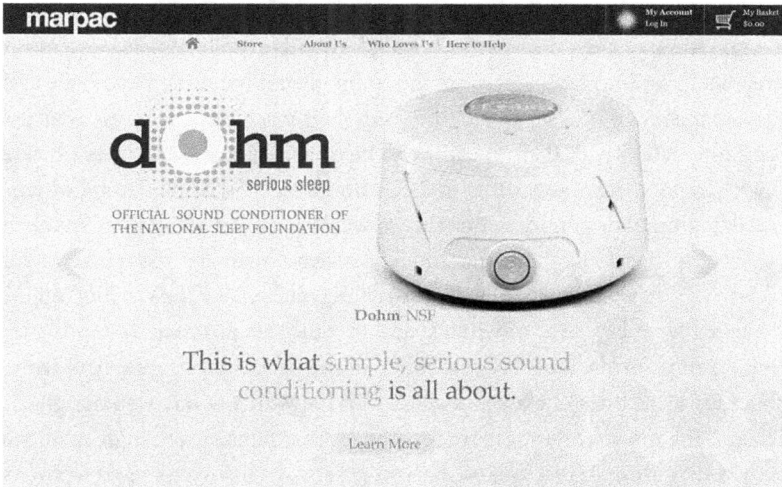

Figure 2.21 In 2012, the Marpac sound conditioner was reborn as Dohm.

Besides connoting a peaceful mantra, the name *Dohm* contains the word *ohm*—the unit of electrical impedance often associated with loudspeakers—and also refers to the sound conditioner's domed shape, which Marpac's recent market research had shown was more memorable to users than the Sleep-Mate or Sound Screen names. The way the new brand name links sound and shape seems quite appropriate, as the machine's distinctive shape is, in fact, an acoustical asset integral to the Dohm's sound.[10] The new brand name marked an attempt to better capitalize on this distinctive and functional form factor, which sets it apart from the electronic, radio-like machines that have come to dominate the market, offering a wide variety of recorded and synthesized sounds. Using the design's age and electromechanical simplicity as assets, Marpac's new website acclaimed the Dohm as "the original, most popular, all natural, white noise sound machine," producing "soothing, all natural white noise."

In addition to emphasizing the domed design, the new Dohm campaign's clean, airy aesthetics imparted an implicit promise of simplicity and peace in a messy, noisy world. This clean, simple, and modern promise, which descends from Bauhaus and International Style architecture and design and is found in American consumer culture from postwar domestic appliances through contemporary media technologies, never seems to lose its futuristic connotations of order and peace. This consumer promise has transcended the physical and entered virtual space as well, as Sherry Turkle reveals in her examination of the "transparency" Apple constructed with its Macintosh graphical user interface. The more the company hid the underlying code and limited the range of users' interaction with their machines, the more users felt their interaction with their machines to be transparent and effortless (Turkle 1997). Today's technological aesthetic is dominated by Apple's trope of emphasizing simplicity and functionality in technology while hiding its enabling complexity. It is an aesthetic that influences web design and the marketing of technology as well. By 2012, Marpac's redesigned website, like that of Apple, deployed large expanses of white space, in which its products rested lightly like Platonic forms. Invisibly embedded in the peace and simplicity of white space are also codes of class and gender. In the words of one web design tutorial: "The more white space there is the more expensive and high-quality a design may seem. If you look at the advertisements in an expensive women's magazine, you will notice that most ads have very little non-negative space. The text is small, leaving more room for background images, and there are very few elements on the page. Contrast that with a direct mail advertisement and you'll see large blocks of text covering multiple images and very little negative space."[11]

Like the rest of the Dohm campaign, the new Marpac website avoids the dated, mail-order aesthetics that dominated their earlier marketing, instead embracing an aspirational, upscale design. The class connotations are important: middle- to upper-class consumers have both the disposable income to purchase a sixty-dollar sound machine and, as evidenced by the professionals who requested a rebranded version of the Sleep-Mate, the desire for its form of technics. Foucault would likely point out that such subjects are also the most instilled with the liberalism that gives salience to technologies of the self—trained in the lifeways of their professional disciplines and responsibilized to the demands of an information economy, their sleep and concentration must be carefully cultivated and protected.

As Marpac marketing coordinator Liz Heinberg explained to me, "The use of white space was definitely intentional. Part of what we are trying to evoke with our website and our packaging is that we are all about simple white noise, a simple solution for sound conditioning. . . . We see the Dohm as creating a *cocoon* of white noise, this little area that is your own private sound environment where you're protected from the outside—and we're trying to evoke that same feeling visually online" (emphasis added).

Heinberg said Marpac did not want to dilute or complicate this affective and sensory appeal with a scientific explanation: "Other companies get the doctor in the white coat to make statements about white noise or brown noise or pink noise stimulating brain function. We ended up staying away from presenting a scientific reason for the success of the Dohm." Instead of appealing to science, Marpac's new design positions white noise as an acoustic analog to white space on a page, a background "absent presence" that helps perfect domestic space through Ihde's technological cocoon.

Tied in with the rebranding effort was a renewed focus on what Sloan, Wallace, and Heinberg see as their product's core selling point, summed up in the Dohm's new tagline, "serious sleep." The term *serious* is rather surprising when placed alongside "sleep," and this unusual combination is deployed in an effort to underscore the sound conditioner's soporific efficacy. This appeal to practicality is where Marpac's marketing parts ways with the sort seen in a yoga product ad. Heinberg explained to me that she did not want to use images of nature or "perfect people sleeping," nor did she want to use the term *spa*, as electronic sound machine competitor Sound Oasis often does. "Sleep is not an indulgence," she said. "We're trying to be more functional." This functionality was summed up in another new motto, "simple, serious, sound conditioning." Although the Dohm name purposely does not seem out of place in an office setting, Marpac has its sights set on a sleep-deprived American populace that is constantly told to take sleep more seriously. Underscoring the seriousness of the product is an endorsement by the sleep advocacy group the National Sleep Foundation. Sloan, who is on friendly terms with Troy Anderson, president of Sound Oasis, expressed an interest in splitting the market with their different strategies—Marpac's "serious sleep" and Sound Oasis's "sound therapy." The rebranding worked for Marpac, which soon joined Sound Oasis products on the coveted shelves and web store of Bed Bath and Beyond. Sales are now increasing at a more rapid pace than they were in the successful decade prior to Sloan and Wallace's purchase of the company.

Heinberg told me that the decision to rebrand was a difficult one and that, out of respect, they had waited to make the brand change until after Dave Theissen completed his final, transitional period with the company. She characterized Marpac's old guard as technological innovators who didn't necessarily name their products in ways that would be "sexy to consumers." Then again, it was because of the old guard's success in domesticating noise, reshaping microperception in the home, and maybe making a macroperceptual dent in the American culture of listening that Marpac can now describe the Dohm as the "original" sound conditioner that generates "natural" white noise.

3

The Ultimate Seashore

Environments and the Nature of Technology

The polynoise of the sea resembles the white noise
of the laboratory.
—**R. Murray Schafer**, *The Soundscape: Our Sonic Environment
and the Tuning of the World*

When new media are introduced, the changes affect the
environment as a whole.
—**N. Katherine Hayles**, summarizing Friedrich Kittler,
Gramophone, Film, Typewriter

In a few boxes, locked behind an aluminum roll-down door in a suburban storage space near Austin, Texas, rest the paper remains of Syntonic Research Inc. (SRI). There are yellowing invoices, photos, and press releases, as well as press clippings, fan letters, and documentation of listening tests—the fossilized impressions of a once-thriving cultural organism. SRI left behind sonic remains as well, imprinted on master tapes stored in a bank vault and on many thousands of LPs, cassettes, and CDs scattered in homes, thrift

environments

totally new concepts in sound · disc 8

SD 66008

SIDE 1: WOOD-MASTED SAILBOAT   SIDE 2: A COUNTRY STREAM

Figure 3.1 Disc 8 of the *environments* series.

stores, and used music shops across the United States (figure 3.1). These re-cordings, known collectively as *environments*, number 22 in total and were released in pairs, with one aural "environment" per side of each record or tape. As SRI's president Irv Teibel (1938–2010; figure 3.2) never failed to emphasize, these were not ordinary recordings when they were released in the late 1960s and early 1970s. Rather than music or spoken word, *environments* sonically conjured *spaces*, such as the beach, a forest, or a heart beating in a person's chest. And it wasn't just the content that was different about these recordings, but also the kind of media practice they supported. Teibel conceived these albums in an era of environmentalism, gurus, and LSD, promoting them as "applied psychology device[s] in recorded form . . . designed to counteract the damaging effects of noise-pollution" and help users achieve alpha-brainwave states of consciousness (1969b). SRI devised its own techniques of playback and listening as well, encouraging the user to

Figure 3.2 Irv Teibel splicing tape in his studio.

read extensive liner notes to properly experience the audio. In fact, according to Teibel, the proper experience of these records involved not listening to them at all.

In this chapter, I investigate the fossil records of *environments*, a cultural production that encouraged its listeners to fine-tune themselves through a cybernetic commingling of nature and audio technologies. These lingering impressions on paper, tape, and vinyl, combined with interviews with Teibel's contemporaries, evoke the sound and shape of Syntonic Research Inc., an entity that grew and thrived through the circulation of records under needles, tape across magnetic heads, and sounds and ideas though human heads. With distribution through Atlantic Records and reviews and articles in publications such as *Rolling Stone*, *Newsweek*, and the *New York Times*, the sounds, ideas, and techniques assembled in *environments* found their way to a large audience. The practices of (non)listening they encouraged would become widespread by the 1980s when New Age music, natural sound machines, and various sound therapies became common. The story of SRI is also the story of Irv Teibel, a charismatic multimedia artist and salesman who merged audio recording, copywriting, photography, biofeedback, and a computer from Bell Laboratories to generate a series of recordings with a cultural influence that has not been properly acknowledged or analyzed.

Teibel's technology distinguished itself in harnessing the noises of nature to do work of the sort previously associated with music. In the nineteenth century, Hermann von Helmholtz delineated a difference between natural noises such as surf or wind and the music of humans that is now taken for granted by acousticians and many musicians: noises are broadband sounds propagated on irregular or aperiodic sets of waves, while musical tones are periodic, that is, made of a limited set of waves that are regular and predictable in their repetitions (1954, 8). Less than fifty years after Helmholtz published this idea, Luigi Russolo advanced his "Art of Noises," which would counter the sleepy predictability of European tones and melodies with a Futurist orchestra of industrial whistles, wheezes, rumbles, and roars (2004). Appearing some fifty years after Russolo's provocations, *environments* (and subsequent natural sound machines and apps) enact an opposite conception and pragmatics of noise. For Teibel, the human predictability of music—even of the snooziest elevator variety—was too demanding of attention and, eventually, too annoying in repetition, for long-term consciousness alteration. Only irregular, aperiodic noise would suffice as a technology of self, calming the distracted mind and letting the user perfect her state of consciousness, because its lack of pattern supplied nothing for the mind to grasp onto. "White noise" from electromechanical and electronic sources, however, was a nonpattern that nevertheless bore human fingerprints, too much resembling what was increasingly called "noise pollution." Instead, Teibel claimed his natural sound devices would restore some natural essence to our denatured condition.

If Russolo's noise was a proto-fascist celebration of industrialization, Teibel's technologically mediated environmental noise was a biomediating product of the music industry with countercultural, communitarian characteristics. Unlike other orphic media technologies in this book, the *environments* series was intended, at least in part, to facilitate copresence with nature and other, enhancing sex and interpersonal communication. For people concerned about the health of the self in denatured spaces of modernity, these technologies promised new spaces of possibility, sonically fabricating a "natural" human preserve. In blending a futurist love of technology with a nostalgia for the lost gardens of Earth, Teibel's work reflects the cybernetic thinking of what has been called "New Communalism" and the "systems counterculture," loose communitarian and scientific movements that moved cybernetic discourse from informatic machine control to integrative ecology (Clarke 2012; Turner 2006). Moreover, in his belief that sound's therapeutic properties could facilitate a less fragmented and more open, interconnected self, Teibel joined the ranks of John Cage and other Cold War–era artists who believed media could foster freedoms that were not only individual, but also democratic (Turner 2013).

In what follows, I explain how Syntonic Research Inc. networked nature, media technologies, and the imaginations of its users to thrive as a space-producing entity. To do so, I study the multimedia text of the first *environments* album, tell the story of its production, and examine listening tests, feedback cards, letters, and other materials that allowed Teibel—and now allow us— to understand the audience reception and use of these most unusual recordings. Teibel's idiosyncratic conception of mediating the self–environment relationship through sound was itself influenced by a cybernetic discourse associated with information technology; moreover, the first *environments* recording—produced with the aid of a mainframe computer—may be the earliest commercial recording to utilize digital production techniques. Nevertheless, I argue that this record series represents a more open, less utilitarian possibility for orphic mediation, one that moves beyond the informatic sleep/concentration binary and into an exploration of self, other, and environment through sound.

Selling Syntonic Sounds

Each *environments* album is a multimedia production combining recorded sound, graphic design, nature photography, and copywriting to facilitate a desired affective response in the user. To use the parlance of LSD therapy, to which *environments* bears some resemblance, the visual textual aspects of the albums make up a virtual *guide* for the user and help structure the *set* (mind-set) to strongly influence the subject's experience within the recording's sonic *setting*.[1] The back of the record jacket and its inner gatefold layout include written claims about the inherent therapeutic qualities of natural sounds. The inclusion of these claims and their accompanying instructions, however, perhaps indicates a certain lack of confidence in such a "natural" audience reaction. In fact, *environments'* liner notes must stand as some of the most highly reflexive and directive texts ever to wrap commercial recordings, drawing far more attention to the act of listening and the apparatus of playback than is the norm in musical album notes. Certainly, nearly all commercial audio formats and products include texts to help the listener identify and appreciate the sounds they contain. However, SRI's great reliance on photographs and directive texts is reminiscent of "The Edison Realism Test," which instructed consumers on how to listen to music on the phonograph in the early 1900s (cf. Katz 2004, 18–19). Just as listening to music in the absence of the performer did not come naturally at first, listening to natural sound in the absence of nature required a degree of cajoling and instruction to facilitate the desired audience reaction.

Fortuitously, the series' creator was more than equal to such a task. Irving Solomon Teibel was barely in his thirties on May 6, 1969, when he incorporated Syntonic Research Inc., a company that would channel the most prominent of his many talents. In the words of his close friend Miriam Berman, whose own *a cappella* heartbeat fills side one of *environments disc 5*, Teibel was "a jack of all trades at a very high level." He was not only a producer of audio field recordings, but also a photographer, graphic designer, advertising copywriter, businessman, and, it should be said, an expert self-promoter. Teibel combined the listening skills and sensitivity of a musician with the technical orientation of a scientist and the carnival claims of a snake-oil salesman. A native of Buffalo, New York, he studied engineering and graphic design before being drafted into the army in 1962. Stationed in Stuttgart, Germany, he worked as a public information specialist, designed the Seventh Army calendar, and experimented with electronic music in his spare time. After his discharge from the army, he moved to London, where he worked as an art director for Young and Rubicam, before moving to New York City in 1966. There he served as associate editor for *Popular Photography* and *Car and Driver*, while experimenting with electronic music and musique concrète (Teibel 1970).

Although it was named to sound like a large and impersonal corporation, SRI was, much like a contemporary electronic act such as Aphex Twin or Deadmau5, basically the alias of one man, who treated audio as an artistic medium and utilized the communicative resources around him to frame and circulate his art.[2] Without fail, Teibel's surviving friends and family assert that he did nearly everything on his own, using only one or two assistants from time to time—though, like Jim Buckwalter before him, he used a number of aliases to make business associates and the public think SRI was a bigger operation than it actually was. As his better-known contemporary Brian Eno did with ambient music, Teibel invented and popularized a novel use for recorded sound and industry distribution channels, adding a new genre of recordings to popular culture. And similar to Eno's ambient music, Teibel's natural sounds could be actively listened to, but were really designed to simply be *heard* as a designed aspect of the lived environment. In fact, Teibel deserves credit alongside Eno as a godfather of New Age music, though neither man appreciated or identified with that genre. Teibel was a purist who generally detested the mixing of environmental sounds and music, but nevertheless, potpourris of Enoesque ethereal music and Teibelian natural noises have wafted through bedrooms, alternative healing centers, and nail salons since the 1980s.

With the success of *environments* far from a foregone conclusion at the time, Teibel deployed his skills as a graphic designer and copywriter to set

environments.
new concepts in stereo sound · disc 1

Side 1: THE PSYCHOLOGICALLY ULTIMATE SEASHORE Side 2: OPTIMUM AVIARY

Figure 3.3 Front cover of
environments disc 1.

the stage for the first record's use (figures 3.3 and 3.4). The gatefold record jacket of *environments: new concepts in stereo sound disc 1* (released September 1969) includes some 1,800 words on the use and uses of its two sides, "The Psychologically Ultimate Seashore" and "Optimum Aviary." The front cover is dominated by the distinctive lowercase series title and his photo of gentle waves lapping a sandy shore in the orange light of dawn or dusk. The top of the back cover exclaims "the most sensuous recordings ever made!" in large type. Beneath this announcement appears a series of statements in quotation marks, each in a different color and font, attributed to subjects of "extensive listening tests," such as: "Better than the real thing." "A gentle, subtle trip." "Amazing!" "Reading speed doubled." "Fantastic for making love!" "Better than a tranquilizer!" "Room seemed brighter."

Under these attention-getters, the back cover's sales pitch begins in earnest, touting the record's use as an aid to "reading, relaxing, sleeping, or just plain concentrating":

> The first of an extensive series, ENVIRONMENTS represents a totally new type of recorded sound—psychologically perfect aural environments which can be left on indefinitely without fatigue or boredom.
>
> The outcome of extensive research on auditory stimulation, ENVIRONMENTS Disc One is not only pleasurable to listen to, but also represents the only effective means of easily coping with the ever-increasing problem of disturbing noise. At normal playback levels (or less), this disc

the most sensuous recordings ever made!

"BETTER THAN THE REAL THING" "A Gentle, Subtle Trip"
"APARTMENT NEVER SEEMED SO PLEASANT BEFORE.." "AMAZING!"
"Great for reading.." "...HAVEN'T FELT THIS GOOD SINCE MY VACATION"
"Can't get over how clear my thinking is" "infinitely flexible.."
"THE HIPPEST RECORD EVER!" "PLAY IT CONTINUALLY..."
"...cured my insomnia!" "...MY FAVORITE RECORD"
"READING SPEED DOUBLED.." "Never heard anything like it!"
"...fantastic for making love!" "NEVER GET TIRED OF IT"
"BETTER THAN A TRANQUILIZER!" "room seemed brighter"

If you've ever had trouble reading, relaxing, sleeping, or just plain concentrating, ENVIRONMENTS will be a source of constant amazement to you. You've never heard a recording before quite like this one.

Above are a few of the many enthusiastic comments received during extensive listening tests conducted prior to the release of this record.

The first of an extensive series, ENVIRONMENTS represents a totally new type of recorded sound — psychologically perfect aural environments which can be left on indefinitely without fatigue or boredom.

The outcome of extensive research on auditory stimulation, ENVIRONMENTS Disc One is not only pleasurable to listen to, but also represents the only effective means of easily coping with the ever-increasing problem of disturbing noise. At normal playback levels (or less), this disc effectively masks most irritating noises to an amazing degree, in much the same way a deodorizer neutralizes disagreeable odors.

You don't listen to this record — you hear it. If played stereophonically, the sound seems to be all around you, creating an unusually sensuous sonic environment. Unlike music, ENVIRONMENTS affects the subconscious without deadening the mind's ability to think.

There are several other unusual features which make these recordings even more unique. For one thing, either side of this disc can be played at any phonograph speed, from 45rpm down to 16 2/3rpm, in full stereo. All that's required is a slight adjustment of your phonograph's tone controls to compensate for the speed change. This amazing capability of variable-speed playback is no mere novelty — the sounds produced at different speeds dramatically affect your respiration, heartbeat, and metabolism. In addition, the unusual characteristics of the disc groove, as well as the use of highest grade pressing materials guarantee extreme durability, thus assuring you of extensive distortion-free playback with minimum wear.

At the slowest speed, each side of this disc will play uninterrupted for an entire hour, more than twice the playing time of any other stereo LP! If you make the slight modification detailed within, this single record is capable of providing a continuous stereo environment which can be left on indefinitely.

Unlike sound effects recordings or other similar sound sources, the superb stereo sound on this disc has been achieved through the collateral use of a specially programmed computer interface. This accounts, in part, for the record's amazing ability to be played at any speed, as well as its ultra-dimensional presence and dynamic range.

Produced by Syntonic Research, Inc.

ATLANTIC RECORDING CORPORATION, 1841 BROADWAY, NEW YORK, NEW YORK 10023

Figure 3.4 Back cover of *environments disc 1*.

effectively masks most irritating noises to an amazing degree, in much the same way a deodorizer neutralizes disagreeable odors.

You don't listen to this record—you hear it. If played stereophonically, the sound seems to be all around you, creating an unusually sensuous sonic environment. Unlike music, ENVIRONMENTS affects the subconscious without deadening the mind's ability to think. (Teibel 1969a)

The rest of the back cover text focuses on the medium itself. Teibel claimed that his records remade the turntable into a different device, a modifiable system that interfaced with the biological system of the user—in effect, a biomedium. "Through the collateral use of a specially programmed computer interface," the text explained, SRI had developed an ocean recording that could be played back at any turntable speed, from 45 revolutions per minute down to 16⅔ rpm. The purpose of this was twofold: first, because "the sounds produced at different speeds dramatically affect your respiration, heartbeat, and metabolism," and second, because it allowed the user, with "slight modification" of the phonograph, to enjoy "a continuous stereo environment which can be left on indefinitely." At its slowest speed, one *environments* album side lasts for an hour (twice the normal maximum length of an LP side), but the inner jacket details methods for getting "continuous playback" from an automatic turntable. There are additional instructions for minimizing record wear by lowering stylus pressure, as well as positioning speakers and changing volume and tone settings for maximum effectiveness.

These *environments'* jacket texts make a set of explicit and implicit claims concerning the interrelations of sound, space, and the hearing subject. They construct a system between the internalities of the user and the externalities of space in which transductions of sound, controlled through the apparatus of the phonograph, are the means through which space and subject fine-tune one another. It is useful to frame this relationship in terms of the three potentials of sonic affectivity outlined in the introduction: sound as mediated by mechanical waves in an environmental medium; sound as transducible, as through electroacoustic mediation; and sound as a medium in itself, through which subjects and objects emerge in modes of affective relation. Around 1960, James Buckwalter's sound conditioner harnessed electrical current to generate mechanical waves that altered the possible modes of affectivity in the medium of sound. Now, in 1969, Teibel was for the first time using the transduction of nonmusical recorded sound to achieve the same goal, a technique that would subsequently be employed by Buckwalter in his analog nature sound machines, as well as by numerous other orphic technology developers.

Much like Buckwalter's patent, Teibel's liner notes portray the external, "ever-increasing problem of disturbing noise" as having corrosive effects on the interior functioning of the self. In response, he provides the self with a means to tune in to a "sensuous sonic environment" and thus enhance its inner functioning. Again, this text presents us with a weak version of the Western liberal subject, not the master of its domain, but distracted, made sleepless, or otherwise affected by its environment. Teibel calls upon the subject to reflect upon and recognize its position in this sonic-spatial system and offers it a new means of controlling the sonic environment in which it is embedded. But while both Buckwalter's Sleep-Mate and Teibel's *environments* do a similar sort of sonic-affective work, the promotional metaculture their inventors use to surround and circulate these background technologies is very different: while the former appeals to a feminized vision of domestic tranquility, the latter appeals to a scientist vision of natural equilibrium.

The systemic relationship between listener and environment that Teibel constructs is reflective of cybernetic theory, long "one of the dominant intellectual paradigms of the Cold War era" when he produced *environments*

(Turner 2006, 27). In 1948, Norbert Wiener had published his book *Cybernetics: Or Control and Communication in the Animal and the Machine*, a lay-accessible presentation of an infocentric paradigm in which mechanical and biological systems were connected to their environments through informational feedback loops, achieving homeostasis (equilibrium) by continuously monitoring and responding to environmental changes. Wiener drew on Claude Shannon's information theory to render biological, mechanical, social, and computer systems analogous, eliding their physical differences by stressing patterns of communication. Communication scholar and historian of technology Fred Turner writes that in cybernetics, "all [of these systems] were simply patterns of ordered information in a world otherwise tending to entropy and noise" (2006, 22). Within the original cybernetic paradigm, the health of all systems is dependent upon *control*, minimizing noise and maximizing information flow and response. If acoustical noise was made informatic in Shannon's information theory, it would become audible once again in Teibel's cybernetics-influenced work.

A cybernetic sense of sonic interrelatedness is embedded in the name Syntonic's pairing of *syn* (together, alike) and *ton(e)*. Teibel's written records indicate that he was looking for a name that would be both imposing and suggestive of psychoacoustics, the science of sound perception. One type-written sheet of paper in the Syntonic archive reads, "Invent a generic name such as Skye & Xerox." Teibel's notes contain dozens of similar names he brainstormed before making his final selection: Simulacranics, Environ-Mental, OMonics, Sonance, and Euphonics, for example. The term "syntonic" had been used in the late 1800s to describe wireless telegraph systems in which pairs of transmitters and receivers were tuned to respond only to one another, but the term had other appropriate connotations as well. In Western music, the tonic is the fundamental pitch in a scale and the chord to which a composition must return to find resolution. In psychology, the term *ego syntonic* indicates thoughts, feelings, and behaviors that are in keeping with the subject's desired sense of self. Of course, a tonic is also a restorative or medicinal elixir, and Teibel never hesitated to market his product as an aural drug, as seen in the pill bottle publicity photo in figure 3.5. The customer in the record shop didn't need to understand the etymology of "syntonic" or the specifics of psychoacoustics to get the point. Teibel's marketing made the logic and feeling of *environments* clear enough to the prospective user before the needle ever dropped into the groove.

In his work on the relationships between technologies and concepts of selfhood, Peter Galison envisions two important lines of inquiry. First, what

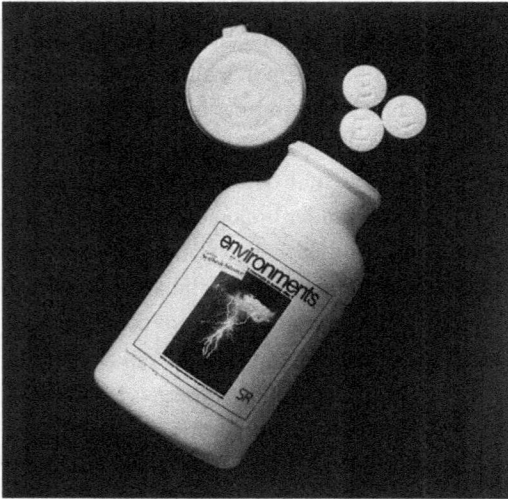

Figure 3.5 A Syntonic Research Inc. promotional photo imagines *environments* in pill form.

a priori notions of self make a new technology imaginable? For example, the creation of the Rorschach ink blot test required a notion of the unconscious that was shared only by a small set of psychologists at the time. Second, how are notions of self *naturalized* through technology? In the case of the ink blot, the use of the Rorschach test disseminated and naturalized the unconscious self that informed its technology (Galison 2004). Similarly, Syntonic Research Inc.'s first record contained an embedded cybernetic conception of the self in sonic environments—and the success of this record helped reshape and spread this sonic self-concept. But how specifically did such a self-concept occur to a nonscientist like Teibel? And what shared macroperceptual knowledge primed his audience to so readily purchase his wares? Answering these questions requires a close look at the development of the first *environments* side, "The Psychologically Ultimate Seashore."

The Cybernetic Counterculture

However hyperbolic the ad copy could be, there was truth in SRI's marketing of *environments* as "new concepts in stereo sound." Beyond repurposing the stereo system as a natural sound machine and opening the public mind to nature recordings' use beyond sound effects records, *environments disc 1*'s "Psychologically Ultimate Seashore" was quite possibly the first commercially successful recording to use digital production techniques. Neverthe-less, the concepts that inform *environments* were not entirely new. Despite the record jacket's claim that the series was "the only effective means of eas-ily coping with the ever-increasing problem of disturbing noise," as we have seen, noise had already been domesticated for use in home and work set-tings. Moreover, recorded music had been used to mask noise since Thomas Edison first tried using the phonograph for that purpose in 1915. By 1967, Stanford industrial psychologist James Keenan was speaking of "The Eco-Logic of Muzak," calling piped-in music a systemic part of the human envi-ronment, "the common stuff of everyday living in the global village" (Lanza 1994, 13, 150).

Teibel was certainly familiar with Muzak. He saved a sales letter a Muzak representative sent to SRI, which pitched the "synergistic effect" that "the scientific application of sound" would have on Teibel's (nonexistent) work-force. The language of this letter is very close to Teibel's own marketing, but with one significant difference. While the Muzak letter appeals to the cor-porate executive's concerns with efficiency and the bottom line, Teibel was pitching his product to a younger generation, one awash in new forms of self-exploration, audio technologies, and environmental concerns. To put it another way, Muzak was an agent of the speed-induced capitalist culture that was fragmenting social and physical spaces, while SRI was positioning itself as an agent of the sonic counterculture. These generational social and technolog-ical currents flow through the story of how Teibel converted a Brighton Beach wave into a digital waveform and then into a vinyl virtual environment.

As Teibel himself once stated, he started the record company "with the help of many friends, from many divergent fields that, by chance, corre-sponded to that particular project" and influenced its artistic, technologi-cal, and psychological pragmatics (Werner 1987). The Manhattan milieu in which Teibel moved in the 1960s was a setting where artists were reshaping physical, technological, and generic boundaries through installations and happenings, mixing media and conceiving of new aesthetic environments. Analog synthesizer enthusiasts were rethinking music in terms of the con-stituent waveforms of sound that Hermann von Helmholtz had discerned a century earlier. Like their counterparts in the sciences, these musicians were armed with technology that treated sound as material to be reshaped, recom-bined, and repurposed. Meanwhile, proponents of psychedelics and medi-tation promoted visions of human consciousness as hackable in one way or another. Fred Turner has called actors such as these "New Communalists," a cybernetics-influenced wing of the counterculture that "turned away from political action and toward technology and the transformation of consciousness as the primary sources of social change" (2006, 4). Bruce Clarke similarly describes the spread and influence of an emergent "systems counterculture" represented by personages and documents such as renegade cybernetician Heinz von Foerster and Stewart Brand's *Whole Earth Catalog*, which connected cybernetics to alternative ways of thinking and living (2012). Such actors believed that "if the bureaucracies of industry and government demanded that men and women become psychologically fragmented specialists, the technology-induced experience of togetherness would allow them to become both self-sufficient and whole once again" (Turner 2006, 4).

"The Psychologically Ultimate Seashore" of *environments: new concepts in stereo sound disc 1* was a sonic ocean in which these cultural streams of sound and self combined. As his friend Miriam Berman explains, Teibel wasn't easy to pigeonhole and moved freely between friends in business, science, and the counterculture. During the 1960s and '70s, Teibel's work and social circles included artists and scientists such as photographers Irving Penn and Richard Avedon, Columbia University molecular biologist and computer graphics artist Lou Katz, and Bell Labs computer music pioneer Laurie Spiegel. "The Psychologically Ultimate Seashore" in fact, developed not through long-term research and planning, but through happenstance, inspiration, and collaboration with two underground filmmakers and a neuropsychologist working at Bell Labs.

Irv Teibel first recorded the ocean in the winter of 1968–69 at the request of Beverly and Tony Conrad.[3] Perhaps best known for his droning, minimalist "dream music," Tony Conrad had performed violin with the groups Theater of Eternal Music and the Primitives, the latter of which included sculptor and drummer Walter de Maria, violist John Cale, and guitarist Lou Reed. (Cale and Reed would go on to name their subsequent band the Velvet Underground after finding a novel of the same name in Conrad's apartment.) Conrad's other claim to fame was his structuralist film *The Flicker* (1966), thirty minutes of pulsing light and clattering synthesized sound known for causing hallucinations, even in audiences bereft of chemical assistance. The Conrads were working on what would be their first film together, entitled *Coming Attractions* (1970). The film opened on the beach, and the sound of the waves pounding the shore was particularly important to Tony. The couple contacted Teibel, whom they knew as a record jacket designer, because he owned a portable Uher reel-to-reel recorder. Over forty years later, Tony Conrad described to me his wintry field recording trips with Irv Teibel:

I explained that Irv and I would need to take the subway to Coney Island. Irv was disheartened at the prospect of this long subway trip; he thought we should stay in Manhattan and simulate the ocean. But I was insistent on recording a real ocean, and we did. But Irv complained again at the beach. I wanted to hold the mikes as close as possible to the crashing waves; Irv wanted to be protected from the cold and bluster, and he was especially impatient when I actually wanted to record by walking out into the waves. "Hey, Tony, isn't that enough?" Irv would call out, recording himself in the act. I wanted as long a stereo take as I could get, but finally we had to fold up and head for home. Irv took the tapes to check the recording quality. The next morning Irv called. "Tony! It sounds fantastic! The recording sounds incredible!"

If, as Conrad recalls, Teibel had been somewhat reluctant about the project, he was thoroughly won over by the sounds it produced. The next day, they went to record bird sounds for the film at the Bronx Zoo. Again, Teibel was not thrilled at the prospect of a long field trip on a winter's day, but was entirely thrilled by the sounds he heard when he got home—so much so, that when Teibel met Conrad to record playing children the following day, he brought news of an epiphany:

> The morning I met Irv at his apartment to record the playground he was very excited. He showed me a complete prospectus that he had designed overnight. It was basically a sales promotion for something that he called Syntonic Research, an invented entity that we would collaborate on. Syntonic Research, his text explained, had established through extensive research that the soothing sounds of the ocean were like a tranquilizer—good for meditation, sex, and effective concentration. We would put out a record, he explained, and sell it as a psychological (and psychedelic) experience. I was startled at the direction this was taking, especially when Irv produced a draft contract for our collaborative enterprise.

The Conrads considered but eventually declined the proposition. According to Tony Conrad, they subsequently had difficulty in obtaining copies of the recordings from Teibel, who was focused on his own plans for them. Teibel began leaving New York, traveling to Cape Hatteras, North Carolina, and other locations to capture better ocean recordings. In the end, the Conrads secured their recordings for *Coming Attractions*. By the end of the year, Conrad saw *environments 1* in stores with "The Psychologically Ultimate Seashore" on side one and "Optimum Aviary" on side two. "The text on the record jacket is almost word for word what Irv composed over-night after that day at the aviary," he recalls.

The entire process, from inspiration through incorporation, production, and distribution, took about a year. Teibel's brainstorming is charted in hast-ily typed and handwritten documents found in the Austin storage space. At the outset, Teibel mapped out the types of releases SRI would produce over the next decade, as well as their proposed effects on users. Conrad's use of the nebulous term "entity" to describe Syntonic Research Inc. is entirely ap-ropos: it was a corporation with very little *corpus*, a research firm whose conclusions were not only forgone, but were reached without employing any researchers. Steve Gerstman, who was briefly SRI's national sales manager before Atlantic Records took over distribution in 1970, told me, "It was all [Irv's] intuition. This was a time when people experimented with drugs and meditation, and he thought this would be a nonchemical means [of achiev-ing this sort of state]." As Conrad's *Flicker* film shows, it was also a time when people experimented with *media* as consciousness-altering devices. Since *environments* wasn't a drug requiring FDA approval, Teibel didn't have to be too careful about his claims. In fact, says Gerstman, Teibel made up the user quotes featured so prominently on the back of the first record, though Teibel attributed these to the first of several *environments* listening tests.

Wave Production

Conrad's narrative doesn't tell us about Teibel's epiphany itself, nor what else may have inspired it besides the magical sounds that came from his Uher tape machine. For these elements of the story we can turn to Teibel's own words, focusing primarily on two sources from the 1980s, a lengthy inter-view and an unrelated essay, in which he reflected back on the birth of *envi-ronments*. In the intervening years, the producer had proved adept at selling the series as a "sonic tonic" for whatever ailed society at the time, from noise pollution to economic stress to the energy crisis of the 1970s (he claimed that *environments* 11's "Alpine Blizzard" lowered the subjective temperature in a room without air conditioning). In both the interview and the essay, Teibel was flexible in his accounts of the series' genesis, reshaping the story for two different audiences. In fact, Teibel seemed to tell the Syntonic story differ-ently every time he was asked about it, rendering a definitive history impos-sible to create. I focus primarily on these two particular tellings because they evoke two different appeals that Teibel was making to potential customers, one based on *nature's inherent perfection* and the other based on *the perfection of nature through technology.*

Teibel's two different accounts reflect two different strands of belief that Turner sees fused in New Communalist ideology. One strand is the belief that self and community could be made whole by turning away from the city and toward nature. In the other strand, self and community are to be found through the use of technology (Turner 2006, 74). On its face, this combination may seem contradictory. However, this technopastoral fusion was made possible by an underlying cybernetic systems approach that had altered contemporary visions of both ecology and technology, so that both were understood as systems that could be fine-tuned for the benefit of mankind and the planet. As we will see, in its synthesis of ocean wave and digital waveform, *environments* itself is a biomedium that embodied just such a fusion. However, in the 1980s Teibel was willing to rhetorically tease nature and technology apart for what he apparently saw as two different audiences: natural sound aficionados and computer geeks. For the first audience, he framed his job as producer as one of carefully *reproducing* nature without altering its essence in mediation. For the second audience, he stressed the synthetic processes through which he *rendered* nature into a usefully mediated form, useful for hacking the human into an improved cyborg state (see figure 3.6).

Reproducing Nature

Speaking with German composer, sound artist, and acoustic ecology enthusiast Hans U. Werner in 1987, Teibel emphasized the soothing connection to the natural environment that made the series possible, while minimizing the mediated and synthetic nature of that connection. Asked by Werner how he had come to combine photography, electronic music, recording, and graphic design in his work, he replied:

> Basically, it is the fact that as a child I had hyperactivity and that I had always been searching for a way that would still the devils in my head. Working on a film back in the late 60s, I found something very interesting. We did a loop on an ocean sound that could be synchronized for a motion picture soundtrack. We have done several hundred loops at this point and all of them were very irritating after a while, but this particular one was quite magical. Everyone who was exposed to it seemed to think that this was something they had not heard on tape before.

Figure 3.6 While Teibel emphasized nature's healing properties, he produced and marketed his nature sounds with a technophilic and countercultural twist.

This got me very excited at that time, as I had been doing a lot of electronic music, and I had never got a reaction like that to my own music. It made me think of some references I had read on how Beethoven often could not listen to his own music. When he had a problem with composition, he would go out into the forest and wander in the woods for sometimes days, listening to the sounds of nature. According to this account, it seemed to have a very calming effect on him, and he felt that there was also a certain religiosity that was very important to his work.

I have never been a religious person myself but I have found making recordings like this gives me a certain communion with religious aspects of my life I have not had before. I wanted to share that with other people.

After a certain period of time I realized the only way I could share it was to start my own record company. (Werner 1987)

In this interview, Teibel positions the sounds of the ocean and woods as a natural salve for the afflictions of the spirit and, more specifically, something that "stills the devils" in his own head. Insofar as technological mediation comes into play in this account of the creation of "Psychologically Ultimate Seashore," it is a matter of selecting a loop of audio that renders the medium and its repetitions as transparent as possible. Later in the interview, the producer compares his method to that of a nature photographer who works "to capture something that can be looked at for a very long period of time." Teibel presents his role as one of carefully curating nature for others without damaging nature's curative properties: "You can cut it, edit it, you can modify it and it still somehow has a basic essence that, if you violate it, you destroy it."

Teibel shows here that he shares concerns with the acoustic ecology community, though his work was in some ways quite at odds with the views of the movement's founding father, R. Murray Schafer. Acoustic ecology grew out of the World Soundscape Project, a Vancouver-based research group founded by Schafer in the late 1960s. In a rhetorical move that showed the influence of systems-oriented ecology, Schafer and his associates used the term "soundscape" to help them address human-made noise. While the term emphasized sound as a spatial component of the environment, it was not meant to stand apart from the subjectivity of the human listener—the soundscape was, in effect, a cybernetic system between the human and the acoustic surround. The Vancouver group aimed to help humans achieve a more suitable homeostatic relationship with their acoustic environment.

For Schafer, who criticized "*audioanalgesia*, that is, the use of sound as a painkiller, a distraction to dispel distractions" (1994, 96, emphasis his), Teibel's recordings would have been part of the problem, not part of the solution. In 1969, the same year as *environments* was released, Schafer coined the term *schizophonia* to describe the allegedly disorienting and deleterious effects of electroacoustic sound reproduction. Schizophonia signified technological processes that rip sounds from their natural contexts and amplify them beyond proportion to imperialistically dominate soundscapes and psyches (90–91). In the words of Schafer's associate Barry Truax, "the mood of the environment becomes that imposed by the electroacoustic sound, and therefore mood becomes a designed, artificial construct. Whether one likes or dislikes the effect is not important to the discussion" (Truax 1984, 121).

Teibel likely would have countered this argument with what he told a *Rolling Stone* reporter in 1972: "We're not saying look, go inside your room, close all the windows, put up soundproof material, make it as pure and sterile as you can, and then bring it all back with one of your [*environments*] records. No, we're saying that people *already* live like that. They live in rabbit warrens" (Ferris 1971).

Though they shared a systems approach to—and a deep appreciation of—environmental sound, Teibel and the acoustic ecologists were of opposite opinions on the type of homeostasis that could be achieved through natural sound recordings. In Teibel's view, the recording reintroduced the natural to the lived environment so that it could reach the interior life of the subject, allowing for "communion" with natural sound's "essence." In Schafer and Truax's view, the recording introduced the artificial into lived space and thus rendered artificial the interior life of the subject. That said, Schafer and Truax were not the Luddites that some of their most forceful passages suggest. Indeed, acoustic ecology has produced and influenced several generations of natural sound recordists and media artists, while Teibel has been cited as an influence by some contemporary acoustic ecologists (e.g., Cummings 2010).

Synthesizing Nature

Three years before the Ulrich interview, Teibel provided a contrasting account of the creation of "Ultimate Seashore" for a book on the history of computers. In "Mother Nature Goes Digital," Teibel highlights the central roles played by an IBM System/360 computer and a Bell Labs researcher who invited him to digitize his sea sounds, Dr. Louis J. Gerstman. From the essay's first lines, Teibel focuses not on natural sound's essential relationship to the human subject, but rather on the technologies, techniques, and manipulations that render that relationship useful: "A good deal of the progress of civilization over the centuries has been a function of gaining control over natural processes so they can be used when we need them. Some examples are windmills, the internal combustion engine, atomic power and Donkey Kong. In 1968, with the help of a computer, I made a modest contribution to this august confluence of imaginative derring-do by putting the true sound of the ocean on a record" (Teibel 1984, 224).

Teibel's humorous opening is at once self-effacing and self-aggrandizing, seeming to intentionally leave the reader wondering whether the author's accomplishment is on par with Donkey Kong or the internal combustion engine. However, the real wonder is Teibel's claim that it took a *computer* to put "the true sound of the ocean on a record." The rest of the essay is a tale of digital audio manipulation that resulted in a sound that was not so much "true" as, if anything, *hyperreal*.

More than just a groundbreaking and popular natural sound recording, "The Psychologically Ultimate Seashore" was the first exposure to digital audio signal processing for hundreds of thousands of listeners. This innovation came thanks to Lou Gerstman, brother of Teibel's aforementioned sales manager, Steve, a neuropsychologist who taught at City College and did research and consulting work at numerous facilities, including Western Electric, Columbia University, the Veterans Administration, and Bell Labs. Primarily an expert in speech processes and disorders, Gerstman's work deployed computers in areas such as voice print spectrograms, the prediction of post-stroke speech recovery, and, most famously, synthetic speech. As noted in his *New York Times* obituary, Gerstman (and John L. Kelly) coaxed not only speech but song from an IBM 704 computer at Bell Labs.[4] In a development that would find its way into popular consciousness, the 704 sang the song "Daisy Bell" to a musical accompaniment programmed by computer music legend Max Mathews, catching the ear of visiting science fiction author Arthur C. Clarke. It was this event that inspired Clarke to write HAL's "Daisy" scene in Stanley Kubrick's *2001: A Space Odyssey*.

Both Buffalo natives living in Manhattan, Irv and Lou met each other when Teibel's brother Phil married Gerstman's cousin Edie. In an interview, Edie's brother, Steve, told me that "Irv and Louie were two characters, two very entertaining guys," imaginative and eclectic thinkers attracted to both the technological and the countercultural. According to Teibel's essay, during one of the pair's frequent chess games (or, perhaps, at a cocktail party, as stated in an SRI [auto]biography of Teibel), Gerstman[5] began musing about his own recent work in psychacoustics, which Teibel understood as "an arcane science seemingly focused on band-aid fixes of airport noise and improving intelligibility of telephonic transmissions" (1984, 224). Noting that many people did not care for the white noise used to mask other sounds, Gerstman recalled reading a passage in Hermann von Helmholtz's work from the nineteenth century. As Gerstman remembered it, Helmholtz suggested that if natural sounds could somehow be captured, they could be utilized to the psychological benefit of listeners. Teibel had just returned from Brighton Beach with his ocean recording, he wrote, "and this casual mention of Helmholtz' musings triggered a 'what-if' that was to have a profound effect on the next decade of my life" (1984, 224).

Combining elements of Teibel's accounts with those of Tony Conrad's, we can synthesize a scene that captures, if not the precise historical details, at least "the essence," as Teibel might put it, of the birth of "Ultimate Seashore": Teibel returns from his beach outing with Conrad and listens to his recordings. He finds a passage of wave sounds particularly transfixing and, using a razor and some splicing tape, loops this section of the recording so that it can play over and over again. The next day, after recording and listening to the bird sounds from the zoo, he plays the ocean loop again. Teibel is still intrigued. The loop is still echoing in his mind that evening when he and Gerstman discuss the (apparently apocryphal) Helmholtz passage over chess (or cocktails).[6] That night, Teibel writes up the prospectus that he would present to Conrad the next day.

And yet for all the promise that Teibel heard in his ocean sounds, there were practical issues that would reveal themselves in the repetitions of that loop of tape, issues that every producer of mediated natural sounds has had to deal with since. It is exceedingly hard to produce a long-form recording of a natural soundscape suitable for continuous listening. As Teibel himself was perhaps the first to point out, the natural sound must be of a nature that one can hear it but not actively listen to it—but lengthy recordings usually contain details that reveal either (a) the specificity of the captured time-space or (b) evidence of the recording medium itself. Examples of the former would include the laughter of children walking by on the beach, a particularly loud bird, or a boat passing by. Examples of the latter include wind in the microphone, a loud wave causing distortion in the microphone preamplifier, or the sound recordist's own hand creating noise on the microphone. Rhetorics of fidelity are common sales pitches for natural sound recordings and machines, but true realism would involve sounds that would draw the listener's attention to the specificities of the setting and the medium, thus diminishing the recording's utility as a technology of the self. For the medium to help the user reshape her own consciousness, achieving a preferred subjective state, it must elide all attention-grabbing specificity. What is really wanted is not realism, but *idealism*: a Platonic ocean or rainstorm to help the user control outward sounds and inward thoughts.

Looping is a key tool in the aesthetics and pragmatics of this audio idealism. Rather than traveling to some isolated locale (where one is still likely to record the sound of planes flying overhead) to record a pristine forty-five minutes of natural sound, a producer can capture a smaller piece of wild time-space and force it to bite its own tail. However, like the long-form recording, the tape loop—or the virtual loop of the repeating digital file—has ways of revealing its own specificity and "mediality" (Sterne 2012). Selection of the loop is critical because, upon repetition, any particular sound that stands out from the rest may be perceived as distracting or even annoying. Moreover, upon repetition, any random succession of audible occurrences may be perceived as a pattern. This effect is particularly common in short loops and can severely undermine the Helmholtzian advantage that Teibel claimed his recordings held over music—the lack of order that allows the mind to tune out natural noises.[7] A final common source of annoyance is recognizable loop points, which result when there is either a gap between the end of a recording and the resumption of its beginning *or* when particular sounds are heard to begin or end at the loop point in an unnatural way.

At their worst, such recognizable patterns and loop points can draw the listener's attention to the artifice of the medium itself, marring the recording's indexicality to nature and diminishing the listener's ability to suspend disbelief and enjoy the recording *as* nature. When faced with producing an LP side's worth of ocean sound, Teibel found these issues impossible to overcome, though in his essay he collapses these problems into a simple issue of fidelity. Everyone knows what an ocean is supposed to sound like, he writes, but each element of the audio signal chain from microphone to loudspeaker introduces distortion. Despite his best efforts, "the inaccuracies of my highly regarded professional equipment continued to prevail, and nearly a year later I had produced a hundred stereo recordings not one of which actually sounded, to my mind's ear, like the ocean I wanted to hear" (1984, 224).

In this sentence, Teibel seamlessly splices together two different types of audio pragmatics, cross-fading from the realist agenda of recording the ocean *accurately* to the idealism of reproducing the ocean that existed *in his mind's ear*. Such a soundless slip between the real and the ideal is not uncommon among audio producers. In fact, the aesthetics of audio "fidelity" rely upon it. Though media are ostensibly the way we reproduce the sonic world, they are also our measure of it, deriving a seldom-acknowledged authority in appraising "reality," precisely because we forget their intentionalities (Gitelman 2006). The techniques and affordances of audio reproduction reshape listening, affecting both how the natural world sounds to the ears and how we imagine it *should* sound in the mind's ear.

Teibel, of course, had no reservations about mediation. He also loved computers and was doubtful but intrigued when Gerstman suggested that his ocean sounds could be improved by the IBM mainframe computer normally used for purposes of speech synthesis at Bell Labs. Speech synthesis (Tompkins 2010), psychoacoustics, the "perceptual coding" embedded in compressed audio files such as the mp3 (Sterne 2012), and computer music (Chadabe 1997) all owe a debt to research done at the birthplace of information theory. In fact, Murray Hill, New Jersey's Bell Telephone Laboratories, was the birthplace of digital audio itself. In 1957, Max Mathews was working on a means to do listening tests of telephone line sound quality. He invented one converter to transduce an audio signal into bits to be processed by a computer and another converter to turn the resulting bits back into sound. The wide-ranging possibilities of digital audio were immediately apparent to Mathews. Luckily, he had a boss, Bell Labs director John Pierce, who had both a love of music and the respect of AT&T management. Pierce gave Mathews and his associates free use of the acoustic research department's mainframe computers after hours. They broke ground in psychoacoustics and speech synthesis by day and created musical software, hardware, and compositions by night.

And so it was that Teibel and Gerstman entered Bell Labs after hours and threaded the Brighton Beach tape onto the reel of a machine for analog-to-digital conversion. The fine details of that night and the next are, unfortunately, lost to time. None of the surviving Bell Labs researchers and composers I spoke to knew the specifics, so we are left only with the somewhat vague account in Teibel's essay. Given the technological constraints of the computer, only two minutes of audio could be processed, which was fine because that was about all Teibel had. The first few attempts to process the audio "yielded little more than noise"—apparently not of the good variety—"as we adjusted such technical niceties as I/O parameters, dynamic range and a random number generator to interface with selected waveforms." Things did not, at first, seem hopeful, Teibel writes.

> Then suddenly we both grew still and listened attentively to the output of the monitor speakers. Rolling out through the grille cloth was a beautiful, tranquil ocean sound I had never heard before. The splice on the loop we were using could not be detected, as an electronic random noise generator reprogramed the waveform parameters with each cycle and created subtle new waves that never repeated. By adjusting bandwidth constraints, we got the sound to grow more and more realistic until what we heard was a serenely majestic ocean sound complete with bubbling surf and a faintly perceived, eerily synthesized foghorn. (225)

The next night, Teibel returned, bringing a variable-speed tape recorder with him. Gerstman and Teibel routed the tape loop through the computer and the output was captured on the recorder. The IBM S/360 was acting as a digital signal processor, digitizing the sound from the loop, making mathematical changes to the digitized waveforms, and then converting the digital signal back into sound to be recorded by the second tape machine. Such real-time digital processing would have been very demanding at the time, and Teibel writes that they set both tape machines at their slowest settings so that it took eight hours to create the thirty minutes of "The Psychologically Ultimate Seashore." "We had, it seemed," wrote Teibel, "created the first digitally produced broadband recording." Through a biomediating series of transductions, they had channeled the most basic of earthly elements through the most advanced emulation of the human mind. Pushing waves through a computer, they synthesized the real into the ideal, the ultimate ocean of the mind's ear.

Listening Tests, Feedback Loops, and Spaces of Possibility

Until 1969, the use of orphic media was to maintain autonomy, building a wall of noise to shore up the boundaries of the self for purposes of individual welfare and productivity. But by thinking in terms of interdependent systems, Teibel created a recording series that he claimed was useful for more than just creating spaces for sleep and concentration. From the first release, he claimed that these records were "infinitely flexible" and suitable for "mental trips" and "fantastic for making love." Like the music of Orpheus, *environments* could be used not just for boundary maintenance but also to open up new spaces of affectivity through sound, new opportunities for sonic engagement between individuals, new kinds of entrainment, new senses of self, other, and environment enacted through vibration.

There is evidence that people actually used *environments* in these ways. As we have seen, Syntonic Research Inc. and its LP series were the result of overnight inspiration rather than painstaking experimentation. Teibel's knowledge of psychoacoustics, meanwhile, was not of a professional level— he simply knew enough to create rhetorical legitimacy by placing references to the psychology of hearing in his ad copy. Teibel did do audience research, however, in the form of feedback cards and listening tests (figure 3.7), learning a significant amount about his users' needs and experiences with his records. And what he learned was rather extraordinary: despite the lack of detailed clinical research on *environments*, professionals such as psychologists and psychiatrists began using Syntonic recordings in clinical settings, while various media producers (often paying a fee) began incorporating

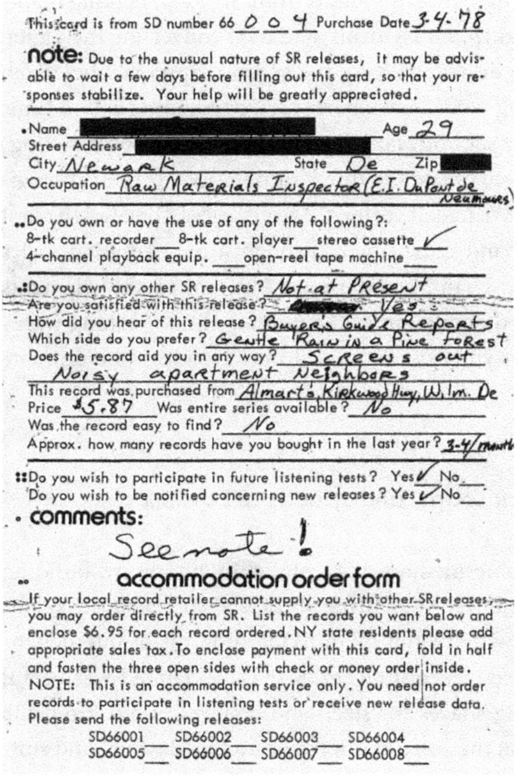

This card is from SD number 66 _0 0 4_ Purchase Date _3-4-78_

note: Due to the unusual nature of SR releases, it may be advisable to wait a few days before filling out this card, so that your responses stabilize. Your help will be greatly appreciated.

- Name ▓▓▓▓▓▓▓▓ Age _29_
  Street Address ▓▓▓▓▓▓
  City _Newark_ State _De_ Zip ▓▓▓
  Occupation _Raw Materials Inspector (E.I. DuPont de Neumours)_

.. Do you own or have the use of any of the following?:
8-tk cart. recorder___ 8-tk cart. player___ stereo cassette _✓_
4-channel playback equip.___ open-reel tape machine___

.: Do you own any other SR releases? _Not at present_
Are you satisfied with this release? ▓▓▓▓▓ _Yes_
How did you hear of this release? _Buyer's Guide Reports_
Which side do you prefer? _Gentle Rain in a Pine Forest_
Does the record aid you in any way? _Screens out_
Noisy apartment Neighbors
This record was purchased from _Almart's Kirkwood Hwy, W.Im. De_
Price _$5.87_ Was entire series available? _No_
Was the record easy to find? _No_
Approx. how many records have you bought in the last year? _3-4/month_

:: Do you wish to participate in future listening tests? Yes _✓_ No___
Do you wish to be notified concerning new releases? Yes _✓_ No___

- **comments:**

  See note!

accommodation order form

If your local record retailer cannot supply you with other SR releases, you may order directly from SR. List the records you want below and enclose $6.95 for each record ordered. NY state residents please add appropriate sales tax. To enclose payment with this card, fold in half and fasten the three open sides with check or money order inside. NOTE: This is an accommodation service only. You need not order records to participate in listening tests or receive new release data. Please send the following releases:

SD66001___ SD66002___ SD66003___ SD66004___
SD66005___ SD66006___ SD66007___ SD66008___

Figure 3.7 An example of the feedback cards enclosed in every SRI release. Some respondents would receive test copies of subsequent releases accompanied by longer listening tests.

Syntonic's ocean waves, rain forests, and country streams into their own artistic works. Teibel's archive is full of critics' reviews and print articles, user feedback cards and tests, and correspondence from clinicians, encounter group leaders, and media producers who used his work. These hundreds of pages of documents provide insight into the reception and use of *environments* in mental health work, spiritual practices, and popular culture. They suggest that, in contrast to Marpac's electromechanical noise generator, *environments* was indeed used in ways not constrained by a utilitarian sleep/concentration binary, ways more in keeping with the spirit of New Communalism.

Picking up where we left off in the story of *environments 1*, the closest thing to a clinical test that Syntonic Research Inc. ever conducted allegedly took place shortly after the ocean recording was produced at Bell Labs. According to Teibel, he took a copy of the tape to a psychology professor he knew on Long Island for testing on graduate students.[8]

A week later I got a call from him. He had done double-blind testing during sleep research and found that the subjects had had quite vivid dreams after listening to the tapes. Many of the subjects had reported that they felt unusually refreshed upon awakening. In addition, experiments utilizing difficult reading matter had shown that comprehension and reading speed in some instances had doubled when the ocean was played in the background. (Teibel 1984, 225)

Teibel attributed the comments on the back of *environments 1*—the blurbs that Steve Gerstman says Teibel made up—to this week-long test of students. Teibel immediately went to work on editing side two from the Bronx aviary recordings, designing the packaging, and finding a manufacturer to create high-quality vinyl pressings for repeated playback. The next test was a market test: the record was stocked at the Harvard Coop, where, according to Teibel, it "outsold the Beatles, especially at exam time" (225).

From there, *environments 1* was an immediate success. Teibel hired Steve Gerstman, who began selling the record to shops along the East Coast, while Teibel stayed in New York and used his marketing skills and contacts to garner reviews and mentions in major press outlets. According to Steve Gerstman, the major breakthrough came on November 1, 1969, when *Rolling Stone*'s "Random Notes" column called the record "an amazing piece of wax" with the potential to "wipe out minds, music, and Muzak—all at the same time," and recommending its seashore sounds for the purposes of "balling and crashing." Teibel's countercultural pitch had succeeded: his noise was perceived not as part of the regulatory mainstream of Muzak and white noise machines, but as a technology of self suitable for the Age of Aquarius. The *Village Voice* concurred, recommending *environments 1* for "speed-reading, love-making, creative expression, and turning on." More mainstream publications reviewed it as well, however. In fact, it seemed that people heard whatever they wanted to hear in *environments*: "sonic tonic" (*Newsweek*), Aldous Huxley's soma (*New York Times*), "acoustical perfume" (*House and Garden*), and acoustic furniture—"part of the room [like] the rug or sofa" (*Home Furnishings Daily*) (Teibel 1969b). The reviews attracted the attention of Neshui Ertegun of Atlantic Records, who offered Teibel a three-record deal. Though Teibel preferred to maintain complete control, he couldn't keep up with demand for the record on his own, and so he accepted the offer to gain access to Atlantic's distribution channels.

Enclosed in each *environments* release was a feedback card similar to those used by Marpac and other manufacturers of consumer electronics and appliances, underscoring the extent to which Teibel viewed his product as "an applied psychology device" rather than a typical record. These cards furnished him with valuable information on the frequency and purposes of customer use and opened up a direct line of communication that circumvented Atlantic channels. The feedback cards also provided customers with a simple means of requesting particular environments for future releases, which Teibel compiled into a list. The final question on the feedback form was an overture for more detailed audience engagement: it asked whether the user would be interested in participating in listening tests by mail.

The listening tests were several pages long and inquired as much into the listener as they did the listener's reaction to the sound. For example, a test was conducted for a meditation-oriented disc of voices continuously singing a single syllable, later released as "Intonation" on *environments 7*. Test listeners were queried on their age, marital status, occupation, experience with meditation, and goals for meditation, followed by a checklist of maladies and concerns such as anxiety, depression, hypertension, speech defects, indecisiveness, and job difficulties. After the checklist, Teibel added the following:

> note: do not be upset if you have answered yes to most of the above. you are not alone. these are the most wide-spread problems of contemporary existence. our research has shown that meditation can be of great assistance in alleviating many of these problems. however, the mere purchase of a book or record will accomplish little. you must want to change. the use of this recording will give you mental and emotional "space" in which to work. how you effect the changes you desire is your responsibility.

In this passage, Teibel's "test" morphs into a directive, a pronouncement that primes the listener to use the recording as a technology of self. Like the electromechanical sound machine, "Intonation" was a technology of responsibilization for the construction of ostensibly agentive individuals in a liberal society that valorized the privatization of solutions for social problems. But where Marpac's machine was positioned as a soothing appliance for the normative home or office, Teibel's listening test positions "Intonation" as a technology of self *in opposition* to the "wide-spread problems of contemporary existence." The responsibilization that Teibel makes "mental and emotional space" for is to be utilized against literally sickening aspects of modern life.

Teibel's spacemaking use of phonography is ambiguous from a political standpoint: will this mental and emotional space be used to nurture a self capable of reflecting upon and challenging the utilitarian social system it inhabits—or does this space merely help the individual perform better within that system? Teibel's directive reflects a techno-libertarian ethos that Turner sees as undergirding both the New Communalist era and the subsequent personal computer revolution of the 1980s: these actors believed that by creating new networks of humans and technologies, they could independently combat the illnesses endemic to the dominant social system. The political outcomes were decidedly mixed, however. While personal computing and the World Wide Web undoubtedly created new spaces of community, they also facilitated the exponential spread of the utilitarian capitalism that they sought to challenge.

The listening tests betray other reasons for questioning the communal, system-bucking potentials of *environments*, namely the class and gender homogeneity of its most avid users and the technophilic, consumerist ideology apparent in many test questions. Most of Teibel's listening tests focused intently on the human and electronic apparatuses that mediated the *environments* experience. The tests for releases such as "English Meadow" and "Caribbean Lagoon" asked: "Have you had a hearing test lately?" "Would you say you are sensitive to sound?" "Please list the audio equipment used for this listening test." "Where are your speakers located?" These questions relate to *environments'* networking of production and consumption, mind and ear, and technological and physiological transduction of sound. Not only professionals working in psychoacoustics, but also hi-fi enthusiasts have long obsessed over the proper articulation of these human and electronic components, as everything from the alleged "golden ears" of experts to the most seemingly insignificant cable takes on great importance as a link in the chain of fidelity (Perlman 2004). Professionals in fields one might associate with this kind of attention to acoustic detail are highly represented among the *environments* listening test respondents. These fields include music, audio and theater production, engineering, and computer science. The other most highly represented field is health care, particularly mental health. In other words, many of SRI's most engaged fans were much like Teibel himself: male, professional, passionate about sound, psychology, and technology. The informed seriousness with which these users took *environments'* potential as a sonic technology of the self is reflected in their lengthy comments on—and, sometimes, frank critiques of—Teibel's audio editing and mixing, the sound quality of the test pressings, and even the quality of the listening test questionnaire as a research instrument. Like the rest of New Communalist movement (and the subsequent "PC revolution"), SRI's user base was middle-class, male-dominated, and probably mostly white—people poorly positioned to see the full scope of inequities in the system they wished to challenge. In this sense, there are overlaps or continuities between the spaces created by *environments*, those created by the "square" hi-fi easy listening and jazz records that came before, and—as shown later—the business-class spaces fabricated by the first consumer noise-canceling headphones. These are spaces of acoustic privilege, most often afforded to those already best positioned by systems of class, race, and gender.

However, despite these critiques and ambiguities, Teibel's solicitation of feedback does provide evidence that many kinds of people did use *environments* for many kinds of purposes beyond the boundary maintenance associated with Marpac's sound conditioners. Teibel's response cards and tests provided him with a large selection of enthusiastic (and authentic) user quotes that he could use on subsequent record jackets and in advertising and press releases. For example, from the one-year period of December 1976 to November 1977, Teibel compiled a list of more than sixty of his favorite user quotes, from people of various work backgrounds and regions of the country, for example:[9]

These "sound" records are used as background when doing therapy and aid in relaxing clients so as to improve the quality of the therapy. —SOCIAL SERVICE CONSULTANT

Your Environments recordings are my way of pulling my nerves together *without* the help of *drugs*. I find after listening to them I am at peace with myself and in complete *control*! Thank you.—BARTENDER IN DISCO

Makes me feel close to nature.—FEDERAL SECURITY GUARD

I recently purchased a Dynaco PAT-5, SE-10, Stereo 400 and Dahlquist D210's. Your discs, with the above equipment, are beyond my wildest expectations of sonic truth.—GARDENER, GROUNDSKEEPER

Research has proven interesting. We do research in the area of meditation via biofeedback and other scientific fields—the "Intonation" and "Dawn/New Hope" are very efficient.—ENGINEER/INVENTOR

Helps considerably to relax after a hot and tiring ball game. Very relaxing.—PRO BASEBALL UMPIRE

These recordings are beautiful—they allow me to go into spaces which one can't ordinarily reach in the present-day urban environment. —COLLEGE STUDENT

When my boat is not on the water, I can still sail.—CONSTRUCTION
WORKER

The sounds appear to affect unconscious mental processes and allow
a full range of mental activity from contemplation to inner peace and
joy.—PSYCHIATRIST, MEDICAL SCHOOL PROFESSOR

It helps create a mood which is very helpful and useful with
females.—STUDENT

I think it helps my plants grow better.—MOTHER

Environments stands alone in this book in terms of the perceived flexibility
of the spaces it fabricated—psychotherapy, biofeedback, closeness to nature,
sex, and even plant growth suggest the opposite of isolation. These are aurally instantiated forms of entrainment, perceived links between self and
machine, self and other, and even plant and machine.

Through his textual and pictorial framing of manipulated natural soundscapes, Irv Teibel succeeded in fabricating *spaces of possibility* through mediated sound. These spaces of possibility could be the outdoor imaginaries
of lone listeners, but they could also be spaces of interpersonal connection
and exploration—liminal spaces where ego boundaries could be weakened
and transgressed, be it through talk therapy, encounter groups, or sex.
Practitioners in psychiatry, psychology, hypnosis, occupational therapy,
and chiropractic medicine wrote to Teibel about the therapeutic value of
his sounds. For a time, "Psychologically Ultimate Seashore" was played at
the beginning of each session of EST (Erhard Seminars Training), a popular
and participatory self-exploration workshop embraced by celebrities such as
Cher, Yoko Ono, Joe Namath, and Diana Ross. Free-form radio DJs broad-
cast *environments* sides to thousands of listeners as a form of "head music."
Environments were received as sonic spaces for the location of the authentic
self and authentic connection with human and nonhuman other.

In a rather remarkable transmission of legitimacy, Teibel had drawn
upon his passing familiarity with psychology and psychoacoustics to create
a pseudoscientific and semifictitious research corporation that subsequently
fed its products and ideas back into "legitimate" clinical settings. Simultaneously, he fed what may have been fake user quotes through the channels
of the popular music industry to facilitate the realization of authentic user
experiences and real quotes for use in subsequent promotions. SRI was a
fully realized cybernetic entity in the 1970s and '80s. It was a network of
sounds, spaces, images, texts, nature, technology, and people that generated
new spaces of possibility for users—and a lot of money for Teibel.

FATWOOD INSTANT FIRE STARTERS. These fatwood sticks contain such high levels of natural pine resin that they ignite with the application of a single match so that you can start a fire in minutes without newspaper or kindling. The sticks are hand-cut from the base of century-old slash pine and, unlike paper or wood that can contain chemicals, these sticks burn cleanly with an intense flame that lasts for up to 12 minutes. Burlap sack holds enough sticks for approximately 45 fires. Weight: 20 pounds.
36204X........ $26.95 Postpaid and Unconditionally Guaranteed

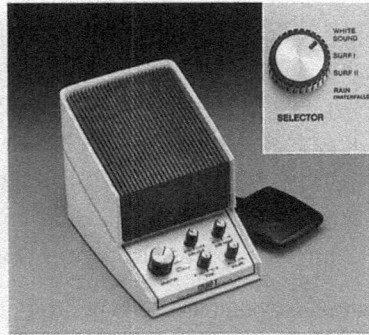

THE ONLY PERSONAL ENVIRONMENTAL SOUND MACHINE. This is the most advanced sleep aid device, and the only environmental sound machine exclusively designed for use also with a pillow speaker (included) so that you can use it without disturbing others. It electronically synthesizes four natural sounds to mask unwanted noise which can disturb sleep or interrupt concentration. Multi-frequency white noise is produced by a unique solid-state micro-circuit which allows for different sound pattern choices: "Rainfall", "Waterfall" "Surf I" and "Surf II" All sound patterns adjust in intensity from light to heavy. Audio amplifier and 5-inch speaker use less electricity than a night light; pillow speaker (3½ x 3 x 1¼ inches). Bass and treble, volume controls. Plugs into household outlet. Height: 7 inches. Width: 5¾ inches. Depth: 8½ inches. Weight: 2.85 pounds.
20706X... $149.95
20701X Without speaker or output jack................ $129.95
Postpaid and Unconditionally Guaranteed   The Only Personal Environmental Sound Machine

Figure 3.8 A Marpac-manufactured "personal" nature sound machine sold by cata-log retailer Hammacher Schlemmer in the 1980s. Despite the name, this machine was far from "the only" offering in a lucrative "personal sensory therapy" mar-ket. Image courtesy of the Browne Popular Culture Library, Bowling Green State University.

Figure 3.9 The website for Sound Oasis, a contemporary leader in the sale of "sound therapy" machines.

Nevertheless, it would turn out that Teibel's approach to recording and perfecting nature sounds would have a more lasting influence than would the more communitarian aspects of his marketing strategy. By the 1980s *environments* had competition not only from other series on cassette and CD (most notably *Solitudes*, by Canadian sound recordist Dan Gibson) but also from analog and digital machines that emulated and/or digitally sampled nature sounds. These latter products included offerings from Marpac, whose analog and digital sound machines would eventually outsell their own electromechanical sound conditioners. As seen in the image of the Marpac-manufactured device in figure 3.8, products such as these were marketed for "personal" relaxation and sleep. Although their marketing would often retain Teibel's appeals to science and health, these products offered the promise of a customized and privatized "Sound Oasis," to use the name of another prominent manufacturer (figure 3.9). While "*personal* sensory therapy" would become a lucrative and recognized product category, the use of orphic media for exploratory *interpersonal* connection would quickly fade.

4

A Quiet Storm

Orphic Apps and Infocentrism

In recent years, noise has come to mean the antithesis of desired
signal in any stimulus or form of energy. . . . Thus it becomes
desirable to designate explicitly the subject matter of this
handbook, acoustic noise.
—**Walter A. Rosenblith and Kenneth N. Stevens,**
U.S. Air Force Handbook of Acoustic Noise Control

Information does not exist, it is a useless notion in biology.
—**Humberto Maturana,** "Interview on von Foerster,
Autopoiesis, the BCL and Augusto Pinochet"

Chris Newby cut a shadowy figure on my screen, lit only by his computer
monitor and the tablet computer he had used to Skype with me from his office on a winter's night. Having so little light to work with, the tablet camera
and video codec had rendered the dark room in low resolution, a patchwork
of shifting blocks of black and gray. As I watched the captured .mov file
of my conversation with him, it occurred to me that the obscured image

Figure 4.1 Screenshots of Lightning Bug.

was appropriate: Newby is the developer of an Android smartphone application that remediates bedrooms around the world every night, lowering their resolution and obscuring their details with a digital scrim. His app, Lightning Bug, performs this act of spatial mediation through sound, enabling would-be sleepers to use digital recordings of natural noises such as rain, thunder, wind, waves, birds, and crickets to mask the sirens, passing trucks, televisions, and other sounds that might otherwise be apparent in their rooms (figure 4.1).

Over thirty years ago, R. Murray Schafer wrote the foundational book of acoustic ecology, *The Soundscape*, in which he described how discreet signals such as a footstep in the snow or the sound of a scurrying animal are occluded in modernity. Deploying the vocabulary of an analog audiophile, he decried how nature's "hi-fi" soundscapes were being degraded by the noise of human technology, resulting in a "lo-fi" signal-to-noise ratio (1994, 43). Orphic apps such as Newby's address the problem of the technological soundscape by *further* lowering the "fidelity" of aural experience. By design, these apps fight the sound of technology with more technological sound in order to fabricate a simulation of silence. Stranger yet, these sonic technologies often use as raw materials the very "archetypal" sounds whose absence Schafer characterized as "a distinct impoverishment": "water, wind, forests, plains, birds, insects, and animals" (10). Schafer praised the sensitivity of the human listener in more pastoral hi-fi times, but it seems that even in our lo-fi milieu something of that sensitivity must remain, judging by the popularity of digital media that mask noise with a quiet storm of comfort sound.

Soundscapes and listening, then, cannot simply be sorted into pre- and post-technological typologies. As Veit Erlmann writes, "generalities, as one often encounters them in the literature on the senses, have no place in . . . charting the cultural production of sensory perception" (2004, 3). Instead, we must turn an "ethnographic ear" (Clifford 1986) toward the specificities of technological thought and practices and their imbrication with "the modalities of attention, thresholds of perception, significance of noises, and configuration of the tolerable and the intolerable" (Corbin 2005, 183).

Over the past three chapters, we have used the filter of orphic media to hear history both dulling and sharpening the senses (Schmidt 2000, 3), generating new aural sensitivities and new means of suppressing and masking sound, as Americans' affectively driven attractions and aversions took shape in new sociomaterial environments. An examination of tinnitus and its orphic suppression showed the auditory system to be self-regulating, constantly adjusting itself in reference to its environmental medium and an ableist and freedom-oriented habitus of listening. The story of the electromechanical sound conditioner revealed ways that military and economic exigencies amplified the speed and reach of technological circulation, leading to the perception of noise as both an unintended consequence and as a domestic solution, a technological cocoon of sensory stability. Subsequently, Irv Teibel's *environments* series reflected the influence of cybernetic, New Communalist discourse—a belief that sound technologies could mediate a better relationship between self, other, and environment. A constant concern throughout these stories has been the relationship between humans and their environment, the former's attempts to control the latter—as a means of self-control—and the unintended outcomes of these efforts.

In this chapter, the rise of ubiquitous digital orphic media serves as the occasion for an exploration of our contemporary "society of control" (Deleuze 1992). By the second decade of the new millennium, the affective use of nature sounds had migrated from Teibel's long-playing records and pricey digital machines on nightstands to inexpensive (and even free) smartphone apps that could be easily used anywhere, by most anyone. But if apps like Lightning Bug are democratizing a certain kind of freedom from listening, why does this form of freedom feel so necessary to so many? Apps such as these proliferate, I argue, because the digital has pushed post-Enlightenment utilitarian logic beyond human limits, amplifying the spatial, temporal, and economic pressures of nineteenth- and twentieth-century capitalism. As Jonathan Crary writes, information capitalism has constructed "a 24/7 environment [that] has the semblance of a social world, but is actually a non-social model of machinic performance," one that "does not disclose the human cost required to sustain its effectiveness" (2013, 9). This human cost is both escalated and obscured by infocentrism, the notion that information is the stuff of life, a discourse that naturalizes the appified control of self and environment.

Information theory undergirds not only the technology of digital apps like Lightning Bug, but also our tacit understanding of the noise we fight with them. As indicated by this chapter's opening quote from a U.S. Air Force technical manual, by the 1950s, a sense of noise as "the antithesis of desired signal in any stimulus or form of energy" had emerged among engineers and was rapidly resonating outward through society. Today, an information/ noise binary has become one of the contemporary West's central discourses, suffusing our notions and experience of acoustic noise with an informatic sensibility and instilling in us the imperative for sonic self-control.

The informatic conception that noise is a disordering disruption of psychic efficiency—and that, furthermore, the efficient channeling of psychic information is the essence of well-being—makes intuitive sense. However, while—or, more pointedly, *because*—these informatic conceptions of sound and selfhood so clearly inform the media practices I analyze, it would not do for me to ground a cultural analysis in these same ideas. One of the most significant insights of cultural studies is that power exerts itself through practical consciousness so that, in Raymond Williams's words, "the pressures and limits of what can ultimately be seen as a specific economic, political, and cultural system seem to most of us the pressures and limits of simple experience and common sense" (1977, 110). Making the pivot that Williams suggests, I regard the informatic conception of noise not as an explanation, but rather as a site for investigation.

Turning an ethnographic ear to the mundane sonic software found on millions of North American smartphones, I will offer a critique of the infocentric and neoliberal understandings that obscure both the digital's human costs and the nature of how we use media in everyday life. These orphic apps are good for illustrating the widespread yet overlooked nature of orphic mediation in contemporary life, but more importantly, they illustrate the ways that media practices can contradict the foundational assumptions and ideologies of the media technologies that enable them. The actual use of apps like Lightning Bug is not informatic, but rather affective, embodied, and used to free us from the material modes of interconnection we find disabling.

In short, we use orphic apps because we are *not* autonomous, informatic subjects—and because we try to live as if we *were*. Laboring in a neoliberal economy of first-order cybernetics, subjects are interpolated as individual information processors who must control self and informational environment in order to achieve a productive state of "flow." In order to counter this inherently noise-corrupted discourse, I draw upon second-order or "neo" cybernetics, a systems theory in which self and world codependently arise without any information being transmitted between them. In this model, the impossibility of informatic transmission paradoxically necessitates our engagement with the world in a relationship that can never be fully controlled. From the vantage point of a noninformatic, non-control-oriented cybernetics, we can better understand how the information economy generates and capitalizes on fearful affects and aversion.

Masking for Autonomous Subjects

Lightning Bug had been downloaded over two million times when Newby and I Skyped in January of 2012. Comments in the Google Play app store indicated that people were using Lightning Bug in order to sleep, relax, deal with tinnitus, and help their children sleep. Speaking from the artifacting darkness, Newby echoed other sound machine and app developers I interviewed in telling me that he uses his own product. Like so many of his customers, he enjoyed the digital refuge of a quiet storm:

> I've always had problems sleeping, since I was a little kid. [Lightning Bug] just helps me mentally get into a place that is more placid and relaxing. So if I'm listening to the sounds of a lake or rain, it reminds me, maybe, of when I was a little kid going to sleep on an afternoon when there was a thunderstorm outside. It takes me back. It helps me connect, mentally, to some event that was more relaxing, more peaceful than the one I'm currently in.

The sounds of rain, brooks, and ocean beaches are found on numerous apps, sound recordings, and tabletop sound machines. Water sounds are a clear favorite among users of such devices, yet there is no universally loved sound, no sonic panacea. Even a single category such as rain generates requests for a multitude of sonic shadings, as another app developer, Todd Moore, explained to me: "If I get asked to make one more type of rain sound, I'm going to go crazy. They want rain on a tin roof, rain on the sidewalk, rain on a tent, rain through trees with wind. Everybody has their own idea of what the perfect sound is."

Just as Orpheus' lyre neutralized the Sirens' captivating song, these orphic applications use digital recordings of rain and other sounds to mask the sounds of users' surroundings. The *acoustical* magic bullet of masking is broadband noise, which contains sound over a wide range of frequencies, thus interfering with the perception of the widest possible variety of sounds. Like Teibel's "Ultimate Seashore," the rainy settings app producers construct—some by editing their own recordings, but many more working with royalty-free loops found on the internet—are among the best "natural" conveyors of broadband noise, which partially explains their popularity. However, the lived experience of noise and silence involves far more than acoustics, as evidenced by the wide variety of rain sounds that Moore's and Newby's customers have asked them to add.

Newby's Lightning Bug is just one of many similar sleep- and relaxation-oriented apps with significant and often passionate user bases. Todd Moore's app White Noise was one of the earliest (figure 4.2). It had already been downloaded over ten million times when it was featured as a "Miracle for 2013" on *The Dr. Oz Show*.[1] Moore told me that he developed White Noise in 2008 in order to use his iPhone as a more convenient replacement for the noisy electric fan that he used to fall asleep. He uploaded his app to the then-new Apple App Store and was shocked by the response he got: thousands of emails, he told me, some of them requesting additional sounds, others just thanking him. In the summer of 2015, a search for "white noise" in Apple's App Store turned up 672 results; Google Play no longer provides numbers, but it reported "at least 1000 results" when I checked in early 2013.[2] While some of these apps don't provide the sort of orphic effect that White Noise does, the majority do. Names such as Sleep Pillow Sounds, Sleepy Time, Sleep Bug, Natural Silences Lite, Rainy Mood, Baby Don't Cry!, Droid Relaxation Machine, Clean Noise, Relax and Sleep, Relax Forest, Peace Noise Generator, and Calm attest to their function. In fact, orphic applications are common enough to have inspired a parody Axl Rose Relaxation app created by the *Late Night with Jimmy Fallon* show, in which Fallon imitates the screechy-voiced Rose singing over the sound of a gentle rain.[3]

As Chris Newby's own desire to "mentally get into a place that is more placid and relaxing" demonstrates, people aren't just using these apps to fine-tune their sonic surroundings. They are simultaneously fine-tuning their own attention and subjectivity, fabricating a preferred experience of self and/or easing themselves into sleep. Still other orphic apps are listed in the "Productivity" sections of the Android and Apple app stores. In 2013, the website and app known as Coffitivity (figure 4.3) generated media buzz by

Figure 4.2 Screenshots of White Noise.

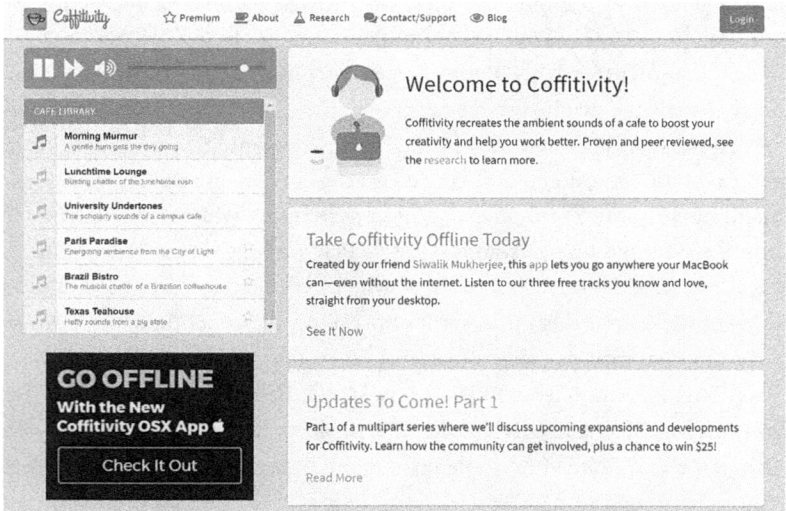

Figure 4.3 Coffitivity, a virtual coffee shop for the ears.

emulating the sounds of coffee shops, inspired by an article in the *Journal of Consumer Research* that claimed "a moderate . . . level of ambient noise enhances performance on creative tasks and increases the buying likelihood of innovative products" (Mehta, Zhu, and Cheema 2012, 784). Noise Machine, White Noise Pro, Noise Killer, Noise Canceller [*sic*], SoundCurtain, Ambiance, Deep Focus, and other apps of this sort feature the same kinds of sounds as the sleep apps, but are marketed for their utility in facilitating productive concentration.

Sleep, calm, concentration—these are presumably the states of a self in control. The economy of orphic apps indicates that these affective states are considered hard to come by and are therefore prized, worried over, and carefully conserved. As many of the app names listed above suggest, *noise* is often conceived as the main threat to sleep, calm, and concentration— and yet also thought of as a vital resource in the defense of these controlled states, a force domesticated by technologies of self-care. As an analysis of sonic culture, the study of orphic media cannot take this noise for granted as a given phenomenological experience or an ontological reality. After all, as David Novak points out, "many languages do not distinguish noise as a general category of sound" to begin with (2015, 125). To understand the noise that Americans fight with orphic media, one must filter it carefully for its constituent parts: noise as a material phenomenon, as a discursive construction, and as something that emerges—and is, in turn, suppressed—in social practices.

The material, discursive, and practical conditions that shape our experiences of noise are today reshaped by economically driven information technologies, discourse, and practices. Writing in the early 1980s, before computer use had spread much beyond computer scientists, engineers, and geeky hobbyists, J. David Bolter predicted, "In the long run, the humanist will not be able to ignore the medium with which he too will work daily: it will shape his thoughts in subtle ways, suggest possibilities, and impose limitations, as does any other medium of communication" (1984, 6). Like the potter's wheel for the ancient Greeks, the computer was already fast becoming a defining technology, "giving us a new definition of man, as an 'information processor,' and of nature, as 'information to be processed'" (13). In information theory, noise is information's evil, yet necessary, twin—and a state of dissolution that threatens those who fail to maintain control. As such, today's widespread noise problems attest to Bolter's prescience: in "the information age," noise has taken on a dark cultural potency.

Writing at roughly the same time as Bolter, James R. Beniger both historicizes and exemplifies the cybernetic turn that Bolter indicates. In *The Control Revolution: Technological and Economic Origins of the Information Society*, Beniger ably dissects a nineteenth-century "crisis of control" that resulted from industrialization's far-ranging material effects on production, distribution, and consumption, as the speed and reach of commodity circulation outpaced human abilities of coordination, spurring a technocratic "Control

Revolution" of information processing, communication, and control (1986). Beniger foregrounds the material and spatial backstory of the information society, tracing a direct line between the utilitarian rationality of nineteenth-century capitalism and the cybernetics of the twentieth century. However, while revealing the historicity of information and cybernetics, Beniger also claims that the true reasons for the rise of the information society can be found "not in the particulars of . . . human history but in the nature of the physical universe" (1986, 31). That is to say, he makes a move often repeated by historians and philosophers of information: infocentrically ontologizing it and recasting all history in its terms (see also Floridi 2010; Gleick 2011).

In the informatic ontology that Beniger recounts—one that has become common sense to most designers of information technology and to many of its users—life is a battle for control between self-organizing information and the entropy that would dissolve it into noise. Drawing on mathematician Claude Shannon, who first theorized information as "a measure of one's freedom of choice in selecting a message" (Shannon and Weaver 1964, 18) and the first-order cybernetics of Norbert Wiener, in which information is the means and measure of any system's communicative self-organization in a "battle between progress and increasing entropy" (1988, 37), Beniger states that all life strives to control itself and its environment in acts of "purposive influence toward a predetermined goal." In fact, the purpose of a life-form or society's very organization is autonomous control. At every level of life, entities process information, material, and energy according to their "programming," defined as "pre-arranged information that guides subsequent behavior," with DNA figured as "the most basic of all control technologies" (1986, 39, 55). As each autonomous agent strives for control, an aggregate system of "densely interconnected programs" emerges. Saving the critic the effort of identifying the economic liberalism that informs this lionization of autonomous control, Beniger cites Adam Smith's "Invisible Hand" of market forces as a primary example of an aggregate system of control (41). As Jonathan Sterne writes, "Cybernetics and information theory do not just promote technical logics; they also promote fundamentally economic and economistic logics" (2012, 77).

For the purpose of understanding orphic media, it is important to re-member the economic context in which the newly productive and disruptive power of noise emerges. Shannon crystallized the contemporary concept of information as part of AT&T's efforts to more efficiently send telegraphic and telephonic messages across long distances. The solution reached was to compress messages into a binary code that eliminated all surplus, leaving only the elements necessary to decompress the full message at the output end.[4] In order to reduce noise in signals containing heterogeneous messages, it was important for Shannon's definition of information to be agnostic as to the message's content—information as a *quantity* completely independent of its material form, meaning, context, or pragmatic import.

Orphic apps exemplify the freedoms that a "lossy" and decontextualizing theory of communication allows. Treating the material world as information, developers like Newby and Moore easily transduce, manipulate, and circulate the sounds of the natural world for use as a sonic utility. Orphic app users are free to extract sonic and affective potentials of rainfall from their soggy material origins, transmitting and recontextualizing these potentials for mobile use as a quiet, controllable storm. An essential aspect of these transductive practices is the ability to discard as unwanted noise any element that is redundant or extraneous to the predetermined goal of control—maximizing "freedom of choice when one selects a message" and positioning the user as "a rational and successful shopper of experience" (Bull 2004, 178). The ability to maximize sonic choice required not only the redefinition of noise as "interference," but also the audiological standardization of hearing (Mills 2011a, 136). The mp3 format that encodes the sound of rain in an orphic app, for example, uses perceptual coding to discard frequencies predicted to be inaudible to the average listener, resulting in a much smaller (and therefore portable and manipulable) file. Fittingly for our topic of orphic apps that mask unwanted sounds by playing back sound files, perceptual coding is underwritten by psychoacousticians' objectification of *masking*—that is, the sounds discarded by an mp3 encoder are those that would otherwise be masked by other sounds present in the recording. Exploiting masking in both perceptible and imperceptible ways, the quiet storm of orphic apps exhibits information theory's simultaneous elimination and domestication of noise. Through the conceptual abstraction and standardization of communication and listener—and the digital technologies this allowed—noise could be "put in its place" and control maximized (Sterne 2012, 95).

Flowing through Noise Corruption

As I replayed my Skype interview with Lightning Bug developer Chris Newby, I noticed something peculiar: many of the sounds he said his sleep-deprived app users requested were precisely the sounds that other users of orphic media try to block out. While broadband noise has been used for decades to mask the sounds of noisy offices, one Lightning Bug user wanted a recording of office sounds because he was always able to sleep at work. Although noise-canceling headphones were originally designed to erase the drone of the airplane cabin, Newby received requests for air cabin sounds in his app. And though snoring spouses have led to the purchase of many a sound machine, Newby received two requests for snoring sounds: one from a woman whose husband frequently traveled for business and the other from a woman whose husband had recently died. Both missed the sound of snoring terribly.

Noise, we have all noticed, is in the ear of the perceiver—and yet we also think of it as an objective reality, a kind of sonic excess or nonsense or hazard. Electrical engineering professor Bart Kosko, in one of many book-length meditations on noise written by scholars in the early twenty-first century, encapsulates the dualistic conception that explicitly and implicitly prevails in contemporary discourse on noise: "[N]oise is a signal we don't like and signals consist of energy and convey information. Noise signals are bad signals or bad sources of energy. But for whom are they bad? Notions of badness vary from person to person. . . . *One person's signal is another person's noise and vice versa*" (2006, 6).

Kosko's definition of noise is dualistic in that it combines the objective (energy, information) with the subjective (not liking)—but it is also informatic in that it reduces acoustic noise to a subset of noise as bad information, merely the *sonic* form of "signals we don't like."

This is not simply the specialized definition of a geek—rather, it is the commonsense definition of noise today. The conflation of sonic and informatic noise speaks to our experience as users of media devices, prone to numerous forms of signal degradation, and it speaks to our experience as consumers of media content, alternately assaulted by noisy, polyvocal cross talk and, perhaps, lured into the algorithmically de-noised refuges of consensus Eli Pariser calls "filter bubbles" (2011). It is also a definition that contains its own dismal inevitable: if noise equals objective signals crossing paths with subjective notions of badness, the explosion of diversity in signals and subjects occurring in a global information economy can only lead to exponential levels of discord, what one author calls "the unwanted sound of everything we want" (Keizer 2010).

Living with and through the powerful technologies that the information paradigm has afforded, individuals intuit information as an essence that penetrates and links everything, entering what N. Katherine Hayles calls "the condition of virtuality" (1999, 19).[5] Implementing a liberal economic, first-order cybernetic vision of information in our digital practices and installing it as an ontology leads inevitably to a kind of "noise corruption" of human experience, due to the fact that human bodies and physical environments can never be fully freed of their contextual specificity—and therefore can never be controlled in the manner of information. For the shopper of experience, with an implicit belief that control is the essence of life, both body and world signal noisily to the contrary. We use technologies based on the binary system of Gottfried Wilhelm Leibniz (1646–1716), a logician with "a full-blown wish for the elimination of everything that is imprecise or ambiguous in human social practice" (Golumbia 2009, 15), yet the more we try to (dis)embody a Leibnizian dream of pure, rational, utilitarian consciousness, the more we are tormented by the noise of our own brute materiality, as well as that of others and our surroundings. In a state of virtuality, the material universe becomes, to use the programmer's parlance, *noise corrupted*— that is, "massively convolved with impractically many broadly diffused and attenuated traces of events that we happen not to be interested in right now" (Fuller 2008, 110n13).

It is in this noise-corrupted milieu that the possibility and necessity of the quiet digital storm arises, as embodied subjects use technologies of the self so they can live *as if* they were informatic. More specifically, we can read the use of orphic apps through the work of psychologist Mihaly Csikszentmihalyi, who conjoins phenomenology and information theory to conceptualize consciousness as "intentionally ordered information" (1990, 26). For Csikszentmihalyi, freedom and happiness depend upon conserving and channeling flows of psychic energy, while distraction, anxiety, or over-self-consciousness are forms of entropy that dissipate attention. To be coherent and whole, one must fight psychic entropy and seek psychic order, or *flow*, in a "battle for the self" (40). In a popular TED talk, Csikszentmihalyi precisely quantifies the problem of attention in informatic terms, asserting that the human brain has a bandwidth of only 110 bits per second, a limited capacity for attending to information that must be conserved and optimized.[6]

Using the flow model, one might conceptualize the use of apps such as Todd Moore's White Noise as "intentionally ordered information" (human consciousness) processing itself through the sound of the smartphone app, effectively off-loading some of its own attention-channeling responsibility in

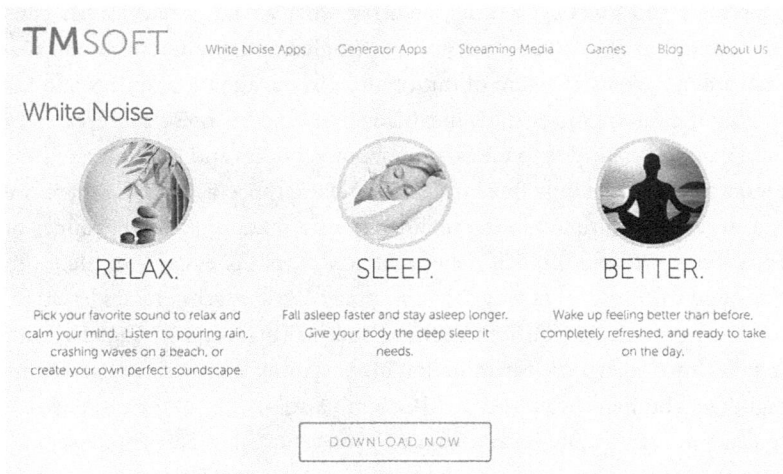

Figure 4.4 Webpage for Moore's White Noise.

a move that enhances self-conservation and optimization. In other words, the acoustical masking power and positive psychological associations of the digital rainstorm in White Noise would divert the flow of attention from entropic thoughts or distracting noises, channeling it into an orderly flow.[7]

The White Noise page of the website for Moore's company TMSoft emphasizes the flow-like combination of relaxation and productivity that White Noise provides (figure 4.4). The top of the page centers on three caps-locked, single-word imperatives: "RELAX. SLEEP. BETTER." These three imperatives are each underscored by a set of subcommands: "Pick a favorite sound to relax and calm your mind." "Give your body the deep sleep it needs." "Wake up feeling better than before, completely refreshed, and ready to take on the day."

"[T]he information we allow into consciousness," Csikszentmihalyi writes, "determines the content and the quality of life. . . . It is attention that selects the relevant bits of information from the potential millions of bits available" (1990, 30–31). The TMSoft website positions acoustic noise in a manner consistent with Csikszentmihalyi's noise of entropic or irrelevant information, harmful to quality of life. In an effort to explain the principle of acoustic masking, the website displays potential sleep interruptions as peaks on a frequency spectrum graph. Following is a reproduction of this webpage, complete with inline graphs.

Lack of any noise interruptions equals a great night's sleep. But just after you enter deep sleep, something outside sets off your neighbor's pesky car alarm. Now your room fills with a very distinct pattern:

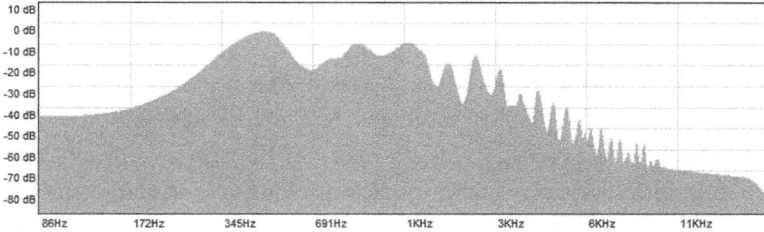

Your brain has been scanning the room all night listening for a reason to wake you up, and that car alarm will do it! Now you'll toss and turn until you hopefully get back to sleep. In the morning you might not remember waking up, but one thing is for sure, you will feel tired because you didn't get a good night's sleep.

Now let's say you fell asleep while listening to white noise. Your bedroom will be filled with all the possible frequencies that your ear can recognize. White noise filling your room looks like this:

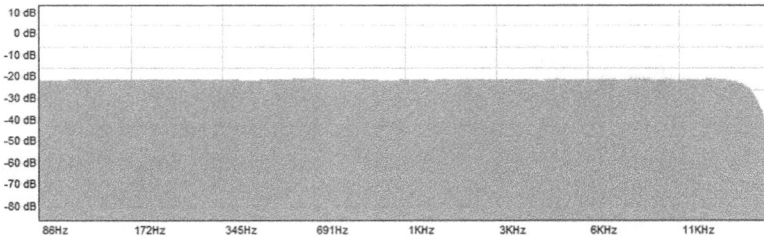

The graph of white noise almost looks like a comfy bed—just add pillow and blanket. OK, let's get back to the evil neighbor and his car alarm. Now when it goes off this time those annoying frequencies will be mixed in with the white noise sound. The end result looks like this:

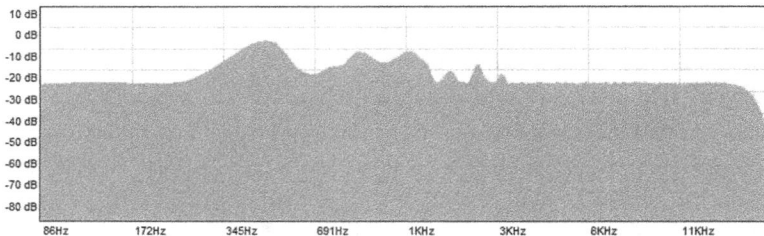

Notice that most of that car alarm's distinct pattern is absorbed by our blanket of pure white noise. Playing white noise audio throughout the night will allow you to stay in deep sleep longer which means you'll wake up feeling refreshed. And if not, it's always the neighbors fault.[8]

TMSoft's lighthearted website copy describes the utility of masking by depicting the sleeper's brain "scanning" its environment for a reason to wake up, selecting the wrong bits of information as relevant and thus diminishing quality of sleep and quality of life the next day. Because it contains information from across the frequency spectrum, white noise obscures entropic sonic "patterns" with a "bed" of sound, aiding in the restful conservation of psychic energy. The website's conceptualization of the self and its sonic surroundings seems rather intuitive in the setting of information capitalism. It positions us as shoppers of experience, vigilantly managing our informatic hygiene, protecting our senses from the faults of neighbors, and treating sleep as an act of "purposive influence toward a predetermined goal": maximizing our paltry 110-bit/second bandwidth of attention the next day.

More than ever, sleep becomes a fraught practice of personal responsibility as unfettered, 24/7 information capitalism fosters what Teresa Brennan calls "bioderegulation," making "humans work harder conforming to the new rules of inhuman time . . . restrict[ing] human interaction and personal contact, and . . . mak[ing] us commute further" (Brennan 2003, 19). As we attempt to flow through the fragmented, hypermediated, ever-stimulating "non-time" of an economy that has divorced itself from rhythms of sun and Earth, we conceptualize sleep "as a variable but managed function" (Crary 2013, 13) to be facilitated by additional mediated inputs. Meanwhile, the TMSoft website's "scanning brain" calls to mind the "sleep mode" of our digital devices, which Jonathan Crary writes, "remakes the larger sense of sleep into simply a deferred or diminished condition of operationality and access" (2013, 13). For informatic subjects, "Off" is never really an option.

Orphic apps might help us sleep, but they never address what keeps us up at night. Like our other digital technologies, these apps participate in a discourse that gives us a sense of control—a feeling that the consumption of technology can generate agency in an inherently noise-corrupted social world. However, just as an orphic app generates its own noise and thus masks certain kinds of dissonance, the informatic discourse of flow masks its own inherent noise corruption in the rhetoric of autonomous control. When discursively positioned as a disembodied information processor and materially positioned in the light-speed flows of information capitalism, the human body can only emerge as noise-corrupted—unable, physically and attentionally, to control itself and its environment as it should. Just a glance at rising levels of screen time and ADHD and falling levels of sleep and outdoor time should give the lie to any notion of individual autonomy in the digital age.

An affective body positioned as a dysfunctional information processor exists in a heightened state of self-surveillance, "scanning" self and environment for a lack of control it always finds—and othering these uncontrolled aspects of self and environment as disabling noise. As the myth of Orpheus and the Sirens reminds us, the problem of control does not *originate* with information capitalism, but it is greatly exacerbated by the discursive and material productions of the control society's "numerical language of control" (Deleuze 1992, 5). Orphic apps function as technologies of the self to help individuals keep up with the demands of control, but they also naturalize this discourse of autonomous control, masking its contradictions in a quiet storm of faux agency. Nevertheless, there exists an alternate ontological conception of our nature as systems—one that embraces cybernetics without reducing the body-mind to information.

Neocybernetics and the Infant Smartphone User

Although Todd Moore's White Noise app was popular from the start, he attributes a huge surge in downloads in 2009 to smartphone-using babies. In that year, the *Washington Post* published the story of a newborn who became accustomed to sleeping to the sound of an air conditioner. When the weather cooled and the baby's parents no longer ran the air conditioner, the baby was unable to sleep. Enter White Noise: "For the next four months, the infant slept with his father's iPhone in his crib and White Noise tuned to 'air conditioner,'" the reporter wrote. "The monotonous buzz kept the baby sleeping soundly and his parents happy."[9] After the article ran, babies became a major source of revenue for TMSoft, Moore told me.

The phenomenon of the smartphone-using baby resists the persistent equivalence between cognition and symbolic information processing promoted by figures such as Leibniz, his student George Boole, and Charles Babbage, not to mention any implicit or explicit definitions of media that center on the development, delivery, and consumption of semiotic content. Although there are many competing theories of childhood development, there is no contemporary psychological theory under which we could construe a newborn's engagement with the sound of the White Noise app as semiotic or representational. Since the time of Jean Piaget, empirical research has shown the development of subjectivity to emerge in interactions between organism and environment, with later, more complex modes of engagement and knowledge construction building upon earlier, simpler behaviors (Fischer 1980). In Piaget's schema of cognitive development, infants do not construct enduring representations of the environment until they have spent at least eighteen months developing reflexes, eye–hand coordination, and an intentional orientation toward objects in the environment (Piaget 1951; Piaget and Inhelder 1969). The sound of the air conditioner, whether directly experienced or transduced through a smartphone, *represents nothing* to the infant—instead, its mediation facilitates a temporary equilibrium between newborn and environment.

As the reader has probably surmised, when a baby "uses" an iPhone, what is mediated is affectivity, the way that subjects and objects emerge in the present moment through their influence on one another. The question at hand is how this orphic perspective might be integrated with cybernetics to provide a noninformatic perspective on the use of digital media. To do so, we turn to what Bruce Clarke calls "the systems counterculture" of the late 1960s and early 1970s, "a loosely collegial group of seminal scientific thinkers whose particular developments of cybernetic ideas and practices led them beyond mainstream doctrines and institutions" (2012, 197). Important among these thinkers was the Chilean Humberto R. Maturana, whose materially focused, cybernetic biology stands in a figure–ground relationship to the informatic cybernetics of Shannon and Wiener. According to Maturana, all life is composed of *autopoietic* systems, which are open to molecular flows from the outside, yet are closed in the sense that these systems can only engage their medium (or other systems) within the constraints of their systemic organization. In the neocybernetics of Maturana, his student Francisco Varela, and his other intellectual descendants, no information is ever transmitted between biological entities, which instead simply respond to the external "perturbations" sensible to their structures as systems (cf. Maturana and Varela 1998, 169). "Information does not exist," Maturana writes, "it is a useless notion in biology" (2007, 45).

In autopoietic theory, systems engage their medium (or other systems) only insofar as the structure of the medium (or system) affects their perpetuation as self-organized system, a dynamic known as "structural coupling." The same can also be said about the system's influence upon its medium—in both directions, interaction is limited by the affordances of the separate structures. At first blush, this might sound like a recipe for stasis, but what is perpetuated in structural coupling is not the present structure of the system, but rather the continued coherence of its self-organization. Moment by moment, the living system changes as it adapts to the changing medium in an evolutionary process of "ontogenic structural drift" (Maturana and Varela 1998, 17–18). Such systems may couple together in multidimensional and recursive relationships leading to complex, multi-cellular life-forms, even though each subsystem relates to the others only on its own terms.

Crucially for our investigation of media and affectivity, "autopoietic systems are both environmentally open to energic exchange and operationally closed to informatic transfer" (Clarke and Hansen 2009, 9). Paradoxically interdependent yet autonomous, autopoietic systems do not operate by communicating messages to one another, nor do they gather information from outside themselves to make an internal model of the medium they inhabit. As we have seen in the automatic gain control (AGC) of the auditory system, the human nervous system, as it interfaces with the outside world, merely responds to the material "perturbations" sensible to its structure as a system (Maturana and Varela 1998, 169).

From an affect theory perspective, Maturana and Varela's perturbations are analogous to Spinoza's "affections," while the changes caused within the system by these perturbations are what Spinoza calls "affects." "The key point is that such systems do not operate by representation. Instead of *representing* an independent world, they *enact* a world as a domain of distinctions that is inseparable from the structure embodied by the cognitive system" (Varela, Thompson, and Rosch 1991, 140). Just as structural coupling yields complex second-order systems such as conscious human beings, so does it enact even more complex third-order relations between such beings, who "coordinate their coordinations" with one another on a meta-relational level, evolving language and the shared objects, entities, and senses of other and self generated in *linguistic* structural coupling.

Through structural coupling, we are able to interact as whole and separate beings operating in an objective world, even as that perceived self and world are mediated by a proliferation of relational, autonomous systems that emerge affectively and enactively. As Clarke and Hansen put it, "to maintain their autopoiesis, (self-referential) systems must remain operationally (or organizationally) closed to information from the environment. On that basis, they can take an 'observer position' to construct their interactions with their environment *as* information. Niklas Luhmann writes with regard to the operation of communication in social systems: 'A systems-theoretical approach emphasizes the *emergence of communication* itself. Nothing is transferred'" (Clarke and Hansen 2009, 9).

In a neocybernetic ontology, the smartphone-using infant is a self-referential system emerging through the creative frictions of environmental perturbation—not an autonomous, preprogrammed information processor controlling self and environment in a quest for "purposive influence toward a predetermined goal" (Beniger 1986, 39). Through Ihde's background relations, the infant's auditory system achieves homeostasis with its technological environment, as AGC calibrates itself to the sound of the air conditioner. When the AC is turned off, the baby's nascent subjectivity is remediated by a new set of sonic relations that decreases its power of sleeping—a "poisoning" in the Deleuzian sense. When the iPhone is placed in the crib, the orphic app White Noise remediates a new set of affective relations that increases the infant's ability to sleep.

The dynamic is the same, albeit more complex, for adult users. While Todd Moore's infant user base exploded in 2009, adult users continued to make requests for their own personal comfort sounds: "Customers were listening to sounds I had never even thought of," he told me. "One lady can't sleep unless she runs her hair dryer all night. She sent me an email and said, 'I'd love for you to add a hairdryer sound. I burn up six a year.'" Worried the woman would burn her house down, Moore added a hair dryer to his app. As the baby grows into an adult—say, one who becomes accustomed to sleeping to hair dryers—the orphic dimension of autopoiesis is complicated, but not supplanted, by representational associations. Enacting a world based on the distinctions that are systemically sensible to us, each of us generates our "affection ideas" about her own sonic state, which in Spinoza's conception are affections themselves—ideas such as "I need the sound of a hair dryer in order to sleep." Thus, our bodies and minds owe their present autonomous state entirely to a history of generative friction beyond individual control.

This accumulation of affect explains why both Moore and Chris Newby have had to design so many kinds of rain scenes in their apps, as the environmental imprints left behind in our physical structures profoundly affect the way we take an observer position on the world and construe it as information. When Newby says his app "takes me back" to when he was "a little kid going to sleep on an afternoon when there was a thunderstorm outside," he is talking about the orphic generation of an environment conducive to the reemergence of a past affective state. To say that the thunderstorm sound *represents* that past moment or has warm connotations does not go far enough. Because we are informationally closed but energetically open systems, we use sound as material, only as we know how—to construct new felicitous relations between self and environment that we think will enliven our viability as an autonomous system.

The claim of informational closure in consciousness has made autopoiesis controversial in the humanities, particularly among theorists concerned with media and affect. In "The Affective Turn: Political Economy, Biomedia, and Bodies," Patricia Clough (2008) argues that autopoiesis is modernist, overly concerned with boundary maintenance, anti-evolutionary, and subject-centered. Clough asserts that in order to challenge the current political economy of the biomediated body, we have to understand that body in terms of flexible flows of information, not informationally closed circuits of autopoiesis. While Clough is far from a genetic reductionist, I would nevertheless contend that the control-oriented, sender-receiver history that informs the conception of the informatic body weakens its potential to challenge a political economy that understands the human body in terms of (patentable) genes. Autopoiesis resists this genetic reductionism, while also providing a foothold for the critique of the information economy by acknowledging that our organizational autonomy is completely dependent upon environmental circumstance—and therefore, control is always incomplete. Moreover, because neocybernetics views information as the construct of specific systems from an observer position, rather than an immanent and transcendent immateriality, it better allows us to denaturalize informatic technologies and practices, revealing the ways that infocentrism injects its inhuman standards into the human environment and capitalizes on our attempts to maintain our boundaries in its spatially, temporally, and socially riven milieu.

Nevertheless, Clough identifies a crucial problem, one that made Varela hesitant to see the notion of autopoiesis applied to social groups: when we focus on boundary maintenance on a personal or social level, we other and dehumanize those outside the boundaries we construct, sowing division, conflict, and warfare. Yet this painful truth only further validates the neocybernetic model, as this kind of destructive boundary maintenance is found throughout history. The problem is, as John Protevi writes, "enacting autopoiesis as a way of social being," not using it as a model for understanding the social (2013, 28). Protevi's philosophy, which synthesizes neocybernetics and Spinozan affect theory, suggests that the health of our individual and social bodies politic depends upon taking an observer position vis-à-vis our own affection ideas—reflexively questioning what *really* enables and disables us and examining our habitual mediating practices of boundary maintenance.

Gaps in the Digital Stream

In the spirit of Protevi's insight, I conclude this chapter by reinserting myself into my ethnographic research on orphic media, reflexively examining once more how sound generated fearful affects in the field and digging into the code of orphic apps to show how an infocentric understanding of media technologies can lead to breakdowns in orphic function. During my field-work on orphic media, I not only studied these technologies, but also came to use them myself. As related in chapter 1, I was suffering from tinnitus related to an acoustic trauma when I began traveling to archives, conferences, trade shows, clinics, and businesses. While on the road, I stayed in various hotels and hostels and often found myself kept awake by noise. Sometimes it was the noise in my head, but more often it was environmental. In retrospect, the problem wasn't really that these places were terribly noisy. In fact, one might say they were too quiet, so that their silence was more powerfully affected—either by my tinnitus or by closing doors, voices, and other occasional sounds that seemingly never failed to wake me.

These material resonances, which might not have woken me on a more relaxing trip, were no doubt amplified by my own mental anxieties: my uncertainty about the project I was embarking upon; my belief that a good night's sleep would be essential to clear thinking at the next day's archive, interview, or observation; my knowledge that I wouldn't have the funding to make this particular trip a second time and so must be efficient in my research, and so on. Or to put it another way, there were the *social* pressures of being a graduate student ethnographer, of precarious finances and status, on the road, interacting with strangers whom I needed more than they needed me. These factors remediated my modality of attention and thresholds of perception, along with the significance of noises and configuration of the tolerable and the intolerable, generating an affective state of noise corruption. From a subjective standpoint, I heard noise keeping me awake; in reality, I was experiencing an unhappy emergence of sonic, spatial, sensory, and social affectivity—one that diminished my power to sleep. Csikszent-mihalyi would say that I was doing a poor job of conserving my informatic efficiency—thus succumbing to noise/entropy—yet it was the affect of a graduate student, the pressure to be the rational, efficient researcher, that was priming my noise sensitivity. The problem was not that I was an inefficient informatic mind, but that I was an affective body struggling to behave like a good Cartesian, Csikszentmihalyian subject.

One night, early in my fieldwork, when it seemed that intermittent hotel noises would forestall sleep the entire night, I reached for my Android smartphone, which was loaded up with the sonic apps that I had just begun investigating. I opened Lightning Bug, selected a "gentle brook" sound, turned up the volume on my phone, and closed my eyes again, hoping my anxious thoughts and any noises would all be swept downstream. But then I noticed a gap. The soothing sonic flow of the gentle brook would periodically cut out—noticeably, repeatedly, and *annoyingly*. Although these gaps lasted less than half a second, they were enough to bring what should have been a soporific background relation to the forefront of my attention. I now noticed the looped nature of this country stream, as it became apparent that the brief silences appeared when the recording reached its end, hesitated, and played again. What was supposed to be the continuous sound of nature now sounded irritatingly fake and repetitious, a form of simulated water torture. I decided to try other sounds in Lightning Bug and then I tried other nature sound apps, all to no avail. The hiccups persisted. I then opened an app that advertised itself as a "white noise generator," only to find that it too was a recording—a white noise loop, with the gap again clearly audible. The copy in Todd Moore's White Noise app website stated, "Lack of any noise interruptions equals a great night's sleep," with "noise interruptions" meaning the noisy interruption of silence. But now these apps had merely substituted an opposite "noise interruption" problem—the silent interruption of noise was keeping me awake. I was incredulous. How could millions of people be using these sounds to sleep? Didn't they hear what I was hearing?

A moment such as this reveals once again that, when it comes to mediation, representation is not everything. The "message" of the country stream was getting through to me loud and clear—I could tell what the sound represented, yet the sound was now worse than useless to me. Surely, as an aural sign (or a constellation of aural signs), the babbling brook and its woodsy ambience held positive connotations for me, but its material purpose was to raise the "noise floor" of my hotel room, lessening the impact of stray hallway sounds while also remaining aesthetically pleasant and perceptually unobtrusive. Even the most unusual comfort sounds—the special requests such as snoring— are repetitive and uninteresting, useful only because their absence would be noticed by the individual whose present nervous structure has emerged through the friction of a spouse "sawing wood." Likewise, noise-canceling headphones or wearable sound generators for tinnitus sufferers must be physically comfortable enough that the user forgets she is wearing them.

Nevertheless, orphic apps *are* built on information technology and the theoretical model this technology embodies. To understand the tension between orphic use and the informatic design of digital media, it is necessary to engage in the "software studies" advocated by scholars such as Lev Manovich (2001, 48) and Matthew Fuller, analyzing "the materiality of software . . . at many scales: the particular characteristics of a language or other form of interface—how it describes or enables certain kinds of programmability or use; how its compositional terms inflect and produce certain kinds of effects such as glitches," like this gap in the audio stream (2008, 4).

When I later interviewed Lightning Bug's developer Chris Newby, I asked him about the gap in the stream. He was well aware of it—in fact, it was the bane of his existence. Yes, Newby loves the sounds of a thunderstorm, yet he nevertheless carefully produces his thunderstorm sounds in such a way that they do not attract attention to themselves, maximizing the steady, broadband "white noise" that is essential to rain's reign as the most popular sleep sound: patternless, masking, and ultimately forgettable. The gaps in this and his other steady-state sounds became a soundless aural irritant, bringing his users' attention back to the app, and they were complaining about it. The bug was not, however, in Lightning Bug's code; it was caused by an interaction between code in recent versions of Google's Android operating system and the hardware of smartphones. Newby thought the problem was specific to phones such as my Samsung Galaxy s2, which divided and executed processing jobs between multiple processing units called "cores." This was a significant problem because multi-core processors were now proliferating in Android devices, due to their speed and information-processing efficiency.

Like other app developers, Newby uses application programming interfaces (APIs), libraries of high-level protocols and building blocks that make it easier to create application software. Lightning Bug needs to decompress various compressed audio files for playback, play the files in looped or unlooped fashion, access the speaker and headphone outputs of any device on which it runs, and interact with hardware volume controls. Writing the code from scratch to control all of these functions on *just one* model of smartphone would be very complex and time consuming; doing so for the many varieties of Android devices would be impossible. Written in the high-level language of Java, Google's Android APIs provide a simplified way to control these functions, translating between developers' intentions and many layers of lower-level code to implement apps on various devices. In a trade-off between ease of development and specificity of control, Google's Android team takes care of the lower-level details, "abstracting away a lot of nuances," as Newby put it, for developers using the APIs. Thus, if Newby writes the simple line of code,

```
Media Player mediaPlayer = MediaPlayer.create(this,
Uri.parse(someValidPath));mediaPlayer.setLooping(true);
```

with "someValidPath" pointing to a compressed audio file such as an mp3, the building block "Media Player" should cause looped playback of that file in his app on any Android device. Media Player is a black box, a bundle of hidden coded functionality, one of many similar media-handling components in a library of APIs Google named StageFright.

Unfortunately for most orphic app developers, in late 2010, when Stage-Fright replaced an earlier library as part of Android version 2.3 (commonly known as Gingerbread), something in the hidden code introduced the gap into audio loop playback on many Android devices. The source of the bug was a mystery to the app developers. Newby was convinced StageFright had changed the way the software handled the decompression and playback of compressed audio. Todd Moore's White Noise did not suffer from the issue, which Newby attributed to Moore's using uncompressed audio in his app. Newby felt that this was not an option for Lightning Bug because the large sizes of uncompressed files would prevent him from using the wide variety of long loops that he preferred. For his part, Moore attributed his lack of issues to the fact that he had developed White Noise's audio handling "closer to the metal," below the API level.

Newby and other developers' educated guess was that, in a dual-core device such as mine, one core would handle the opening of the compressed audio in chunks of several seconds at a time, while the other core handled temporarily storing the decompressed audio in a section of RAM called a buffer. Splitting up jobs in parallel processes like this is more efficient from an information-processing standpoint, Newby told me; it works extremely well for decompressing photographs and video, for example. However, he surmised, due to the temporal and looped nature of his audio, slight timing inconsistencies between the two cores were leading to gaps in the audio stream—and there was no way for a developer to fix this at the API level.

In July 2011, one of Newby's competitors, Charles Syperski—maker of an app called Sleepy Time—filled out a bug report on the Android Open Source Project Issue Tracker.[10] Newby and Syperski decided to get their customers involved by sharing with them the link to the bug report. Eventually, 877 people upvoted and commented on the report; they complained that the bug had ruined apps that they depended on nightly, raising its profile among Gingerbread bugs that needed fixing. Six months later, Google closed Syperski's report without comment, marking it "Released," which indicates that "this bug has been fixed, and is included in a formal release."[11] But the gap in the stream remained. Newby had to hire another programmer with expertise in working with audio below the API level. He released a fixed version of Lightning Bug only to have to repeat the process all over again when Android's 4.0 Ice Cream Sandwich release reintroduced the audio gap issue. Not only had Google failed to fix the audio loop problem, but their new OS release had broken Newby's own workaround.

The most maddening thing was what a seemingly simple issue it was—looping audio was one of the most basic functions an audio app developer could need. And not only would subsequent versions of Android fail to solve the problem, but they would break Newby's workarounds, forcing him to spend time and money on yet another fix. Meanwhile, subsequent posts to the Issue Tracker were also seemingly disregarded.

Newby is an admirer of Google and is very reluctant to criticize the company, but it wouldn't be hard to argue that this persistent bug reduced Lightning Bug from a possible full-time job for Newby to just another app in the Play store. In 2012, Lightning Bug had some two million "installs," but by 2016 that number had only increased by 500,000. Meanwhile, newer players with competing products have found enough success to hire small teams of engineers. Today, Newby says he made the mistake of obsessing over fixing the loop problem when he should have been porting his product to other platforms, such as web browsers and Apple's iOS.

The independent developers in this case found themselves the victims of a second gap, this one between the institutional scale and logic of Google and their own smaller-scale agendas and power. "Big screens and fast processors are what's important" to Google, Newby told me, while quality control around looping audio was not. And there was a communication gap as well. Like Newby and Syperski, I was unable to make contact with the admins who changed the status on these bug reports. Not only was it seemingly impossible to alter Google's agenda, but it was impossible to find out why. Contrary to commonplace fantasies about technologies of communication, the seemingly infinite scalability of information networks creates communication gaps as well as bridges.

Newby found himself the victim of various contingencies of specifications, operating at the microprocessor scale up through the multinational corporation. In his study of the mp3, Jonathan Sterne writes that such specifications operate "as a code—whether in software, policy, or instructions for manufacture and use—that conditions the experience of a medium and its processing protocols. Because these kinds of codes are not publicly discussed or even apparent to end-users, they often take on a sheen of ontology when they are more precisely the product of contingency" (2012, 8).

In the case of the gap in the stream, my orphic experience of the medium was being disrupted by obscure protocols not apparent even to the app programmers themselves. Sterne argues that audio formats evolve in a tension between efficient compression and aural verisimilitude, usually understood as synonymous with "hi-fi" or "high-definition" audio. In this case, a loss of verisimilitude resulted from a *temporal* conflict between the efficient transmission and decompression of data. The failure of the Android phone to provide a continuous white noise sound seems especially ironic considering that "white thermal noise" was central to the theorem that allowed Shannon's message-sending paradigm to be applied to the "continuous messages" of voices traveling over telephone lines (Shannon and Weaver 1964, 22–24).

However, the protocols by which the Android operating system, multicore processing, and audio compression operate are not organized around the creation of steady-state sonic spaces; instead, these informatic and institutional logics privilege the efficient sending of messages and visual content over audio quality. This information-efficient design leads to a glitch in the smartphone's actual sonic-affective use. Therefore, the gap in the stream is not merely a lack of audio verisimilitude; it is also a gap between the informatic idealism of digital media and the material practices of digital users. The lossy efficiency of digital discourse attempts to discard as noise the very creative frictions that underwrite our perceived autonomy.

Part III. Cancellation

I can't even listen, you wildin'

I'd much rather sit here in silence

—**Drake,** "The Language"

Bose QuietComfort and the Mobile Production of Personal Space

> All I could think about was, "My gosh, there must be some way of
> separating things that you don't want from things that you want."
> —**Amar Bose**, *Cancelling Noise*

A series of white male faces appears on-screen, business "road warriors," men of action facing the camera in their natural domain—the airport. With enthusiasm tempered by an almost solemn sense of wonder, each offers a one-word testimonial between cross-fades: "Fantastic." "Quality." "Wow." The object of their admiration, and the product on display in this advertisement, is the Bose QuietComfort Acoustic Noise Cancelling Headphones. Cut to another white businessman as he leans back in his airline seat, headphones on, eyes closed. The other passengers fade into nothingness, dematerialized by the magic of QuietComfort phase cancellation. In another Bose ad, a business traveler wearing headphones reads the newspaper in-flight as the surrounding cabin fades into an abstraction, a white line drawing that suggests purity and stillness (figure 5.1).

Figure 5.1 Bose headphones cause the shared space of the aircraft cabin to disappear in a TV ad.

The United States–based Bose Corporation is the original developer and best-known marketer of noise-canceling headphones, which are designed to dramatically reduce the wearer's perception of ambient sound. Conventional headphones use passive noise reduction, which blocks or muffles the passage of sound waves into the ear canal. Noise-canceling headphones add tiny microphones and signal processing to produce an out-of-phase copy of the aural environment in an attempt to negate its phenomenological existence. Bose QuietComfort and similar headphones have become increasingly popular since their introduction for consumer use in 2000 and are a common sight in airport electronics boutiques and on the ears of travelers. Reviewers and users affirm that the headphones offer clearer audio from portable media in noisy environments, but the devices' marketing, reception, and history of development suggest that their primary function has more to do with conflicts of sound, space, and self in an increasingly mobile modernity.

Noise-canceling headphones offer air travelers not only the reduction of noise but also the production of personal space. The babel of airport throngs and the roar of the jet engine exemplify the noise generated in a

United States where space is reconfigured to maximize speed and circulation. Screaming babies and screaming turbines signal the fact that, even as we speed through the air toward our goals, our freedom is constrained by physical and social forces. Air travel is a moment in which people with diverse backgrounds, beliefs, and bodies crowd together in unusually close proximity. With the pure, white lines of its dematerializing aircraft cabin and its fading fellow travelers, the Bose ad campaign offers the promise of turning physical spaces and others into phantoms—in effect, tuning out shared space and difference. In the face of the discomfort and forced togetherness of travel, people are encouraged to employ noise-canceling headphones as orphic media, carving out an acoustically rendered sense of personal space that Bose has marketed as "a haven of tranquility."[1]

Having explored the historical constructions of space, self, and technology that have motivated orphic media use since the 1960s, in this chapter I shift to the ways that orphic media shape *social* relations when people are encouraged to believe that, in Margaret Thatcher's words, "there is no such thing as society." Here, I use noise perception as a problematic to explore the orphic remediation of public and quasi-public spaces between the 1980s and the teen years of the new millennium, an era characterized by neoliberalism and increased (physical, if not class) mobility. Neoliberalism is the currently prevailing idea, famously espoused by Friedrich Hayek and associated in the United States with Ronald Reagan, that a global free market, unhindered by government regulation, is the ideal site for human self-actualization. Under neoliberalism, freedom is an individual matter, and relations with others that do not result from individual choice are seen as impinging on that freedom. The type of self constructed in this boundary-maintaining ideology has Western antecedents in the work of Adam Smith, René Descartes, and others who portrayed the self as a rational mind that deploys techniques and technologies in pursuit of individual goals. But what does it sound like when such selves cross paths or crowd together in pursuit of their different goals? In such cases, the friction between individualism and difference generates noise in the *social* sense—noise as *othered sound*. Like any type of othering, the perception of noise is socially constructed and situated in hierarchies of race, class, age, and gender. As these categorizations have always represented fraught social boundaries in America, it should come as no surprise that the separations of noise cancellation came to reinforce these lines of discomfort and power. Therefore, the white line drawing that surrounds the white business traveler in early Bose headphone advertising does not delineate an ideologically neutral field; rather, it limns a perfect representation of what Jennifer Lynn Stoever calls "the sonic color line"—the border between "proper" and "improper" ways of sounding and listening that establishes white, male practices as "default, natural, normal, and desirable" (2016, 12).

Noise-canceling headphones have a special historical relationship to air travel—in fact, they were conceived in flight. Tracing this history, I examine marketing, news reports, and reviews to show how Bose's noise-canceling headphones were positioned as essential gear for the mobile rational actor of the global market, the business traveler. Though the spaces of the cabin and air terminal have been shaped for business travelers, representations of air travel and the discourse of business travelers indicate that they remain paradoxical spaces in which the pursuit of freedom impedes its own enjoyment. Rather than fight the discomforts of air travel as a systemic problem, travelers use the tactic of orphic mediation to suppress the perceived presence of others. I will conclude this chapter by suggesting that noise-canceling headphones go beyond our normal understanding of sound reproduction devices in that they remediate the acoustic environment, turning it into a database of content for the filtration of material and social difference—a sonic interface that remediates the sonic color line, affecting audible difference in a separate but unequal manner.

Social Construction of Noise Cancellation

Bose's QuietComfort brand name conjoins the aural and the tactile—not to mention the aural and the psychological—into a single sign, connoting a quiet respite from physical and interpersonal entanglements. Of course, people have long been able to alter their experience of their sonic surroundings by donning a pair of headphones. However, with noise-canceling headphones, orphic mediation becomes an explicit and primary function in audio technology, as the power button offers an (imperfect) on/off interface with the soundscape. It might be argued that this new form of "soundscaping" is merely a technological advance in the application of acoustical principles. However, a brief look at the historical context of QuietComfort's development uncovers some of the ways that sociocultural beliefs and difference permeate the construction of sound, space, and media technology.

On May 19, 1978, Dr. Amar Gopal Bose (1929–2013), inventor, CEO, and majority stakeholder in the privately owned Bose Corporation, had just plugged a pair of headphones into an airplane armrest for the first time. While he had been excited to experience the sound of this new form of in-flight entertainment, he was disappointed by what he heard. The noise of the jet airplane forced him to turn up the headset volume to the point of distorting the classical music he had hoped to enjoy. "All I could think about was, 'My gosh, there must be some way of separating things that you don't want from things that you want,'" he later explained. It was then that Bose took out a pen and paper and did the calculations that proved the possibility of active noise cancellation.

As an amateur classical violinist with a PhD in electrical engineering from MIT, Bose worked at the intersection of the social worlds of music and science, bridging gaps between the cultural and functional expectations of each, and thus occupying the role that sociologists of science and technology have called the "go-between" or "intermediary" (Hennion 1989; Pinch and Bijsterveld 2004). Fusing expertise in both electrical engineering and psychoacoustics, Bose proved particularly adept at designing products that utilize, alter, negate, or simulate the relationship people perceive between sound and space. Bose products that calibrate this relationship include small "Wave Radios" that are said to sound like much larger sound systems, car audio systems that automatically change music equalization to compensate for road noise, and a computer system that produces acoustic simulations of aural spaces, allowing architects and others to "hear" a concert hall and speaker system before they build it.

However, the social worlds of music and science were not the only important cultural influences on Bose's development as a designer of audio technology: he attributed much of his experimental drive to his early experience of racism. It seems poignant that Bose found a way to engineer sound to tune out difference in tight spaces, allowing for less friction and greater productivity, as Bose himself used audio technology to overcome racism and find empowerment in the global marketplace. The son of a white mother and a Bengali father, Bose grew up in the 1930s and 1940s in a white Philadelphia suburb. He spent much of his boyhood repairing radios in the basement, his refuge from the racist verbal and physical abuse he says awaited him on the street (Pais 1996). In the black-and-white causality of acoustic equations on paper, Bose eventually found an idealized, predictive, and apparently raceless space. His work in fabricating space through sound stands as an example of the idealist spatial practices Henri Lefebvre describes, in which engineers and designers conceive and design space in a conceptual framework (1991, 38). By embracing this scientific rationalism, an idealist view that sees physical space as something to be abstracted, shaped, and perfected, Bose was able to reshape his social world as well. He left behind the neighborhood racism to become an MIT professor and the founder of a corporation with over eight thousand employees and more than $2 billion in annual sales (2010).

As in the case of Apple's Steve Jobs, journalistic accounts of the Bose Corporation often center on the figure of Amar Bose. Such "heroic individual" narratives make technological innovation a matter of individual excellence; like noise-cancellation technology, these narratives suppress the presence of numerous others to foreground the rationality, independence, and agency of the individual.[2] Read in isolation, the Bose biography threatens to obscure the depth of the social inequities that make it so exceptional. Moreover, the rationalism that Bose used to overcome racism is not without its own racial history. The objectifying cultural turn of the European Enlightenment spawned colonialism and Orientalism, as well as modern science,[3] and though they apply a rhetoric of objectivity, scientists and technologists are never "above" the politics of the social milieux from which they emerge. The historian of technology Rayvon Fouché, for example, alerts us to the racialized aspects of seemingly neutral technologies:

> Technology is often thought of as a value-neutral "black box" for inputs and outputs. Critical studies of technology have opened the black box, but there are many hidden compartments that still need to be explored. . . . We need to reassess and expand our study of technology to examine how racially marginalized people, such as African Americans, interact with technology. . . . This is difficult because race and racism, in relation to technology, have always been hidden in a mysterious place of "unlocation" (2006, 658).

Fouché provides examples of African Americans who repurpose technology in ways that make black people more audible, visible, and empowered as a *group*. Bose, who was often mistaken for—and persecuted as—an African American by whites, followed a different trajectory, finding his own *individual* technological empowerment by excelling in the white-dominated social worlds of academe and entrepreneurship, engineering expensive products for middle- and upper-class audiophiles.

More importantly, noise cancellation seems to have been socially constructed to effect a variation on Fouché's "unlocating" of difference, employing ostensibly neutral technology to distance otherness in the crowded, allegedly democratic spaces of modern travel. Bose noise-canceling technology was first used to diminish engine and wind noise in the two-way communications of pilots' radio headsets, functioning as a communication-facilitating device. However, in Bose's marketing for its one-way, retail headphones, "separating things that you don't want from things that you want" took on social as well as sonic significance. As seen in the fading passengers of its commercials, Bose markets the QuietComfort brand to consumers as an isolation—rather than communication—device. In particular, the headphones caught on with those exemplars of neoliberal agency, Bose's fellow business travelers.

Spaces of Circulation, Sounds of Otherness

Bose headphones' popularity with business flyers is underscored by the tongue-in-cheek opening paragraph of a review in the flagship British edition of *Business Traveller*, a consumer magazine published in ten countries, including the United States:

> On a recent trip to New York in business class, I realised that I didn't fit in. I was wearing the same uniform as everyone else (either a suit, with no tie, or chinos and a blue shirt and jacket), I had the same traveller's paunch, and I still got excited by the champagne selection in the lounge. But once on board, everyone pulled out a pair of noise cancelling headphones. I had none. I was clearly an imposter and should find another cabin in which to travel.

Well-fed, dressed in masculine attire, discerning in matters of champagne and electronics, the "everyone" of business class presented here is far from diverse—and quite similar to the succession of road warriors who give their testimonials in the Bose commercial mentioned earlier. The market research firm Mintel reports that men are more than twice as likely as women to travel for business. The average air traveler is between thirty-five and fifty-four, college educated, and relatively affluent, possessing "the disposable income needed to pay for added convenience, comfort customization and lifestyle appeal" (Mintel 2008, 2010).

Indeed, the road warrior's recent use of noise cancellation to fabricate personal space is part of a longer history in which public space has been customized for his convenience, comfort, and tastes. The business traveler has become an important economic engine, market category, and recognizable social type for whom specialized magazines, websites, luggage, electronic devices, frequent flyer programs, and other products have been developed. Saskia Sassen points out the "uncontested claim" international business travelers have made on global cities, noting how they "have reconstituted strategic spaces of the city in their image," creating homogenized and exclusive spaces of "airports, top level business districts, top of the line hotels and restaurants, a sort of urban glamour zone" (1996). The spaces of the airport and airplane are also configured to include special areas for these first class, executive, or business passengers.

Such spaces are not, of course, democratic, but rather reflect the tastes and needs of the travelers they are meant to attract. Such travelers are, in fact, "at work" when in the airport or in the air and often expect—or are expected—to be productive at such times. In these spaces designed to promote the efficient and friction-free circulation of economic agents and capital, there is an effort to suppress the unfamiliar, idiosyncratic, and potentially uncomfortable. In short, any kind of difference, any deviation from the normative expectations of the mobile business class, including noise, may be perceived as counterproductive. In the airport and airplane, the forces of market capitalism create what Lefebvre calls *abstract* space, a type of space that "functions 'objectally,' as a set of things/signs and their formal relationships," smoothing out natural, historical, and cultural differences that threaten to slow the flow of goods and capital (1991, 49).

But what does abstract space sound like? Over the years, postmodern theorists, critical geographers, media scholars, and others have described the condition of contemporary space as degraded by speed, illusion, abstraction, and visual distraction, but they have rarely framed the spatial problematic in terms of sound. Other scholars, however, have shown that since the Enlightenment, sound, like space, has been rationalized and abstracted for exchange, circulation, and expansion. As Leigh Eric Schmidt writes, "the Enlightenment changed the senses. Like any cultural regimen of perception, it dulled and sharpened simultaneously" (2000, 3). The sharpening included focused, critical, and technological listening practices such as the physician's auscultation through the stethoscope, while the dulling involved "the quieting of all those heavenly and demonic voices by which 'superstition' had for so long impeded the advancement of knowledge" (5). These techniques and technologies were designed to shore up the rational credentials and boundaries of the subject by better objectifying and controlling the objects of audition, leaving little room for resonances of unreasonable nature. In his characteristically polemical style, R. Murray Schafer describes "imperialist" and "synthetic" dynamics in the modern soundscape, analogous to Lefebvre's abstract space, as the microphone and loudspeaker alter the aural for the purposes of time-space compression and semiotic exchange (1994, 91).

These spatial histories are built into the intentionalities of noise-canceling headphones, as mobile orphic media designed to help individuals navigate abstract sonic spaces by further abstracting the relationship between space and sound. Emphasizing siren-silencing over sound's communitarian potential, noise-canceling headphones help to craft subjects capable of selecting "messages" circulating in shared acoustic spaces.

However, headphones are not the only sonic spaces designed for the road warrior. Like the visual aesthetics of interior design or the feel of leather chairs, aural architecture is an important aspect of Sassen's environments tailored to business-class mobility.[4] In his aural analysis of the Mall of America, Jonathan Sterne details the important role programmed music (Muzak) plays in the production of commercial spaces and the circulation within these spaces. The use of different types and volume levels of music in the mall's hallways, stores, and parking lots builds, encloses, and divides the acoustical space, managing and coordinating the relations between different parts of the mall. "Music programs correspond to the demography of the Mall's *desired*, rather than *actual*, visitors," Sterne writes, noting, "the Mall desires an affluent (and usually white) adult middle-class population" (1997, 43). Airports, which have come to look more and more like upscale shopping malls, have in some ways come to *sound* like them as well. Listening to airports suggests that, regardless of the demographics of actual users, the mediated sounds found there skew toward the tastes of older, wealthier, and predominantly white listeners—be it CNN, classic rock, jazz, or New Age music. Executive lounges represent even more rarefied sonic spaces in which thick walls and acoustical tile block out the noise of the many in the terminal.

So why then, if the aural environment has in many ways been tuned for their ears, are business travelers so eager to tune it out with noise-canceling headphones? There are several reasons for this, many of which are tied to the successful proliferation of human and capital mobility under neoliberalism. First, not all sounds that are custom designed for a particular audience are designed to benefit those listeners. Sterne points out that in the use of programmed music, not only is music commodified—the *listener's response* to that music is commodified and sold to store and mall owners by music programmers. Likewise, many of the sounds of the airport are designed to attract, distract, and open the traveler's wallet, in effect trying to pull mobile subjects into human and capital flows that they may wish to resist. In the face of the commodification of aural attention, orphic mediation through headphones may function as a defensive tactic for travelers, creating a sonic refuge from what Margaret Morse calls "nonspace"—space that privileges exchangeability and convertibility above all else, reducing all things to signs and measuring all things according to exchange value.[5]

Second, business travel is not the only kind of air travel to expand since the 1970s. Much of the noise, crowding, and delay that characterize contemporary air travel are unintended consequences of neoliberal deregulation's success in—to use the common conflation of consumption and political representation—"democratizing" air travel. Instituted in 1978 under Jimmy Carter, deregulation led to increased competition, drops in ticket prices, and the hub-and-spoke system of stopover (rather than direct) flights, which created greater cost efficiency but also cascading effects of delays in cases of bad weather or mechanical issues. The wisdom of air deregulation, with its mixed results of increased passenger numbers, cheaper fares, industry destabilization, and customer dissatisfaction, is debated (e.g., Siddiqi 2003), but ubiquitous news stories on holiday delays and "air rage" suggest that many flyers do not perceive their increased mobility as a source of freedom.

Despite their being molded in some ways for a privileged class of traveler, the air terminal and the cabin are still strange spaces in which one is implicated in flows and stoppages not of one's choosing. Modern transportation puts us in close proximity with diverse strangers while leaving the rules for interaction largely up to negotiation and interpretation. In such circumstances, it is little wonder that many people choose to retreat from sociality through books, newspapers, and media devices. Anne Tyler's 1985 novel *The Accidental Tourist* contains the following prescient passages, which highlight orphic media's utility in minimizing contact between the business traveler Macon Leary and another passenger:

> On the flight to New York, he sat next to a foreign-looking man with a mustache. Clamped to the man's ears was a headset for one of those miniature tape recorders. Perfect: no danger of conversation. Macon leaned back in his seat contentedly. . . .
>
> The man beside him took off his headset to order a Bloody Mary. A tinny, intricate Middle Eastern music came whispering out of the pink sponge earplugs. Macon stared down at the little machine and wondered if he should buy one. Not for the music, heaven knows—there was far too much noise in the world already—but for insulation. He could plug himself into it and no one would disturb him. He could play a blank tape: thirty full minutes of silence. Turn over the tape and play thirty minutes more. (2002, 26–7)

In this scene Tyler crystallizes the conflicting relationships between free-dom, otherness, and selfhood in the spaces of mobile capitalism. If it is only through the other that we know who we are, then interacting with others is always a presentation and renegotiation of the self—a process that might be felt as fatiguing or even threatening to the constant traveler. Technology, however, comes to the rescue, creating "insulation" between the "Middle Eastern" and American travelers, containing the "ethnic" sounds of the for-mer and potentially protecting the latter from the "noise in the world."

In such situations, noise is the sound of otherness, sound that a white, male "accidental tourist" does not wish to integrate into himself or be integrated into. In the cabin, both the jet engine and conversation can be perceived as noise. In her protagonist's imagined listening to the blank tape, Tyler fore-shadows Bose's web marketing of its noise-canceling headphones, which of-fers "a quieter world" and "the tranquility you desire"; in her use of the word *insulation* to describe this effect, she also foreshadows Bose's marketing of the production of quiet as the production of personal space. Tyler provides us with an alternative reading of the electronic shops now found in every airport: do they sell technologies for in-flight entertainment or boundary maintenance?

QuietComfort for the Neoliberal Self

As seen above, though space has been reshaped in many ways for the busi-ness traveler, the inertia of circulation nevertheless involves physical and social forces that can affect one's sense of being a free and individualized self. Bose's message that QuietComfort soundscaping offers a sense of physical and psychological space has been well received. Reviews and journalistic ac-counts of QuietComfort have been remarkably consistent with the narrative encouraged by Bose's marketing, suggesting that users understand these de-vices as self-preserving tactical aids in their navigation through noisy spaces filled with others. These pieces also construct an image of self that is similar to the portrait scholars have painted of the self in neoliberalism, one that is autonomous, reflexive, and self-managing.

An examination of ninety-six newspaper and magazine reviews and arti-cles published in the United States, Canada, Australia, England, and Ireland between 2001 and 2009 reveals that all mention air travel, with many follow-ing the same crisis-resolution pattern: an opening description of airborne horrors leading to the presentation of Bose headphones as technological solution. Former *New York Times* consumer technology critic David Pogue, for example, uses this pattern to frame his comparison of Bose and other noise-canceling headphones, beginning with the following list of travails: "As you may have heard, air travel this summer isn't going to be pretty. You'll be crammed in, delayed and bumped—if you're lucky. If you're unlucky, your flight will just be canceled. Fortunately, not all of this misery is out of your control. Take, for example, the noise-canceling headphones that Bose began making popular a few years ago" (2007).

It is notable that the foregoing indignities are spatiotemporal rather than aural in nature. Being "crammed," "delayed," and "bumped" suggests a self impeded from its rightful free movement through space. The headphones are suggested as a way to control at least some aspects of this "misery." In the next paragraph, Pogue takes an aural turn, describing the technology of phase cancellation and the relief it can bring as "the roar of the engines is magically subtracted from the sound that would otherwise have ground away at your well-being for six hours." While there is presumably some playful hyperbole at work here, there is also the clear implication of a self that must protect itself through technology. The implied reader is not a wide-eyed adventurer but a savvy and world-weary accidental tourist, guarding his well-being through technologies of the self.

This mobile self-manager of Pogue's review, navigating the throngs and waiting out the delays, resembles what scholars have referred to as the neoliberal self. Recounting the critiques of neoliberalism offered by Barbara Cruikshank, Nikolas Rose, and Wendy Brown, Ilana Gershon notes that each scholar refers to a "reflexive relationship in which every self is meant to contain a distance that enables a person to be literally their own business" (2011, 539). As their own businesses, such subjects must manage and care for their own skills and assets while negotiating their dealings with other autonomous agents, be they individuals or corporations.

If the neoliberal self is responsible for reflexively developing its assets and creating strategic alliances, it must also conserve and protect those assets, strategically avoiding or severing unwanted ties. As spaces where multitudes of these free agents must negotiate with one another, the airlines, and the Transportation Safety Administration, sites of air travel become paradoxical spaces where too much freedom for too many becomes a freedom that crams, delays, bumps, and grinds. In these spaces where freedom proves illusory, orphic media provide at least an illusion of freedom, offering the ability to disconnect from the networks of sound and sociality in which one is implicated.

Significantly, the very presence of a technological "solution" to this problem of conflicting freedoms reinforces the essential neoliberal belief that problems must be solved individually and within the market rather than addressed as systemic issues: individual consumption, rather than collective action, is the site of social agency. Obscuring the systemic nature of travel woes by making them a matter of personal responsibility also encourages passengers to perceive their problems in the form of irresponsible fellow passengers. This perception is on display in one long-running and "most-viewed" thread in the *Business Traveller* forums, titled "The fattest person I have ever sat next to."[6] The initial post is little more than a link to an image of a very large man who is somehow seated in a coach-class seat despite being twice its width. The next poster complains about "subsidizing" fat passengers' weight in ticket prices, notes fat people's larger carbon footprints, and suggests weighing people, since airlines already weigh luggage. Other posters concur, with one suggesting screening passenger size with a metal cage like the one used to limit the size of carry-on luggage. The thread spools out in a succession of complaints about "rude," "smelly," "greasy," "chatty," and "ugly" flyers. These posts overwhelmingly portray travel woes as a problem of difference, as others fail to conform to norms of behavior, class, appearance, hygiene, race, or nationality. It is forms of difference—not, say, overcrowded planes with undersized seats—that are understood to burden these travelers. It is also telling that both problems and recourse are framed in market language: subsidy, prices, surcharges, taxes.

Where the airlines fail to surcharge these nonconforming bodies off of the plane, the market supplies the dematerializing properties of noise cancellation, which offers not only the intramodal affective mediation of fighting sound with sound, but also the cross-modal mediation of sonically muting visual and haptic affectivity. The Bose advertisement's fantasy of fading fellow passengers is, in fact, only half the equation: by facilitating the shift of attention to the virtual space of a stereophonic soundscape and/or computer screen, orphic technology allows users to disappear their *own* bodies as well, a phenomenological shift that reconfigures subjects' relations to their surroundings. In this shift, hearing takes on something like the imperious and objectifying perspective usually attributed to vision. Writing in the 1980s, Michel de Certeau, for example, uses the view from the height of the World Trade Center to explore representational spatial practices in which the powerful define and contain the other (1988). The politics of orphic mediation, however, reflect *controlled listening's* utility in moments when the powerful wish to define, disappear, or make themselves socially inaccessible to the other. Like sight, sound dominates.

Close readings of ads, reviews, and articles uncover what sorts of selves are to be dominant and dominated through Bose headphone use. In the *Business Traveller* review mentioned earlier, Bose headphones signify one's belonging in business class. Similarly, another Pogue review explains that the wearer will "strike . . . fellow passengers as a savvy, experienced hard-hitter who knows all the tricks in the travel game" (2009). Other reviews and articles cite the headphones' popularity with "the travel set," mentioning the destinations of Paris and Phuket, Thailand (Kellner 2009), or voice concern about "a tool for one to obliterate the sound of the many" (Walker 2008), an objection that nevertheless affirms the status and exclusivity the devices project. As previously described, Bose commercials introduced QuietComfort primarily (though not exclusively) through a white, male, middle- to upper-class perspective[7] (figure 5.2). When the white business traveler reclines with eyes closed and his fellow travelers fade away, or as he opens the informational shield of the newspaper and the cabin becomes a white line drawing, these techno-utopian visuals suggest spaces cleansed of racial, class, and gender differences, places where a pure Cartesian self can meditate and envision, undisturbed. In such a sublime space, Adam Smith's rational actor can be his most rational, with the differences and conflicts that complicate a libertarian view of free markets and free selves held at bay. The normative self in the QuietComfort discourse, then, is white, male, rational, monied, and mobile.

And what is the noise that this normative self seeks to diminish or eliminate? Nearly all references to noise in the advertising and print discourse fall into one of two categories: the sounds of transport and the sounds of other people. The first category includes noise from jet engines, trains, subways, buses, automobile traffic, road noise, and car horns. This is to be expected, both because Amar Bose first conceived these headphones for air travel and because active noise cancellation works best on droning, lower- to mid-frequency sounds (which describes all of the sounds mentioned except for the car horns).

However, although active noise cancellation is less effective in suppressing transient, higher-frequency sounds, *voices*—particularly women's and children's voices—are referenced in reviews almost as often as the sound of the jet engine. Against the peace and logical geometry of the Bose commercial's abstracted air cabin we can contrast "the most rambunctious child's shriek or a woman complaining to her significant other" (Kellner 2009), "a

Figure 5.2 "Road warrior" images from Bose ads.

crying baby and a nervous, talkative flier" (Heptinstall 2005), and the "annoying coworker in the next cubicle . . . or, ahem, a nagging spouse" (Saltzman
2006), all of whom are portrayed as noise sources in (male-written) newspaper pieces. These voices are emotional, distracting, and annoying—generally
too young, feminine, and irrational to silence themselves. This theme is also
present in the imagery of a Singaporean print ad campaign for the Bose QuietComfort (figures 5.3–5.5), as described in an advertising magazine: "The
campaign features mime artists in situations where people would typically
make loud, unwelcome sounds (shouting, crying and pain-induced yelling),
silently acting out the scenes. A woman sits comforting two sobbing babies
in one shot, while a couple have a heated argument in another. In the final
shot, a man appears to be in agony as he waxes himself."[8]

Again the primary noisemakers hail from the domestic realm: aggravat-
ing babies and a fighting couple. The unwelcome scream of the self-waxing
man is a humorous deviation from the women and children theme, though

Figure 5.3 A Bose mime ad campaign depicts noise as domestic.

Figure 5.4 A Bose mime ad campaign depicts noise as feminine.

Figure 5.5 A Bose mime ad campaign depicts noise as irrational.

it is worth noting that he becomes a noisemaker in the act of "feminizing" himself.

In this discourse, the rational, normative agent must protect himself from the inchoate sounds of the jet engine, woman, or child. This gendered marketing and reception of QuietComfort points to these devices' place in a longer history of masculine-coded audiophile products. As home audio equipment has long been used to construct a masculine refuge in the shared domestic space of the home (Keightley 1996), noise-canceling headphones are used to construct a mobile office or den by actively diminishing the audible evidence of the shared space users inhabit. The woman and child are others who bind the self-regulating, corporate self, limiting the number and variety of alliances available to it. QuietComfort shields the rational actor from types of communication that distract from the pleasures of production and consumption.

It can be argued that another type of irrational other lurks between the lines in both the advertising and the critical reception of noise-canceling headphones: the terrorist. The original QuietComfort headphones were released to market in the year 2000, the year before commercial passenger jets were used as missiles to attack the Pentagon and World Trade Center. The widespread consumer use of noise-canceling headphones, and the cultural conception of personal space that is attributed to wearing them, have developed during a decade in which air travel has been dominated by the nebulous threat of terrorism. A sense of danger and suspicion has become attached not only to air travel in general but to one's fellow passengers and even to one's self, as checkpoints, screenings, wandings, and pat-downs become the norm.

In the attacks of September 11, 2001, racial, ethnic, and religious differences of the sort that an idealized free market promised to render irrelevant became explosively visible. The psychological and symbolic import of destroying the centers of U.S. military and trade power were clear, but no more important than the blow struck to air travel as the symbol and embodied enactment of mobility and freedom. Shuffling through homeland security, shoes in hand, the business traveler became more temple supplicant than road warrior—an intolerable affront to the freedom of class privilege that was eventually remedied with TSA Pre✓ fast lanes. Though the terror felt by travelers has receded, the uneasy atmosphere that lingers in its wake gives us other ways to read Bose newspaper article headlines such as "Far from the Maddening Crowd," "Headphones to Make the World Go Away," and "Hear No Evil—Wherever You Are." In such a setting, cultural difference is not only devalued as impinging on the enjoyment of travel—it is also seen as a threat that costs "us" money, dignity, and freedom of mobility. In spaces seemingly threatened by irrational, suicidal others, the rational neoliberal self has all the more reason to produce personal space through audio technology.

Diversity and the Sonic Interface

I have described how the intentionalities of noise-canceling headphones channel a set of social, historical, and technological dynamics that have influenced the production of public space in American capitalism. In putting on a pair of QuietComforts to block out the sounds of others and better concentrate on a spreadsheet or movie, the road warrior creates a small field of Lefebvre's abstract space, in which difference is minimized so that the informatic circulation of texts and commerce can be maximized. This orphic technology, like the more exclusive spaces of the air terminal and the cabin, has been developed with the business traveler in mind. Business travelers, however, are not the only consumers of this technology today, and I want to conclude by beginning to consider what happens when diverse selves put on devices that dial down difference, a question that I will consider more fully in the next chapter. For now, I want to posit the idea that, just as these headphones are *reflective* of a rationalist European history, their intentionalities are also potentially *productive* of particular ontologies and social relations.

The use of headphones with portable media devices is, of course, nothing new, and many others have considered the spatial and phenomenological effects of the Walkman and iPod. What sets noise-canceling headphones apart is that they do not merely block out the aural world but *mediatize* it in order to cancel it out. These devices meet Lev Manovich's definition of new media, in which content and interface are no longer one (as in the "old" media of film or painting), but instead the user accesses a database of information through a separately designed interface (2001). The power button on noise-canceling headphones is a new media interface designed to turn the aural world into a database of content that can be selectively accessed. If this perhaps sounds like hyperbole, consider the development of a smartphone app that further refines this interface with the aural world. Awareness! The Headphone App uses the iPhone's microphone to monitor environmental sound, "gating" (filtering out) all sound below a volume threshold set by the user. The app's description in the iTunes Store explains the advantages in distributing the responsibility of listening to the iPhone: "Perfect for exercising at the gym, jogging outside, awaiting a boarding call at the airport, or even listening to a podcast while watching kids in the playground. You control how much outside sound is heard and when. No need to remove or re-adjust your earphones, even with noise cancelling or noise isolating headsets." Without the faintest hint of irony, the description goes on to assert, "Awareness!' could save your life, stop you missing a flight, or just let you listen & talk."

Understanding just how such new media devices position diverse users as objects and subjects requires what Lisa Nakamura calls a theory of "digital racial formation" (2009). Nakamura considers the subjectivities that white, male-designed web interfaces impose on diverse internet users—a line of questioning we might extend to the interface QuietComfort forms with the sound of lived space. This line of questioning acknowledges that individuals' subjective horizons are profoundly shaped by the media they utilize and works to locate racial formations in the black boxes of media technologies.

In putting on noise-canceling headphones, diverse selves put on the Western perceptual and affective praxis that has been built into their technology, a praxis that attempts to construct an on/off interface with the aural environment and the space one shares with others. Though this interface technologically quiets the perceived noise of difference, it does not affect all differences equally. No matter the cultural background of the wearer or the content of the media being listened to, the headphones cast people who culturally value talk as noisemakers, discouraging sociality between strangers, coworkers, and even family members. When Amar Bose sat in an airplane and dreamed up a way of "separating things that you don't want from things that you want," he was thinking of sound, not culture. This act of separation *is* a form of culture, however: it is a technological practice that separates us from things—and people—before we have a chance to know whether or not we want them. To the extent that the use of noise cancellation is the norm in spaces of transit, the cultural value of circulation suppresses the cultural value of embodied copresence; in addition, whatever opportunities these spaces offer for intercultural interaction will be minimized.

This problem is exacerbated by the fact that racism and sexism already profoundly influence the ways we listen to one another, encouraging us to reflexively hear as noise the dialects, slang, accents, music, and audible behavior of nonwhite, non-male, and non-middle-class people. Stoever's book *The Sonic Color Line* centers on the historical processes "enabling some listeners to hear themselves as 'normal' citizens—or to use legal discourse, 'reasonable'—while compelling Others to understand their sonic production and consumption—and therefore themselves—as aberrant. Essentially," she continues, "one's ideas about race [and, as Stoever readily acknowledges, gender and class] shape what and how one hears and vice versa" (2016, 14). As this chapter has shown, when the "normal" perception of noise is already suffused with unexamined race, class, and gender ideologies, the production and use of noise-canceling technologies can never be neutral. It is important, then, to reckon with the potential for the sonic interface of noise cancellation to remediate sonic color, class, and gender lines into discriminatory walls of sound.

This last point may be particularly relevant for academics, many of whom, like other neoliberal subjects, fly frequently and often work in transit. In fact, two readers of earlier versions of this chapter read it while in flight: one wore noise-canceling headphones while doing so and the other wished for a pair as a baby cried. I am writing this very sentence high above the American Midwest, foam plugs firmly lodged in my ears as I ignore the person beside me in favor of an imagined scholarly audience. It is perhaps ironic that cultural scholars—who so often seek to amplify everyday, marginalized, or silenced voices—also treat the voices around them as noise.[9] However, deadlines are deadlines: academics, under ever more pressure to earn our keep within the corporatized, neoliberal university, increasingly travel within the aural architecture of the mobile ivory tower, where we are "free to think." Attending to my own practices here in economy sensitizes me to the economic abstraction of my own aural experience—and even generates some empathy for the pressures felt by the swells up in business class, whose freedom and mobility indeed come at a cost. The purpose of listening to our own listening as a social practice is not to preemptively condemn technologies such as noise cancellation, but instead to learn *when* we use them, *why* we use them, and what kinds of social amplifications and reductions result. What affective configurations of selfhood and social space are emerging from our increasing reliance on these technologies?

In recent years, noise-canceling headphones have escaped business class and crossed the color line, as both Bose and other manufacturers—especially Apple's Beats Electronics—market noise-cancellation to younger, more racially and economically diverse demographics. Now the most high-profile form of orphic mediation, noise cancellation is spreading around the world and integrating itself into the technological praxis of diverse global cultures. Therefore, in the next chapter I will study the Beats "Hear What You Want" advertising campaign, examining how the "black noise" (noise from an African American aural perspective) depicted in these ads differs from the "white noise" that the Bose ads promised to control, looking for clues as to how orphic practices might change (or stay the same) in different socio-cultural contexts.

6

Beats by Dre

Race and the Sonic Interface

Loudness is something racialized people cannot afford.
—**Liana M. Silva**, "As Loud as I Want to Be: Gender, Loudness,
and Respectability Politics"

I'm not tryin' to hear that, see?
—**Positive K**, "I Got a Man"

Let's return to the sounds and images this book began with: the 2013 commercial in which Beats headphone–wearing NFL player Colin Kaepernick remains unaffected by the wild gesticulations and verbal abuse of an opposing team's fans outside a football stadium. *Hush* opens with this ad from Beats Electronics' "Hear What You Want" campaign because it powerfully displays how individuals use orphic media in attempts to sonically control themselves. The soundtrack to the ad, Aloe Blacc's song "I'm the Man," perfectly thematizes the affectively self-constructive and self-defensive potentials that noise cancellation can offer; in fact, according to Blacc, Beats cofounder

Jimmy Iovine conceived the "Hear What You Want" ad campaign as soon as he heard the song.[1] Blacc's chorus lifts the melodic and lyrical hook "You can tell everybody" from Elton John and Bernie Taupin's romantic ballad "Your Song" but replaces the subsequent phrase ("this is your song") with the mantra, "I'm the man, I'm the man, I'm the man." The verses feature another repeated and equally solipsistic phrase: "This is my world." Paired with images of an athletic hero under siege, the lyrics speak to the power of sound as a technology of the self: By controlling the sound of my world, I can compose and amplify the song of myself.

What I have yet to consider in any depth, however, are the racial politics that contribute so much to the cultural power of "Hear What You Want": Colin Kaepernick is African American, while the majority of the jeering football fans depicted in the ad are white. And, of course, only a couple of years after shooting this commercial, Kaepernick would deploy silence in a very different way, fighting racial injustice by initiating the most widespread and consequential silent protest in professional sports history. In the last chapter, I explored how race influenced the invention and marketing of Bose noise-canceling headphones, ending the chapter by suggesting that we think of it as an interface with the sonic world, one potentially embodying its own digital racial formation (Nakamura 2009), a rationalist, European, post-Enlightenment technology with a tendency to remediate the sonic color line (Stoever 2016) as a wall of sound. In this chapter, I want to develop and complicate this idea, examining the multistability of this interface—its multiple potentials for differently positioned subjects. Tricia Rose points out that in hip-hop, turntables, mixers, and samplers are *technologically* "revised in ways that are in keeping with long-standing black cultural priorities, particularly regarding approaches to sound organization" (1994, 63). In the case of Beats headphones, exponents of hip-hop culture altered the *discursive* construction of noise cancellation in accord with their cultural priorities for organizing sound. These different potentials within the same technology exist due to sound's already mediatic nature, the differential politics of meaning and possibility that emerge in the intermediation of sounds, silences, and subjects.

Today, noise-canceling technology is no longer the possession of a privileged few—and understanding the intersections between race, culture, and mobile audio technologies will be increasingly important for media scholarship, given the dynamic growth of the headphone industry into new, diverse markets in the twenty-first century. Companies such as Apple, Grado Labs, JVC, Panasonic Corporation, Philips, Pioneer Corporation, Sennheiser

Electronic, Shure Incorporated, Skullcandy, Sony Corporation, and Ultimate Ears are enjoying huge profits and investing heavily in research and development in a product category that was worth over $3 billion in the United States in 2015 and is projected by Grand View Research to reach an astounding $17.55 billion globally by 2022. While not all of these headphones and earphones will use active noise cancellation, most have sonic-isolation capabilities well beyond those common in the Walkman era; furthermore, the report suggests that "enhanced noise cancellation capabilities" will be a major reason for increasing earphone adoption, along with the proliferation of mobile devices and increased disposable income in emerging global markets (Grand View Research 2015). How will noise cancellation be understood and practiced in these diverse socio-cultural settings? What kinds of sounds will be othered? In which spaces will orphic practices thrive, find contestation, or be prohibited?

As a case study, I examine the moment when Beats helped push noise cancellation across age, class, and color lines by using black athletes to advertise its Beats Studio Wireless Headphones. How did African American executives reimagine Bose's sonic practice of "separating things that you don't want from things that you want" for Beats' younger, more economically and racially diverse market? As Jimmy Iovine has asserted, he and Beats' cofounder, Andre "Dr. Dre" Young, had already "sold half a billion [dollars'] worth of product before we paid for one ad," mainly by partnering with cell phone and laptop makers and by putting their conventional (non-noise-canceling) headphones on the ears of taste-making athletes and musicians.[2] The new campaign, then, was designed to introduce Beats' new technology of silence, not its already familiar technology of music reproduction. Just as Bose's white "road warrior" hero figure was positioned in opposition to particular kinds of "white noise," the African American athletic heroes of the "Hear What You Want" campaign fight "black noise," depicted as the social friction that threatens to wear down the successful man of color.

Where Tricia Rose broke ground in studying hip-hop as "black noise" that empowered marginalized populations through the reorganization of sound, this chapter studies a different kind of "black noise": disempowering sound and discourse from an African American point of audition, noise to be avoided, ignored, or overcome. In order to better situate racialized technologies of silence in their social context, I will compare Beats' depiction of heroic silence to African American athletes' *actual* use of silent protest during the national anthem in the 2016 and 2017 NFL seasons. The "Hear What You Want" campaign depicted *strategic quietude* as a *prudent tech-*

nology of self-care in a racist America, refashioning the social construction of orphic technology for black users, while also maintaining Bose's affective detachment of self from social dissonance through sonic separation. In real life, however, some of the same athletic stars from these commercials deployed—and debated—*the use of silence as risk-filled political action*, an affective *engagement* with the political that shook the NFL and the American political landscape.

Hip-Hop and Affective Control

Like other orphic media manufacturers discussed so far, Beats Electronics has its own creation myth, this one a meeting in 2006 on Venice Beach between two friends and business associates, white rock producer and music executive Iovine and black hip-hop producer, performer, and label owner Young. Dr. Dre was a founding member of the Compton rap group NWA and the man who introduced Snoop Dogg and Eminem to the world, while Iovine was the chairman of Interscope Geffen A&M Records, which distributes Dre's hip-hop label Aftermath Entertainment. In a story Iovine has repeated with minor variations numerous times, Dre tells Iovine that his lawyers have suggested he put his name on a line of athletic shoes. Iovine responds with something to the effect of, "Fuck sneakers, let's make headphones and speakers." It was an inspired decision for that moment in the history of the music business. Selling media technology diversified Dre's and Iovine's fortunes at a time when the internet was turning music into a low-margin commodity.

When the pair partnered with accessory maker Monster Cable to produce the first Beats by Dre Studio headphones in 2008, the move worked in part because it invested Dr. Dre's cultural capital—as a sonic-perfectionist producer with impeccable taste—in a product category then dominated by the poor-quality earbuds that came bundled with iPhones, iPods, and other media players and smartphones. True, audiophiles would sneer at the sound quality of Beats by Dre headphones, especially frowning upon the hip-hop aesthetics of their boosted bass frequencies (though it should be noted that audiophiles enjoy disparaging Bose products as well). Nevertheless, for many consumers, Beats Studio introduced them to a new standard of sound quality and a new fashion sensibility, as the company's designers reimagined the staid, clinical aesthetics usually associated with over-the-ear and on-ear headphones, transforming them into colorful adornments for the head. From the start, Beats Electronics steadily grew its portion of the headphone/earphone market into a new luxury goods category, prompting a $309 million, 50.1 percent share capital investment from smartphone maker HTC and an expansion into various kinds of headphones, earphones, and wireless speakers, as well as an online streaming music service. By 2014, Dre and Iovine had severed ties with both Monster and HTC—at a moment when market research firm NPD Group was claiming Beats accounted for 59 percent of the high-end, $99-plus American headphone market (Ng, Dou, and Karp 2013). In one survey, 46 percent of teens indicated that they planned to buy a pair of Beats as their next headphone purchase (Richter 2014). In August of that year, Apple Incorporated made the largest acquisition in its history, purchasing Beats Electronics for $3 billion in cash and stock.

Beats and Apple were well suited to one another. On a business level, the partnership allowed Apple to profit from the fact that its earbuds had never approached the quality of the products they came bundled with, while also supplementing its flagging music download sales with new revenue from Beats' music streaming service. The two companies were also somewhat alike: They had not invented the mp3 player, smartphone, or audiophile headphones, but they used industrial design and marketing to expand sales well beyond the mainly white, male hobbyists and technophiles previously associated with these technologies—turning digital devices and accessories into aspirational luxury goods. While neither company had reshaped its respective market single-handedly, the media hype that surrounded the iPod, iPhone, iPad, and Beats by Dre headphones gave the powerful impression that they had.

Beats differed from Apple in one significant way, however—by making its association with African American culture and celebrities the centerpiece of its marketing strategy. While Beats has partnered with non–African American musicians such as Lady Gaga and David Guetta and has gotten plenty of unpaid promotion by giving away its products to celebrities of all races, for the most part the company's image has relied upon paid endorsement deals with black musicians and athletes such as Nicki Minaj, P. Diddy, Kendrick Lamar, Kobe Bryant, Cam Newton, and Serena Williams. The Beats by Dre brand identity is literally synonymous with Dr. Dre's identity as a sonic architect of hip-hop, a genre of black music that has proved indispensable to the contemporary marketer. Dre and Iovine's former colleague, African American advertising executive and former Interscope President of Urban Music Steve Stoute, writes enthusiastically in his book *The Tanning of America* (2012) that hip-hop's combination of "authentic," outsider identities and aspirational celebrations of material goods made it a perfect commercializing force. Hip-hop, writes Stoute, is a "mental complexion" that young people can all buy into through brand consumption, regardless of their own race.

Of course, hip-hop is only one example in a long history of African American musical culture's commodification (Burnim and Maultsby 2014), while Beats follows a long line of products sold through the use of racialized black identities. As musicologist Alex Blue V notes in his study of Beats, "The use of black male athletes to sell headphones can be seen as an extension of . . . a problematic history, beginning with black people being sold as products, transitioning into a fascination with black bodies as other, primitive, and natural that allowed white advertisers to market their products as natural and authentic" (2017, 89), an insight that, we note, both agrees with and offers a critique of Stoute's. But there is an important divergence from historical precedent where hip-hop and Beats are concerned—in hip-hop, African Americans retained for the first time a much greater level of aesthetic and financial control. In contrast to the histories of blues, jazz, and rock and roll, in hip-hop, black people have managed to retain power as arbiters of authenticity in a mainstream musical genre, allowing a select few black tastemakers and trendsetters like Dr. Dre to profit enormously, not only from music sales but from relationships with corporate purveyors of clothing, cars, beverages, and electronics. In fact, shortly after Beats' sale to Apple was announced, a video leaked in which a celebrating Dr. Dre called himself "the first billionaire in hip-hop."

Moreover, the assertion of African American control of capital has itself been a central lyrical message in hip-hop since the 1990s—and Dr. Dre was one of the important navigators of this entrepreneurial turn. As Eithne Quinn evinces, the "gangsta" ethos that Dre and his NWA compatriots brought into the genre was pointedly about black men capitalizing on their own success as "ruthless," self-interestedly agentive individuals, succeeding financially by any means necessary in an urban environment of malign neglect and police brutality. "In the mixed-up, no-guarantees world of neoliberal America," Quinn writes, "gangsta rap was energized politically by the rejection of collective protest strategies and the embrace of a ruthless drive for profit" (2013, 16). Jeff Chang marks the completion of this hip-hop transformation in West Coast rap's turn from 1980s pre-L.A. riots protest songs like NWA's "Fuck Tha Police" to post-riots party music, as epitomized by Dr. Dre's 1992 solo debut, *The Chronic*, which "seemed a heaven-sent balm, a handshake extended by capital to the kids" (2012). As a solo artist, Dre now couched his verbal menace in "G Funk," his new, mellow strain of George Clinton's mid-tempo "P Funk," a subgenre less overtly political than gangsta rap. Hip-hop had always functioned as an "apparatus" in Laurence Grossberg's sense of the word, with DJing, rapping, breakdancing, and graffiti providing black and brown youth with affective resources for the production of black spaces, oppositional identities, the experience of bodily pleasure, and perseverance in racist America. Now, in the 1990s, the apparatus was perfected for export beyond the confines of neighborhoods like the Bronx and Compton, in part because it spoke so well to the precarious economic environment and neo-liberal ethos that *all* young people needed to navigate.

Like all party music, G Funk was a rhythmic, melodic, timbral, and vi-brational vehicle for affective transmission, making heads nod and bodies groove—and its lyrics were also reflexively *about* the affective states that can be achieved through music, drugs, drink, and sex. One thing that made gangsta rap and much subsequent hip-hop different, however, was the de-gree to which it was also about the control of capital. The chorus of Dre's smooth G Funk anthem "Gin and Juice" is a celebration of combined affec-tive and commercial control, as the producer and his new protégé Snoop Doggy Dogg cruise the L.A. streets in a classic car:

Rollin down the street, smokin' indo, sippin on gin and juice
Laid back. With my mind on my money and my money on my mind

In its confluence of smooth vehicular mobility, weed and gin–smoothed af-fect, and monetary rumination, "Gin and Juice" provides the perfect mix of business and pleasure, a theme song for an "always on" neoliberal work cul-ture in which we are encouraged to "love what you do and do what you love." *The Chronic* "was the product that finally and seamlessly closed the gap be-tween the vanilla exurbs and the chocolate inner cities, Chang writes—"a brand-conscious 'G' Thang ready for easy consumption" (2012).

Through both *The Chronic*'s lyrics and its music, Dre performed a sense of individualized affective control perfect for the neoliberal era—a stance on everyday life that Beats' design and marketing teams would build into the social meaning and use of headphones. Awad Ibrahim (2007) describes hip-hop in terms of "mattering maps," Grossberg's affective "investment portfolios" that "'tell' people how to use and how to generate energy, how to navigate their way into and through various moods and passions, and how to live within emotional and ideological histories" (Grossberg 2014, 82). Tall and fit, with a deep, authoritative voice and a firm command of studio pro-duction and business dealings alike, Dre embodied a complex of powerful affective possibilities, ways of imagining and comporting oneself in the world—both for people of color and for those Stoute calls the "mentally tan." As Ibrahim emphasizes, these affective investments are "complexly contradictory," as they can empower individuals while also naturalizing harmful and divisive ideologies such as misogyny, homophobia, and (we might add) neoliberalism (2007). Similar to his music, Dre's line of headphones would offer both boom and flash: Their technology offered a means of sonic-affective control while also *representing* that kind of control through their eye-catching design and high price tag, a way of making it through everyday life while also telling others that you have made it. At the same time—and, again, like the music itself—the headphones would have a way of obscuring their own socially isolating individualism. Beats by Dre made room for a party of one.

Tuning Out Haters

In 2013, Beats' black chief marketing officer, Omar Johnson, helped shift the capitalization of African American affective control into a new market by overseeing the use of athletes to sell the company's new line of noise-canceling headphones. During the years of hip-hop's ascendency, the United States also saw black athletic superstars rise to new levels of prominence; like star rappers onstage or in the cypher of a rap battle, athletes are exemplars of controlled excellence on the field or court. As a former Nike ad man, Johnson saw the potential of marketing noise cancellation through the lens of players' struggles to maintain affective control before and after a game. Johnson's team interviewed the athletes who would be featured in the ads, learning how they used the headphones in their own roles as road warriors to create spaces of pregame and postgame calm so they could perform better under pressure in distracting environments far from home. These television and web commercials conjure a kind of black noise as social discomfort, presented from the subject positions of lone, exceptional black men in America.

The casting of Colin Kaepernick as a lone athlete walking a gauntlet of enraged, mostly white NFL fans, for example, needs to be understood within the context of his being a quarterback of color. Seeing an African American in this position as the helmsman of an American professional football team had until recently been a rarity; Kaepernick's ascension to this coveted role was immediately met with a *Sporting News* column on his tattoos, dressing its racism up "objectively" in a corporate suit:

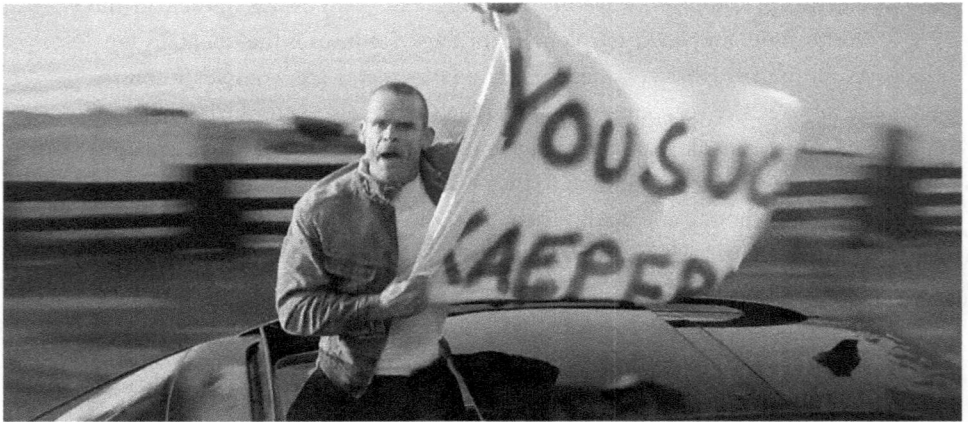

Figure 6.1 A white hater berates Colin Kaepernick in a Beats "Hear What You Want" ad.

San Francisco's Colin Kaepernick is going to be a big-time NFL quarterback. That must make the guys in San Quentin happy.

Approximately 98.7 per cent of the inmates at California's State Prison have tattoos. I don't know that as fact, but I've watched enough "Lockup" to know it's close to accurate. I'm also pretty sure less than 1.3 percent of NFL quarterbacks have tattoos. There's a reason for that. NFL quarterback is the ultimate position of influence and responsibility. He is the CEO of a high-profile organization, and you don't want your CEO to look like he's just got paroled (Whitley 2012).

Questions of mental fitness also followed Kaepernick online and on sports talk radio: Was he a true strategist or just a "raw talent"? Did he have the "mental toughness" to lead the team in high-stakes games such as the playoffs? (Corsello 2016).

The "Hear What You Want" ad portrays this discourse as noise that Kaepernick needs to cancel out in order to perform well on the field. It opens with a "white-sounding" voice over a black screen, compressed and equalized to sound like it comes from a radio or television speaker: "Can he handle it? Can he handle the pressure? This is the big question with quarterback Colin Kaepernick. I've been talking to a lot of fans and they keep saying, 'We can get to him.'" Fade in on an image of the quarterback looking out the window of the team bus en route to the game. A car is traveling alongside and a white man with close-cropped, verging-on-skinhead hair is standing up through its sun roof, shouting at him and holding a bedsheet flag that reads, "You suck Kaepernick" (figure 6.1).

Figure 6.2 Garnett tunes out the hate as away fans hurl eggs and a racially tinged epithet in a Beats "Hear What You Want" ad.

This kind of black noise is central to the narrative of the "Hear What You Want" campaign. Echoing Steve Stoute's ideas on hip-hop and advertising, Omar Johnson stresses that "truth and authenticity" are central to his marketing campaigns, in contrast to other brands that "are actually afraid of the truth" because "truth has a little dirt on it, it's not always clean or politically correct" (Beer 2015). Black noise comes through loud and clear in the first of the "Hear What You Want" ads, in which NBA player Kevin Garnett watches a white TV commentator call him "over the hill." Seconds later, as his team bus navigates the gauntlet of enraged, egg-throwing away fans (figure 6.2), a white man calls him a "big gorilla motherfucker."

Another of the "Hear What You Want" ads capitalizes on the outspokenness of one of the NFL's most controversial players, Seattle Seahawks cornerback Richard Sherman. Hailing from Dre's gang-associated home of Compton, with long dreadlocks and a reputation for "trash-talking" players on opposing teams, Sherman has been villainized by many fans and commentators through use of the racially coded word "thug." The Monday after Sherman berated 2014 NFC championship opponent Richard Crabtree in a live postgame television interview, the word "thug" was uttered on TV 625 times, more than on any other date in the previous three years surveyed (Wagner 2014). Others in the media countered the "thug" accusations by pointing out that Sherman has never been arrested, had a 4.1 GPA in high school, and chose to attend Stanford for its academics when he had his pick of several illustrious football universities. P. L. Thomas wrote in a blog post during the controversy, "Each time these justifications are used, I recognize a level of racism and condescension not unlike the use of 'thug'—not toward Sherman, but toward a hushed suggestion of those real thugs (he grew up in Compton) with whom Sherman is being unfairly confused." What many in white America find threatening about Sherman, Thomas wrote, is his *bravado*, his verbal refusal to contain himself and stay in his place (2014).

Following Johnson's "truth and authenticity" strategy, the Beats Sherman ad went straight to the heart of the controversy, appearing only days after the Crabtree incident. Instead of running the gauntlet of enraged fans, Sherman appears in a locker room, surrounded by a tight scrum of mostly white reporters. Beats noise-canceling headphones are mounted on the player's head, but not yet pulled over his ears. Softball questions come first: "The atmosphere is electric—what's it like playing for these fans?" "How important is home field advantage for you?" Sherman fields the questions easily, though he barely finishes a sentence before the next question is shouted at him. Then the tone of the questioning becomes ambiguous ("Do you really think you're the best corner in the league?") and increasingly aggressive ("Would you say your trash talk is a distraction to your team?"). The reporters begin to badger him, asking if he plays dirty or has a problem with aggression. One white reporter leans over to another and mutters, "He thinks he's so fucking untouchable." "Did you fight a lot as a kid?" a black woman asks. "Not everyone from Compton's a gang member," Sherman replies calmly, remaining unruffled by the increasingly rude line of questioning.

Then, from off-camera, a male voice that can only be described as "white sounding" asks *the question*: "What do you think about your reputation as a thug?" Silence, except for the clicking cameras capturing Sherman's long stare at the unseen reporter (figure 6.3). Sherman looks down, sighs, and shakes his head: "I don't have that reputation." Now so many questions are being shouted at him that he can't even answer them. "Thank you, guys," he says, turning his back on the reporters and pulling the headphone cups over his ears as Aloe Blacc's "I'm the Man" drowns out the crowd.

Protest and Quietude

The "Hear What You Want" ad campaign was more than a commercial success—it was politically prescient, generating market heat from the same affective energies that would soon ignite a conflagration of sports and ra-

Figure 6.3 "What do you think about your reputation as a thug?" Sherman, head-phones at the ready, prepares to tune out a racist line of questioning.

cial politics in the United States. Yet at the same time, by elevating silence's personal utility over its political potential, the ads missed the activism that was to come by a mile. Reflecting on the meaning of "Hear What You Want," Omar Johnson said to a reporter,

> Think about Richard Sherman ... and all the commentary and things people wouldn't really address: Is he articulate? Is he a thug? Is he this? Is he that? All these things people had in their head but wouldn't say. Our spot catalyzed those conversations. And we've done a few spots like that to start those conversations, which music has been doing for decades, across races, ages, and cultures. (Beer 2015)

Johnson's comments seem rather strange. After all, people *were* saying the things they had in their heads about Sherman. That's the premise of the commercial—that Sherman had to contend with unceasing and racially coded public criticism of himself and his actions. It is not white reticence, but a surfeit of racially coded white bluster and opinion that powers the ad's appeal to silence.

More importantly, unlike his representation in the Beats ad, the real-life Sherman has not shied away from explicitly identifying the racial subtext of this discourse. In fact, even as the "Hear What You Want" campaign ramped up, Sherman, Kevin Garnett, and other African American athletes were actively challenging the racism they quietly tuned out in Beats' ads. During the same week that his ad aired in 2014, Sherman told one reporter he believed that "thug" had become an "accepted way of calling someone the n-word nowadays" (Bandini 2014). Later that year, Garnett joined several other black players in violating the NBA's dress code, wearing T-shirts reading "I CAN'T BREATHE" on the court before a game—a silent protest against of Eric Garner's July 17 death from a police chokehold in New York City.

But, of course, the contemporary athlete most associated with political activism for racial justice is Colin Kaepernick, whose silent protests have had extraordinary political repercussions. During the 2016 season, the quarterback's quiet refusal to stand for the pregame national anthem and, in his words, "show pride in a flag for a country that oppresses black people and people of color," generated enormous controversy and widespread media coverage, "fueling," a *Time* magazine cover claimed, "a debate about privilege, pride, and patriotism" (Gregory 2016; Wyche 2016). While Kaepernick sat down during all of the San Francisco 49ers' preseason games in 2016, it wasn't noticed by the sports press until after the third game on August 26, when a photo circulating on social media generated fan and media commentary. In an eighteen-minute video shot two days later, Kaepernick responds to the controversy by providing a remarkable, impromptu locker room disquisition on race in America. The video resembles Sherman's Beats ad in more ways than one, as a tight scrum of mostly white reporters pepper Kaepernick with questions about indicting police, respecting the military, distracting his teammates, and putting "the focus . . . on you and not the issues." "It wasn't something that I really planned as far as it blowing up," the quarterback said when asked about his motivations. "It was just something that I personally decided, 'I just can't stand for what this represents right now.'" However, Kaepernick continued (and subsequently repeated several times), it was good that his refusal to stand had "blown up" in public consciousness because it was raising awareness of injustice and leading to conversations about race in the United States.[3] One of those conversations was between Kaepernick himself and white military veteran and football player Nate Boyer, who had written the quarterback a thoughtful open letter in the *Army Times*, stating, "Even though my initial reaction to your protest was one of anger, I'm trying to listen to what you're saying and why you're doing it." Kaepernick attempted to listen in turn, inviting Boyer for a private discussion in which they arrived at the "middle ground" of showing respect for the military by "taking a knee" rather than sitting during the national anthem. "Soldiers take a knee in front of a fallen brother's grave, you know, to show respect," Boyer said in a later interview (Brinson 2016). Thereafter,

African American players across the league, as well as amateurs and professionals in other sports, began to kneel or raise their fists during the anthem before games.

These athletes' silent protests derived much of their meaning and affective power from the ongoing racial dissonance circulating on social and other media: police violence against black people made visible, the attendant activist response of Black Lives Matter, white "backlash" to BLM, the overtly racist 2016 presidential campaign of Donald J. Trump, and the meme-powered rise of "alt-right" white supremacists during that campaign. The protests were reenergized in 2017 as the NFL season opened in the wake of the white supremacist Unite the Right Rally in Charlottesville, Virginia, on August 11 and 12. This event, which included a march of torch-bearing white men chanting racist slogans and a vehicular assault on counterprotestors that left nineteen injured and one dead, prompted only a belated and apologist response from now-President Trump, who drew false equivalence between the avowed racists and the antiracist counterprotestors. Explaining his refusal to stand for the anthem at a preseason game the day after Charlottesville, veteran Seattle Seahawks defensive end Michael Bennett said, "We're fighting for what America is built on: That's the freedom, the equality, the justice for all and the liberty, and those are the things that I'm actually trying to remember and honor when I sit down for the flag" (Martin 2017). Thirteen days later, Bennett was himself the victim of alleged brutality at the hands of Las Vegas police, who mistakenly suspected him of firing a gun at a prize fight. Bennett later posted an emotional open letter on Twitter, claiming that police put a gun to his head and threatened to "blow [his] fucking head off." "All I could think was, 'I'm going to die for no other reason than I am black and my skin is somehow a threat,'" he wrote, adding that this kind of profiling is why he sat down for the anthem.

But while silent protest seemed to be captivating public attention in a way that the athletes' words about inequality and injustice never had, its effects were more like an affective chain reaction than the start of a thoughtful conversation about race, as many reacted instantaneously, according to the conditioning of their identity positions. Numerous white fans and commentators took offense as soon as they became aware of the kneeling players, which led to a media narrative that Kaepernick's protest was the cause of falling NFL television ratings. In a press conference on September 6, Richard Sherman expressed concern about this turn of events, while still also expressing his support for his teammate Bennett, Colin Kaepernick, and the cause of racial justice. What Sherman disagreed with was the *tactic* of not standing for the anthem. "[Kaepernick's] heart was pure, he was trying to do the right thing," Sherman said. "But in our society, you've got to find the right way to do the right thing *so people don't close their ears.*" Sherman, the so-called thug, seemed to apply his Stanford education in communication to the situation, noting that the communicative action of kneeling was generating a reaction so loud that it drowned out the message the players meant to convey: "You might as well be saying, 'blah blah blah blah blah.' Because people are just seeing you kneel during the national anthem, and they're taking that and *closing their ears.* And that's unfortunate" (Lyles 2017, emphasis added).

Donald Trump, for his part, had no interest in Sherman's type of nuanced analysis, but instead seemed thrilled to serve up the renewed black protests as red meat for his white political base. At a Friday-night Alabama rally on September 22, Trump used the TV cameras to show the NFL's white team owners how they ought to respond to kneeling black players: "Get that son of a bitch off the field right now, he's fired. He's fired!" he shouted to the crowd's audible delight. "NFL ratings are down massively, massively," because "people like yourselves turn on television and you see those people taking the knee when they're playing *our* great national anthem," Trump told the white audience, leaning hard into the word "our." In fact, although NFL ratings had declined by 5 percent year over year, by week seven of the season, the league was doing better than network TV as a whole, which was down 8 percent over the same period (Pallotta 2017).

The next day, Richard Sherman released a measured video critique of Trump's performance on Twitter. Opening with a sigh and the words "Well, a very interesting time we're living in now," Sherman calmly contrasted Trump's lack of criticism for white supremacists with his attacks on those "protesting the injustice and bigotry and racism that has plagued our great country for so long, and [who] are trying to make a difference to make our country even better" (Tsuji 2017). That Sunday, in response to Trump's divisive commentary, the silent protest spread across the entire league, with even white players and staff kneeling, linking arms, or staying in the locker room for the national anthem before the day's games. The meaning of these varied gestures, however, was less than certain: Was the message still one of racial justice? Or was it anti-Trump? Pro–free speech? Pro-player? Pro-NFL? In the weeks and months that followed, it would become clear that NFL ownership and management were far more concerned with circling the wagons around their business interests than with fighting racial injustice.

Dishearteningly, the racial and political identity of the listener continued to be strongly predictive of the way the protests' message was received. In one poll, 65 percent of white respondents disapproved of the NFL anthem protests, with 49 percent strongly disapproving; 74 percent of black respondents approved, with 50 percent strongly approving. Sixty-seven percent of Democrats approved of the protests, while just 11 percent of Republicans did. Where most blacks and Democrats perceived a struggle for racial justice, many whites and most Republicans were outraged by what they saw as the denigration of the American flag and military. In October, Vice President Mike Pence briefly attended an Indianapolis Colts game, seemingly with the express purpose of leaving the stadium as soon as any players took a knee. Some players did protest, and Pence replied in kind by departing. The withholding of participation around the national anthem could go both ways.

While this new front in the culture wars had nothing to do with headphones, it had everything to do with listening, affect, and a sense of self-preservation. In his locker room discussion, Kaepernick emphasized that he simply *couldn't* stand for the anthem and maintain his moral sense of self, while Boyer's *Army Times* letter describes the pride and tears the anthem and American flag conjured within him before one game and the hurt he would have felt if a teammate had refused to stand in that moment. Where one man heard a sacred hymn to country and personal sacrifice, the other heard a painful irony in "the land of the free" and, perhaps, a call to resistance in "the home of the brave." Taking a knee offered a silent, visual performance of African American listening, a solemn means of expressing the affective dissonance of black noise.

From a cultural studies perspective, these two different reactions could be mapped onto Stuart Hall's dominant-hegemonic and oppositional readings of televisual content, with Boyer using an interpretive framework that aided the "institutional/political/ideological order imprinted" on the national anthem, while Kaepernick "detotalizes the message in the preferred code in order to retotalize the message within some alternate framework of reference," engaging a "politics of signification" or "struggle in discourse" (Hall 1999, 513, 517). Yet this picture is incomplete, too suggestive of a dispassionate interpretation, reason, and, as *Time* put it, "a *debate* about privilege, pride, and patriotism." It does not fully capture the deeply felt, embodied experiences of dissonance and resonance that made it impossible to stand for the anthem—or impossible not to.

Here we must reckon with the orphic aspect of music—its potential to stir, invigorate, incapacitate, unite, and divide individual bodies and assemblages of them. Writing on the affective potentials of popular music, Gil Rodman suggests two different understandings of affect: "(1) as a phenomenon that exceeds signification (for example, how music feels, rather than what music means); and (2) as a way to explain how (and how much) particular music matters to the lives of its fans (for example, that fans invest time, money, energy, emotion and identity into 'their' music)" (Rodman 2015, 53).

While popular music and patriotic music are not the same, both open up an orphic vector of intensity, a politically significant force that exceeds signification, charging given individuals with differing experiences of im/possibility and dis/empowerment. This form of affectivity is at once pre-personal, interpreted as personal emotion, and strongly tied to group identities as different sounds, songs, and genres articulate with different identities in ways that seem natural to us. All of these levels of affectivity are involved in Kaepernick's inability to stand and Boyer's inability not to. The difference lies in the fact that white American listeners have long assumed the correctness of their unexamined reaction to sound and have judged both the sounds and the listening of African Americans by its standard, while the latter have had to engage what Stoever calls "an aural form of Du Boisian double-consciousness . . . internal projections of how the white listening ear hears and understands them" and then to decide whether to conform to the dictates of that ear or to critique and challenge them (2016, 213).

In this case, however, both Kaepernick and Boyer exhibited the ability to "listen across difference" (Dreher 2009), advocating for the importance of listening to the other's views, imagining the other's affective investments, taking the risk of opening themselves to the other's point of audition, and thereby reaching the compromise of taking a knee. But the opinion polls reflected exactly what Sherman's internal white ear heard with such clarity. For most whites, the affective power of the national anthem—its tattered promise of shared identity in a polarized country—made the silent protest too repellant for them to listen to its message. For many, the very fact that the flag and anthem were called into question by black people inspired a newfound (though not necessarily insincere) reverence. What was once a last-minute opportunity to grab a beer or hot dog was now an irresistible clarion call to join the battle of white identity politics.

And while the impasse wasn't *about* headphones, there was a way in which headphones provided a perfect embodiment of it. "Hear What You Want" wasn't the only big sports-and-headphones marketing ploy of 2014—that was also the year that Bose outbid Motorola to become the NFL's official headphone and headset sponsor, giving its noise-canceling products new visibility on the heads of officials, coaches, and staff, but also generating headlines such as "NFL Fines Colin Kaepernick $10,000 for Wearing Beats by Dre Headphones," as players refused to give up their prized Beats (Macatee 2014). The symbolism of the majority-white officials and coaches wearing Bose while the majority-black players preferred (and were disallowed from wearing) Beats couldn't be more apropos. This remediation of the sonic color line was suggestive of two incompatible modes of defensive listening—one fighting the black noise of white racism and the other, the white noise of black silent protest. Ironically, even as Omar Johnson's commercials starring NFL players misrepresented the political power and consequences of silence, their sounds and images presaged what would come to pass by the end of 2017. The white haters of the ads had now materialized on the streets of Charlottesville; the black athletes were indeed besieged, trying to perform athletically amid the vocal political disapproval of much of the NFL's majority-white fan base; and Kaepernick and (to a lesser extent) Sherman were at the center of it all.

But unlike the character he played in his Beats commercial, Kaepernick did not achieve victory over the maddened crowd—instead, he was the victim of the most spectacular case of blacklisting since the McCarthy era. In March of 2017, Kaepernick opted out of his contract with the San Francisco 49ers to become a free agent, a move that would normally allow a quarterback of his stature to play the market of NFL teams for a more lucrative deal. Instead, not a single contract was offered to him, while lesser players were hired. Teams made excuses for not signing the former NFC champion, but the real reason was clear. Before Kaepernick entered free agency, he stated that he had already made his point and would not protest during the "Star-Spangled Banner" in his 2017–18 season. However, by then the protest had already grown much larger than Kaepernick, while he continued to symbolize the movement. Owners and coaches, fearful of the vehement disapproval that would come from the president and so many others, would not go near him. In the end, Kaepernick's use of silence made him both more powerful and more vulnerable than the man depicted in the Beats ad.

This contradiction between reality and representation arose because, while Johnson said his commercials were about starting conversations, in fact, they sold the ability to shut those conversations down. In contrast with the real-life Richard Sherman, a man with a degree in communication and a loquacious, fearless public persona, the man in the ad chooses to disengage from the media noise of a still-racist country. Instead of demanding the freedom to be heard, he puts on the ability not to listen. He disengages from the ego-dystonic discourse of public life and finds solace in the ego-syntonic sounds of Aloe Blacc, whose song updates the protest soul sound of the 1960s for the neoliberal individualism of the 2010s.

Viewed together, the Kaepernick, Garnett, and Sherman ads present a stark and lonely vision of black masculinity in the United States. We see these men not with their teammates, nor with their families or friends, but alone in the liminal backstage spaces of the stadiums in which they play, where they are hounded by haters and doubters. In order to be the heroes we see on the field and the court, these ads tell us, they must first contend with this hate and doubt on their own. In order to be exemplars of athletic control, they must first control their own affectivity. The idea is not to overcome racism socially but to cancel it out electronically. In this sense, "Hear What You Want" positions noise cancellation in the same way that gangsta repositioned hip-hop, as an individualist technology of self-advancement for men of color.

Yet it would be too simplistic to criticize these commercials for elevating individualism over social justice. Whatever one thinks of these ads' politics, Johnson is right when he attests to their truth and authenticity. The images of white fans and reporters shouting rudely and threateningly in the faces of black men—in acts of sonic aggression the latter could never safely reciprocate—attest to philosopher Robin James's claim that while "white supremacy grants white people the ability to be understood as expressing a dynamic range [of sounds] . . . white supremacy paints black people as always-already too loud" (2014). As both Stoever and Blue note, the murder of seventeen-year-old Jordan Davis by middle-aged white man Michael Dunn for playing hip-hop exemplifies the perils of being loud while black in America. "Loudness," writes sound scholar Liana M. Silva, "is something racialized people cannot afford" (2015). As we have seen, even silent protest caused many whites to, in Sherman's words, "close their ears."

But it is not only the direst threats that make quietude an important strategy for the racialized self. What person of color has the time or energy to challenge every microaggression or to educate every misinformed or prejudiced individual she meets? How many people feel they have the financial wherewithal to make waves over structural racism when work is scarce and easily taken away? How many of the social and physical spaces that the average person of color moves through seem to offer even the *possibility* of some kind of collective action against injustice? In such circumstances, people find ways to control their own affectivity to get through their days, beating black noise on their own.

It is also possible that privileging protest as the only legitimate response to racial injustice may, in fact, reinscribe the stereotype of black people as always already loud. Blue suggests an alternate reading of the Beats ads in which the athletes are less resistant to outside forces than simply indifferent, using quiet to cultivate a self on its own terms rather than in opposition to white power. Drawing on Kevin Quashie's book *The Sovereignty of Quiet: Beyond Resistance in Black Culture* (2012), Blue resists the formulation in which blackness is loud, communal, public-facing, and oppositional, noting how noise cancellation can nurture black culture's vital yet less recognized contemplative tradition:

> By reading black culture through a frame of quiet, we make space for black subjectivity without assuming that it is always subaltern and that all actions are in protest. Quiet exposes beauty, power, joy, fear, chaos, and peace. It demonstrates an expressiveness that is not subject to the public, and herein lies the sovereignty to which Quashie refers. The athletes become quiet, empowered subjects, able to express a subjectivity that the public cannot mold and cannot control (2017, 101–2)

Through Blue's frame we can reinterpret the "Hear What You Want" campaign as reclaiming the calm, complexity, sensitivity, and quietude so long denied in representations of black men in the United States.

We Are All Road Warriors

The Beats campaign also speaks to dynamics of disaffection that involve Americans of all races these days. As so many spaces we inhabit have been abstracted for the fast circulation of capital above all else—and as inequality grows—the production of personal space for individualized affective control "just makes sense." This is one reason the black athlete's outsider position is so identifiable to "mentally tan" white youth who have never had to contend with the racism these ads depict. When spaces are organized around the circulation of capital to which most have little access, disaffection grows ambient. This is the genius of setting "Hear What You Want" on the highway, outside the stadium, and in the shadowy space of the locker room, rather than under the bright lights of the game. Many can relate to the outsider position these images convey, the precarious feeling of being on one's own, trying to control oneself and survive in the liminal spaces at the edges of the spectacle.

Although the Bose and Beats ads discussed in this book look and sound radically different, they both sell a similar conception of a neoliberal male hero preserving himself in a noisy world through technological progress. As socially organizing principles, technological progress and neoliberalism are productive of certain types of freedom. It may be fair to say as well that, at least for those with the technological aptitude of Amar Bose or the artistic and entrepreneurial abilities of Dr. Dre, the contemporary American meritocracy is less racially oppressive than it was in the past. But beyond their refusal to acknowledge the structural inequalities that invalidate their conflation of free markets and democracy, proponents of technological and neoliberal progress also fail to understand these dynamics as culture—a type of culture that shuts down diversity in less overt ways. Neoliberalism accepts all comers, as long as they subsume their differences in the name of capital circulation. Like hip-hop, culturally diverse ways of being in the world are encouraged when they can be commodified and consumed as media, but are rejected as disruptions to the smooth circulation of capital when practiced in lived spaces such as airports, airplanes, or city streets. Paradoxically, the "libertarian" market often encourages us to quiet down, headphone up, and keep our noise to ourselves.

It is apparent from the foregoing chapters that the globalization of noise cancellation is a complex phenomenon—a contingent interplay between the microperceptual intentionalities of subjects and those of media technologies, both of which are shaped by, and feed back into, macroperceptual histories that yield the virtual possibilities of the present moment. When Sony released the first Walkman in 1979, its designers included two headphone jacks in a concession to their understanding of Japanese macroperceptual conditions, fearing that isolated public listening would be frowned upon in an ostensibly collectivist Japanese culture. The designers were to some extent correct—and yet the social opprobrium that emerged around the Walkman was not enough to override the intentionalities of the device. Few people used the second headphone output and it was soon dropped from Walkman designs, as private listening became commonplace in Japanese public spaces (du Gay et al. 1997, 59). Conversely, ethnographic fieldwork has found that in the ostensibly individualistic United States, middle school students routinely fight the individualizing intentionalities of stereo earbuds by sharing them with friends, one apiece, in enactments of friendship and shared musical pleasure (Bickford 2014).

Chastening examples such as these remind us that we cannot rely on any kind of determinism—technological, economic, or cultural—to make blanket predictions of locally situated media practices. The best we can do is attempt a blurry snapshot of the virtual possibilities in a given moment—the modes of relation that emerge from the use of specific media in specific cultural contexts. When it comes to audio media, mapping these modes of orphic control requires knowledge not only of the technologies involved, but also of what Steven Feld calls the "acoustemologies" or distinct sonic epistemologies of different cultures (1990); as Don Ihde points out, different cultures can use the same technology for different practices and/or carry out similar practices with different technologies (1993, 40).

On the other hand, as Ihde would be the first to remind us, technological intentionalities can and do translate across cultures—particularly in a global context that is, in fact, *constituted* by technological practice and infrastructure. As David Novak writes, it is useful "to challenge the comparative models of exchange that represent circulation as something that takes place *between* cultures" and "privilege the concept of feedback to emphasize that circulation itself *constitutes* culture" (2013, 17, emphasis his). For Novak, feedback is a "condition of subjectivity" in an era of global flows—and like the sonic feedback of a speaker's output cycling back into a microphone's input, culturally mediating feedback circuits can create disruptive (and potentially productive) dissonances.

As seen in the use of noise-canceling headphones, as well as in the NFL protests, the power and stakes of silence derive from listeners' situation in media circulatory systems that provide unprecedented control, yet always seem beyond our control. The collective protest that critiqued racial injustice and activated different affective responses in listeners of different races nevertheless circulated mainly through the same types of personal screens and earphones. The same technologies circulated similar information yet radically different experiences of social feedback to individual media users, depending on how the protest was felt to expand and diminish each individual's power to act and be acted upon. Despite our differences in race, ethnicity, gender, and class, we are nearly all road warriors in America today because the electronic highways of information capitalism run through our eyes, ears, and bodies day and night. It is the elusive intentionality of controlling ourselves by controlling those flows that noise-canceling headphones promise, and it will be fascinating to learn from ethnographers whether and how this kind of freedom through personal regulation is exercised in Mumbai, Jakarta, and Johannesburg.

Conclusion

Wanting What We Hear

Anecdotal evidence of the increasing cultural, economic, medical, political, and military importance of sensitive listening and orphic media abounds. Scanning the media in a single month, July 2017, we find numerous examples: During the first week of July, *In Pursuit of Silence*, a documentary concerned with "our relationship with silence, sound and the impact of noise on our lives," enjoys an extended-run Los Angeles premiere. Meanwhile, the second-biggest-grossing film in the United States is not a tent-pole superhero movie or animated feature, but a mid-budget, R-rated crime story about a getaway driver with an iPod fixation and ringing in his ears. Like scores of other contemporary films, Edgar Wright's *Baby Driver* deploys a combination of high-pitched noise and muffled diegetic sound to represent its protagonist's acoustic, physical, and psychological trauma—a "tinnitus trope" that went from nonexistent in mid-1990s Hollywood film to inescapable by the new millennium (Hagood 2015).

Baby's auditory system is marked by the traumatic event that eventually led to his reluctant life of crime; his omnipresent earbuds supply a soundtrack to manage his awareness of both the noise in his head and the dangers and consequences of his immoral acts in the world. Mediated music sets the pace for the mobile mayhem Baby cuts through the city streets, as it also buffers

Baby—socially and affectively—from the menacing and ever-changing cast of independently contracted maniacs he works with. That sound media's orphic utility is the central conceit in a mainstream Hollywood movie speaks to how common and intuitive this kind of mediation has become.

So does the music industry's biggest public controversy in July 2017: As first reported by the website Music Business Worldwide, the streaming service Spotify is larding some of its most highly trafficked playlists with the work of "fake artists," in order to reduce royalty payments to musicians and record labels. The playlists in question are typically instrumental in more ways than one: "Chill," "Dinner," and "Focus" playlists, which have hundreds of thousands or millions of followers each.[1] Spotify can pay pseudonymous studio musicians to produce the music because listeners of these playlists are not interested in specific artists or songs, but rather the orphic utility they offer. "Spotify loves 'chill' playlists," reporter Liz Pelly writes, "they're the purest distillation of its ambition to turn all music into emotional wallpaper. They're also tied to what its algorithm manipulates best: mood and affect."

Looking across the various streaming services, one finds the utilitarian spirit of Muzak healthier than ever. Apple Music, for example, has an "Activities and Moods" page featuring target-affect categories such as "Motivation," "Focus," "Chill," and "Workout," each of which contains approximately twenty different playlists (figure c.1). But streaming services out-Muzak even Muzak itself by establishing an affective feedback loop with their listeners: "These algorithmically designed playlists," writes Pelly, "have seized on an audience of distracted, perhaps overworked, or anxious listeners whose stress-filled clicks now generate anesthetized, algorithmically designed playlists" of calming, middle-of-the-road music.[2]

Stories of sonic affect, sensitive listening, and orphic technology dot the news media as well this month: An article in *Harper's Bazaar* titled "How City Noise Is Slowly Killing You" claims that "big-ticket 'digital detox' packages, free from the beeps and rings of modern gadgets, are proliferating across luxury resorts," and reports that an international noise abatement program called Quiet Mark has convinced more than seventy technology brands to lower the noise levels of their products. The *New York Times* examines the 420,000 noise complaints the city received in 2016 (more than double the number lodged in 2011), prompting a subsequent *Times* column on the best noise-canceling headphones, white noise machines, and earplugs for New Yorkers.[3]

Tech journalists, meanwhile, are enthusing over the new Here One wireless earbuds, designed to let users customize their sonic environments

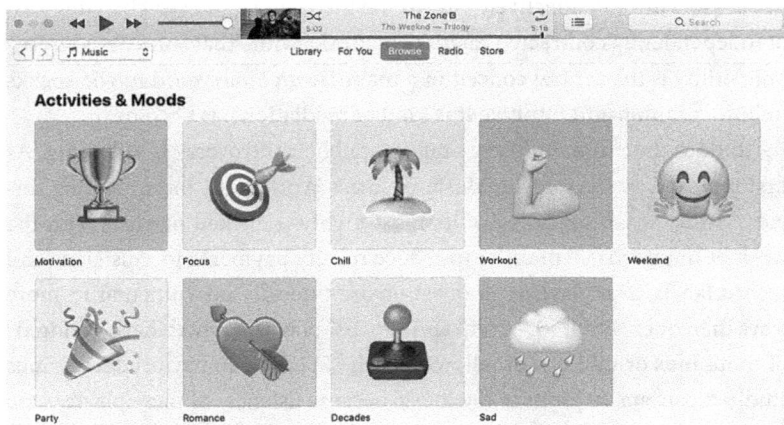

Figure C.1 Apple Music's "Activities and Moods" categories.

through amplification, noise cancellation, targeted filtering, and even special effects. One journalist presaged the tenor of these reviews in a podcast recorded while the product was still in development, gushing, "This is what I want. I want to never take them out. I want to hear only what I want to hear . . . I want to live in my own filter bubble!"[4] The July 2017 issue of the audiology trade magazine *The Hearing Review* bears the headline "Forecast: Turbulent Seas of Change" and features an article titled "Is the Sky Really Falling?" The issue is dedicated to what its editor calls "the turmoil that our industry finds itself in": Due to the combination of technologies like Here One and government deregulation, consumers are potentially able to remediate and customize their hearing on their own, cutting the audiologist out of the picture.

Lest we imagine this arbitrarily chosen month found us in an unusually heightened state of aural anxiety, a check of the previous month reveals stories such as an *Atlantic* piece on the "over 2,200 anti-wind groups" who claim the inaudible low-frequency noise of wind farms cause "wind-turbine syndrome," inducing "panic, sleep disturbance, headache, tinnitus, dizziness, nausea, and visual blurring." And moving forward to August, we learn that anonymous sources in the U.S. State Department are blaming a powerful yet inaudible "covert sonic weapon" for hearing loss and neurological damage among its Cuba-stationed diplomats. The Trump administration will soon use this unknown and acoustically improbable weapon as a reason to eject Cuban diplomats from the United States. (Subsequent research will identify Russian-funded microwave radiation attacks as the probable cause of the diplomats' symptoms.)[5]

In all of these varied examples from the summer of 2017, we find people trying to remediate sound in order to maintain control. In the more benign cases, individuals merely treat sound in a utilitarian manner, while in the more troubling scenarios, affects of fear, paranoia, and rage suffuse sonic engagement. It is a seeming contradiction: People are overwhelmed by real and imagined sounds beyond their control, even as technology provides them with unprecedented control of their aural experience. And by confining these examples to stories of *literal* listening, I have elided 2017's truly unavoidable stories of mediated fear, paranoia, and rage: (1) the Trump administration's blatant, Twitter-led rejection of listening across racial, class, gender, and national differences, and (2) the factional and algorithmically monetized online antagonism and hysteria that once fed into—and are now fed by—Trump's election. Similar to the experience of sound, access to political discourse has never been so individualized or controllable, yet the experience of it often feels completely out of control.

A central purpose of this book has been to explain this impasse of mediated control in literal and figurative listening. Using the example of sound, which gets into our bones while still exceeding our grasp, I have examined how the pursuit of happiness through control produces certain kinds of freedom, but also new assaults and sensitivities. An examination of tinnitus and its orphic suppression (chapter 1) showed the auditory system to be self-regulating, constantly adjusting itself in reference to its environmental medium and an ableist, freedom-seeking habitus of listening. Tinnitus, hyperacusis (sound sensitivity), and misophonia (sound phobia) are signature infirmities of our time, representing most acutely how the desire for freedom from the maladies of body and world can actually exacerbate them—turning our listening into aversion, fear, anger, and suffering.

The rest of the book examined the cultural, economic, and material contexts that have tended to encourage control through orphic media practices. The story of the electromechanical sound conditioner (chapter 2) revealed ways that military and economic exigencies amplified the speed and reach of technological circulation, leading to the production of noise—as both an unintended consequence and as a domestic solution, a technological cocoon of sensory stability. Subsequently, Irv Teibel's *environments* series (chapter 3) reflected the influence of cybernetic, New Communalist discourse—a belief that sound technologies could mediate a better relationship between self, other, and environment.

But cybernetics also inspired infocentrism, a noise-corrupted discourse that produces at once the responsibility for controlled attention and a distracting informatic din, leading to the use of "flow"-facilitating smartphone and computer applications such as White Noise and Lightning Bug (chapter 4). While Teibel's recording series was designed to open up communitarian spaces of possibility, it was the utilitarian sleep/concentration binary found in Marpac's marketing for the sound conditioner that would come to dominate orphic media use in the temporally and spatially fragmented environments of neoliberal capitalism. In the new millennium, noise-canceling headphone brands such as Bose (chapter 5) and Beats (chapter 6) would market the promise of remaining unaffected by tuning out racial, gender, and class difference, sonically fabricating the sensation that "there is no such thing as society."

Today, we are entering an era of algorithmic listening, in which Claude Shannon's "freedom of choice when one selects a message" and Amar Bose's "separating things that you don't want from things that you want" find their most sophisticated expressions of control. If these technologies are to be developed and used in ways that strengthen, rather than weaken, our listening abilities, we will have to find understandings of self, media, and freedom that transcend individual control. For this reason, after taking a look at the near future of orphic consumer technologies and their implications, I will return to the noninformatic cybernetics of autopoiesis, an affective ontology that helps us reflect upon the closed nature of our listening abilities while also emphasizing the ability—and necessity—of listening through that closure.

The Hearable Future

If the future of personal audio technologies (and the threat to the profession of audiology) can be summed up in one word, it is, unfortunately, "hearables"—the ungainly portmanteau that refers to wearable computer technology ("wearables") for the ears. Continued processor and battery miniaturization, refinements in digital signal processing and wireless technologies, and the deregulation of the hearing aid market are affording a convergence between audiological "prescription media" (Mills 2012) and consumer devices, offering individuals new, prosthetic means of controlling their own aurality. According to one industry analyst, hearables promise to make "the ear . . . the new wrist," and are predicted to generate $5 billion in revenue by 2018 (Hunn 2014). Of course, some skepticism is warranted regarding such predictions—by 2018, Doppler Labs, maker of the Here One hearables was out of business, the victim of mismanagement and lackluster battery life. Nevertheless, hearables are an increasingly significant part of what I have called "the silicon sonic turn," a (re)turn to imagining the ear and voice as the ultimate human–computer interface (HCI), as represented by the voices of Watson, Siri, Alexa, and Samantha, the talking OS in the movie *Her* (2013). As wireless computers in human ear canals, hearables may be better than wearables at the HCI skill set: unobtrusively housed in the body and enabled with sensors and bone-conduction microphones, they potentially offer better biometric monitoring and activity tracking, as well as the simple, vocal control of one's smartphone and the internet of things (see Hagood 2018).

More importantly for this book, hearables also create a more sophisticated auditory interface with the world, an "augmented reality" (AR) that changes the affective possibilities of acting and being acted upon through sound. Hearable manufacturers such as Doppler Labs and Braggi promise far more than audio playback and voice communication, touting features like noise cancellation, amplification, equalization, digital effects (such as echo and reverberation), language translation, and even selective filtration or enhancement of specific sounds—changing *what* and *how* users hear. Through these prosthetic abilities—some implemented in first- and second-generation products, some still in research and development—hearables blur the lines between prescription and consumer media. As *The Hearing Review* notes, consumer and professional audio companies like Dolby Labs and Bose have rushed into this space, developing audiological technologies and successfully lobbying regulatory agencies to loosen restrictions on the over-the-counter (OTC) hearing device category, sending waves of panic through the audiology industry ("NASEM Committee Looks into OTC Hearing Device Regulations" 2017). Yet, as indicated by advertising in *The Hearing Review,* this convergence is also being initiated from the other direction, as hearing aid manufacturers tout their use of technologies such as Bluetooth to better integrate hearing aids with smartphones and the wider consumer media ecosystem.

Doppler Labs' Here One earbuds wirelessly pair with its smartphone app to offer what the company marketed as "Real World Sound Control, [letting] you hear what you want and tune out what you don't so you can control your audio experience in every environment." Although the implementation did not live up to the hype in the first-generation product I used, Doppler was nevertheless selling the dream of moving beyond binary, on/off noise cancellation to the selective cancellation of *specific* sounds the listener doesn't want, as "Here One learns your unique hearing preferences and optimizes the way you hear the world."[6] Such hearables confront us with the possibilities and foreclosures of *algorithmic listening*, as information technology begins to both learn from us and choose for us, extending to the sensory world the same kinds of selective logics that have been applied to cultural work (Striphas 2015), social media (Bucher 2012), and news (Anderson 2011). Like the journalist who exclaimed "I want to live in my own filter bubble!" many consumers intuit and enthusiastically anticipate the aural applications of these logics.

The *filter bubble* is, of course, the cautionary term coined by Eli Pariser to describe "the new internet" that algorithmically predicts the relevance of information for individuals based on their past online behaviors—"new," according to Pariser, because it produces for each of us a completely individualized internet, in which we neither choose nor know what information has been excluded from our purview (2011). To describe an analogous phenomenon in the realm of AR audio engineering, Joseph Klett uses the term *baffling*, a "material and symbolic confusion [that] insulates the listener from common acoustic space while rearranging their perception of what is meaningful in that space" (2016, 112). The baffled state of the listener in an immersive audio application is algorithmically constructed through (1) the "personalization" of sound for distinct listener bodies, (2) a "disorientation" in which a fixed stereo or surround soundstage is supplanted by dynamic relationship between a mobile listener and virtual sound objects, and (3) a "translocation" in which the acoustic characteristics of one space are transposed onto another. Echoing Pariser's concerns, Klett argues that "immersive audio processes *subjectivity in independent relation to a non-local space*" rather than "a generic auditory space for all listeners to hear," embodying a "cultural filter" that privileges "personal differences rather than a shared experience of common phenomena" (123, emphasis in original).

The effects that Pariser and Klett describe are the logical outgrowths of digital logics and practices designed to generate freedom through sorting and control, algorithmic phenomena that, as Deleuze notes, simultaneously surveil, sort, and control aspects of *users*, generating specific parameters of ability—bubbles of freedom that also constrain (1992). As Tarleton Gillespie writes, all algorithms encode "specific assumptions about what knowledge is and how one should identify its most relevant components" (2014, 168); this "knowledge logic" is embedded in Claude Shannon's definition of information as "freedom of choice when one selects a message," as well as Norbert Wiener's cybernetic vision of freedom through control. The much-touted "openness" of the internet, Alexander Galloway notes, is dependent upon this strategy of control, in which standardized protocols such as TCP/IP (Transmission Control Protocol/Internet Protocol) allow heterogeneous types of knowledge become "content" accessed through standardized interfaces (Galloway 2004). In the words of Wendy Chun, "software produces users," encouraging us to cede it power in exchange for a more utilitarian engagement with the world (2008, 21). Just as the controlling logics of digital musical instruments position musicians as *users*, encouraging them to scroll through endless menus in search of the right sound (Theberge 1997), AR audio imposes an interface logic on the audible world, a *reduction* of reality (Galloway 2012) to the infocentric model of menus and choices. For society to implicitly accept this identity between control and freedom, Chun argues, is to cheapen the latter, deploying a "gated community" logic that works to constrain our engagement with the world and with one another (2008, vii).

Then again, the filter bubble and baffling are not sui generis technological effects of digital life, but rather evolutions of long-studied cultural and cognitive processes. After all, what is the ideology critique of cultural studies if not the interrogation of automatic and unnoticed "knowledge logics" that keep certain kinds of knowledge beyond our ken? And aren't we always already baffled, as our ideologically informed and habitually patterned auditory subconscious continuously discards the vast majority of what we hear, while at the same time the prefrontal cortex mixes these inputs with virtual objects and acoustics of our auditory imagination? Utilitarian logic, capitalism, and digital technology did not invent self-centered attraction, aversion, and drive for autonomous control; rather, they more efficiently exploit these aspects of being human.

Whether it is affect-oriented playlists, filtering hearables, or discursive filter bubbles, orphically algorithmic technologies encourage us to experience our habitual affective reactions as rational and self-sustaining choices. The purveyors of these technologies profit from flattering us as agentive, rational, and individual shoppers of experience in order to surveil, model, and monetize us as what Deleuze calls "dividuals" or clusters of data to be controlled. As John Cheney-Lippold explains, algorithms sort us into "measurable types," which are designed to predict our future actions while also "structur[ing] our lives' conditions of possibilities," constraining our future freedom of action (2017, 35).

By default, algorithmic listening keeps us in our comfort zones, diminishing the diversity of our experience and thus diminishing our sensory and cognitive flexibility and resilience. As discussed in chapter 4, when life is structured as a battle for autonomous control through the consumption of good information and the avoidance of entropic noise, listening becomes hypersensitive and noise omnipresent. Ironically, reason and agency diminish as we tend to either turn away from discomfiting inputs or fixate on them obsessively as threats that need elimination. Oddly enough, the latter option provides a sense of comfort too, as technology feeds our confirmation bias, presenting a filtered world that never requires us to recalibrate our senses, opinions, or reactions. Without promoting false equivalence between their politics, when the American right and left call each other "snowflakes" and "brainwashed by Fox News," they both point toward and enact this underlying process.

Listening through Closure

A neocybernetic approach to our media use is useful for stepping outside the ideology of freedom through control that underwrites our algorithmic capture as dividuals. In this autopoietic conception, biological and social systems do not process information found in the outside world: while these systems are open to *molecular* flows, they are closed to *information*, instead responding only to external "perturbations" sensible to their structures as systems. Engaging with the environment as their systems allow (a process called "sensorimotor coupling"), sentient systems *construct* information, generating a sense of self and world. The sense of self arises for an important reason: Like any animal, humans must be able to distinguish between the perturbations that arise as a consequence of their *own actions* and those that derive from other changes in the environment. In hearing, if one fails to recognize that turning one's head changes the perceived position and timbre of sounds, one will attribute these audible changes to the environment itself, creating confusion and danger in future actions. *Thus, a sense of self and not-self is enacted in everyday perception and action.* In the words of Evan Thompson, "sensorimotor I-making and sensorimotor sense-making arise together and are inseparable; they're dependently co-arisen" (2015, 334). Here we find the generative paradox of affective cognition: to sense is to sense not-self, yet it is only through this affective relation to not-self that a sense of self arises. Therefore, the system that *others* owes its emergence to that which is *othered*.

Returning to the myth of Orpheus on the *Argo*, we can concretize neocybernetics in sonic terms. The Argonauts row through the medium of the ocean, but they also dwell at the bottom of an ocean of air, a gaseous molecular medium that presses down upon them, both constraining and enabling their structures as autonomous systems, as well as sonically mediating their perception of the space around them. As the rowing bodies perturb the howling, churning, and creaking media of air, water, and wood with the oars in their hands, each man enacts a vibrational sense of self, other, and environment through hearing and touch. Each Argonaut's aural world is mediated by sonic relations that extend "below" individual consciousness (air molecules, inner-ear cilia, neurons), "alongside" it (the rowers' rhythmic, technological entrainment with one another and with Orpheus' timekeeping *keleustes* chant), and "above" it (cultural and political patternings of sound and listening) (Protevi 2013, 41). There is no perception of sound that does not simultaneously express the subject's dependent co-arising with all three of these levels of affectivity, yet in a given moment we perceive and understand only a fraction of what affects us.

Autopoiesis, therefore, provides a biological and phenomenological framework for understanding a fundamental problem for humanity—we perceive and engage others and the world but can only do so as it "makes sense" within our systemic limitations. And yet, as Bruce Clarke and Mark N. B. Hansen emphasize, it is this very closure—the ultimate unknowability of the other and the world—that necessitates the outward-reaching growth and affective cognition of systems. In the bittersweet model of autopoiesis, structural closure necessitates affective openness—the impossibility of informatic transmission necessitates reaching out, listening out, and trying to make sense. As tools to enhance, dampen, and alter our "alongside," affective relations with a sensed self and a sensed world, media technologies are integral to the actions we take, as we navigate our productive yet irreconcilable differences with one another. Therefore, at their most fundamental level, media are not tools for representing or defending what we already are, but are rather tools for becoming what we will be in relation to the not-self.

This truth is something many already sense but have trouble making peace with. The modern history of orphic media coincides with the widespread realization—a sinking feeling, really—that scientific discoveries and socio-technical realities have rendered obsolete the notion of the rational, autonomous, liberal subject. Timothy Melley describes an "agency panic" that takes hold in American culture during this era, "'conservative' in the sense that it conserves the traditional model of the self in spite of the obvious challenges that postwar technologies of communication and social organization pose to that model." Tracing a new "culture of paranoia" in American postwar fiction and popular culture, Melley characterizes agency panic as "a nervous acknowledgement, and rejection, of postmodern subjectivity" (2000, 15). Chun, meanwhile, asserts that the conflation of freedom and control in the postwar era "produces and is produced by paranoia that stems from the attempt to solve political problems technologically. To be paranoid is to think like a machine" (2008, viii).

Merging Melley's and Chun's insights yields an American history much like the one in this book, in which individuals respond to a perceived loss of humanity by becoming ever more cybernetic and informatic, attempting to engage the world through a controllable interface in order to regain an autonomy that never was, ironically constraining their possible future actions within the logics of knowledge and practice the interface affords. In this way, we enact the great danger our autopoietic bodies present to diversity and social cohesion: in our tendency toward boundary maintenance and sticking to our conditioned sense of comfort and safety, we perpetuate and exacerbate divisions of race, gender, class, sexuality, and political view that have emerged through history—building walls and failing to listen across difference.

One final example of orphic media's recent digital evolution may represent the apotheosis of paranoid listening: the "hearing protection/enhancement device" (HPED), branded by one manufacturer as Tactical Hearing. Marketed to law enforcement officers, military personnel, and hunters, HPEDs represent the militarization of both professional audio production and hearing aid technologies. These digital earplug devices—such as Tactical Hearing's T-4-16-HD and Etymotic's EB15 High Fidelity Electronic BlastPLG (figure C.2)—combine active noise cancellation, amplification, and compression to offer firearm users both enhanced "situational awareness" of quiet sounds and hearing protection from gunfire and explosives.

While protecting police, soldiers, and gun owners from hearing damage may be, in many cases, a laudable use of technology, it also instantiates a power differential in the act of hearing, providing gun owners and agents of the state protections and enhancements that unarmed civilians do not have; this is especially problematic since mediated sound has already been weaponized by military and law enforcement agencies (Goodman 2010). HPEDs, which can enhance human hearing up to eight times—allowing one to embody a "surveillance state" while also maintaining a safe, auditory defensive crouch—perfect autopoietic boundary maintenance through orphic media. HPEDs help listeners in "hearing like a state," constructing as information anything relevant to "situational awareness" while compressing or gating as noise anything else, thus representing a personalized breakthrough in the history of military noise control described in chapter 2.

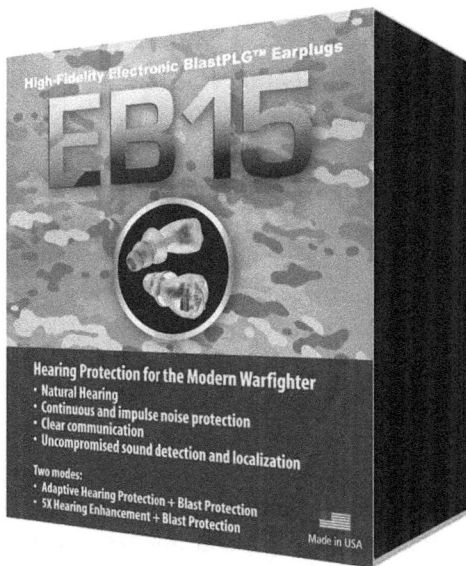

Figure C.2 Etymotic's EB15 High-Fidelity Electronic BlastPLG.

HPEDs and other orphic media suppress more than noise, however, in that they further inhibit situational awareness of affective connections and possibilities below, alongside, and above the listening subject. As Deleuzian sound machines, orphic media use the sub-subjective molecular sound field as material for the creation of new affective assemblages; as transductive attachments to our auditory systems, they integrate with our neurophysiology and our personal habits of listening; as media that renegotiate our real-time relations, they involve others' spaces alongside the user; and as marketed technologies with instructions, advertising, presets, and interfaces, they implicate their users in ideological, economic, and political systems that extend far above the individual. Today's orphic media admit few of these interconnections, however, and in fact encourage us to ignore their evidence. As personal technologies, they encourage us to tactically locate, isolate, and eliminate "noise" as independent from the listening subject, never critically examining orphic media's roles in the ontogenesis of a sound-sensitive self. But, as seen in the neurophysiology of tinnitus, embodying freedom of choice and the ideology of ability as a habitus of listening primes us for auditory suffering. Using these and other media technologies uncritically weakens users' repertoires of listening modes and develops habits that oversensitize individuals to the noise of others, both literally and figuratively.

Hearing a Freedom beyond Control

Understood for what they are, orphic media can be valuable. They allow users to navigate the "paradox of control" in which individuals are expected to manage noise conflicts with neighbors on their own but are given little or no civic power to control local traffic, aviation, and industrial noise (Bijsterveld 2008). And it is no minor feat that these technologies help us find coherence in the fragmented space-time of contemporary life. But while it is sometimes healthful to recoil from sound, our ability to thrive as self-organizing bodies and societies also depends on what Kate Lacey calls adventurous listening, "listening out for voices that are unfamiliar or uneasy on the ear" (2013, 197), engaging with sounds as they are, without preemptively sorting them into habitual categories of good, bad, and irrelevant and denying ourselves the uncomfortable "perturbations" that can stimulate growth and change. As Reb Anderson writes, "If you don't trust interdependence, then you normally try to get out of the world of delusion. You try to fix the situation by your own personal efforts. But trying to get out of the world where you suffer because you believe yourself to be independent only reinforces that same world" (2001). Orphic media are sold as such a "fix," functioning as a technological fetish that "protects a fantasy of utility or wholeness, compensating in advance for this impossibility" (Dean 2009, 38). When used as fetish, orphic media reinforce the systemic conflicts between sound, space, self, and sociality they ostensibly elude.

To move beyond self-defeating tactics toward orphic media that strengthen our powers of audition, we could extract the informatics from our cybernetics, acknowledge our boundaries, and listen *through* them. Unlike information, a sound can never really be transmitted. I can never hear the same sound as you because our positions in space, our apparatuses of hearing, and our past experience of sound and its meanings differ. Sonically, we are incommensurate because there is no objective sound to be heard, only individual hearings in separate courts of perception, where each judges alone. We are bounded sonic systems that never receive but only *produce* information. Nevertheless, if I listen affectively, I may be able to hear how we are also united in sound. When your voice resonates through my boundary walls, I may hear myself hearing the sounds you initiate, sensing how I become a new self in response to this perturbation. I may also sense how my hearing brings a new *you* forth—an expression of you that only *my* experience can contain. Our mediating boundaries, in fact, make us one.

Recently, a number of writers have considered this sonic interplay between inner and outer, self and other. Lisbeth Lipari uses the term *interlistening* to indicate the inseparability of speaking and listening and "to describe how listening itself is a form of speaking that resonates with echoes of everything we have ever heard, thought, seen, touched, said, and read throughout our lives" (Lipari 2014, 9). John Biguenet writes that there is no such thing as silent reading, only "an act of hospitality toward another's mind, in which we silence our voice in courtesy to the voice of another's consciousness, a voice that alternates with our own in conversation" (2015, 56). Dominic Pettman argues that the odds of our survival as a species would be increased by extending this hospitality to the environment at large, developing a "sonic intimacy" that internalizes the sounds around us as the voices of the world.

As inspiration for this sonic intimacy, Pettman suggests we need an "anti-Orpheus" figure, one who "would not seduce the environment through song but would rather allow himself to be seduced by it, through listening" (2017, 88). However, as already discussed in this book, the mythical Orpheus *is* an open and dedicated listener who allows himself to be aurally captivated by even the minute vibrations of a spider spinning its web; thus, his use of sonic techniques and technologies is grounded in—and fosters—a sonic intimacy with the world. It is this sacred aspect of Orpheus that has been forgotten in orphic media development and use, the practical awareness of the interplay of perception through which we come to contain—and be transformed by— that which we perceive as external to us. The kinds of listening practices described by Lacey, Lipari, Biguenet, and Pettman help us to value what we perceive as it is—*wanting what we hear* instead of hearing what we want. A "wanting" that connotes not avarice, but a welcoming in. As the great guru of intimate listening, Pauline Oliveros, understood early on, this kind of welcoming requires practice—the exercises and techniques she developed to support "deep listening" may be our best guide so far for exploring "the vastness and complexities" of the aural world discarded by the lossy processes of informatic listening (2015, 56).[7]

There is no inherent reason why orphic media cannot support and expand this kind of deep listening. In his study of ambient music and video, Paul Roquet suggests thoughtful forms of these media "might teach us to read the air itself as a site of subjectivation, providing a resource for recognizing how the atmosphere is tuning our affective lives. To learn to read the air in this way is to embrace the weak, partial, and embedded agency of the environmental self" (2016, 183). Roquet points to musicians such as Eric Satie and Haruomi Hosono, who inject humor, irony, and ambivalence into their ambiences, encouraging us to engage critically and creatively with our senses of calm and unease. Might our technologies of sonic control be bent toward a similar purpose?

Unfortunately, there is no easy aural remedy for widespread cultural hyperacusis and misophonia. But if an avoidant desire for a technological fix to sonic conflict is the problem, maybe we can recalibrate our expectations toward practical, experiential, and critical engagement. Perhaps a better future of orphic media lies partially in sound technologists becoming more like Orpheus, grounding themselves in techniques of affective listening. Rather than engineering the narrow freedom to hear what we want, they might dream up technologies to help us free ourselves from the habits of attraction, aversion, and indifference that shape our listening—sonic technologies for a freedom beyond control.

Notes

1 Also, Peter Doyle has written a wonderful analysis of the sonic territorialization that record producers perform through the use of echo and reverb (2005).

2 This is not for lack of trying! My research into these more complex devices is ongoing and I plan to publish an analysis of them that builds on the work on orphic media presented here.

3 Critics of this line of thinking have correctly pointed out that the development of information science was marked by a careful concern for the material technologies and bodies it endeavored to connect (Mills 2011b). However, this history is also marked by a tension between those such as Claude Shannon, who was reticent about applying the concept of information too broadly and those such as Norbert Wiener, the father of cybernetics, who would spread information as far and freely as possible. There is no argument but that the second camp won: genetics, psychology, and economics are but a few of the fields that have been remade in information's image, leading eventually to this immaterial presence occupying every corner of the imagined universe.

4 For example, Anahid Kassabian, who studies musical technologies similar to those in the present book, draws on distributed computing to describe sonic affect in terms of "distributed subjectivity": "a nonindividual subjectivity, a field, but a field over which power is distributed unevenly and unpredictably, over which differences are not only possible but required, and across which information flows, leading to affective responses. The channels of distribution are held open by ubiquitous musics. Humans, institutions, machines, and molecules are

all nodes on the network, nodes of different densities" (Kassabian 2013, xxv). While this paradigm attempts to challenge the cognitivist Enlightenment liberal subject, it unintentionally reinstates it by conceiving sonic affect in terms of information processing. Conceiving of music as sonic information that is merely processed differently by different freestanding "computers" misses the essential point that bodies of listeners and bodies of music are *produced* in their specificity only through their interaction. Affectively speaking, there is no a priori information transmitted between senders and receivers because no two people ever hear the same sound; rather, different sounds and subjects are produced through modes of interaction, according to different circumstances of vibration, spatial position, neurophysiology, enculturation, and so on.

5 Although clearly the mantra-like repetition of the sutra box and the minimalism of the music of the Buddha Machine both foreground the orphic aspects of sound over the representational potentials of audio media.

6 Rainymood.com is a single-serving site (sss) that does nothing but play a rainfall sound while simulated beads of water roll down the computer screen. White noise, of course, has its own connotations and thus still holds some semiotic function—in fact, for many people white noise connotes the ability to get a good night's sleep. Nevertheless, the utility of digital white noise and rain-sound products is not the transmission of entertaining or edifying representations.

7 Eugene Thacker uses the term *biomedia* to describe both information technology's reframing and reworking of organic bodies and the already informational nature of these bodies that allow them to be mediatized in these ways. I too assume an underlying molecular contiguity between life and media but, as discussed below, I do not reduce this relationship to the immaterial concept of information, focusing instead on the material, machinic potentials of affective resonance.

8 The outer ear, for example, can be thought of as a kind of funnel that collects acoustic energy, while the tympanum (or eardrum), stapes, and cilia of the ear transfer this energy along progressively finer scales. Noting that early sound transcribing and recording technologies were inspired by the human tympanum, Jonathan Sterne refers to the mechanism of the energy transfer model as *tympanic* (2003, 22).

9 Transduction has proved to be a productive model for sound and media scholars who wish to emphasize ontological contiguity in sound's mediation rather than assuming that mediation implies a distancing from reality, as seen in much postmodern theory (Helmreich 2007; Sterne 2003). When sound is transduced from energy into signal, there is no ontological shift from materiality into representation, nor from reality into hyperreality, for that matter (Hagood 2014).

10 Here, I take inspiration from Truax's model of "acoustic communication," in which sound mediates meaningful relationships between listeners and their environments, rather than being mediated by the linear transmission of energy or

signal. This is Truax's intervention, making a move from the linear, objectivist orientation of the engineer to the three-dimensional, subjective experience of acculturated and emplaced listeners. Truax's intention in this move is similar to the intentions of practice theory, performance studies, actor–network theory, and similar contemporary frameworks in anthropology, sociology, and cultural studies—to understand sonic experiences and phenomena as they emerge in the context and actions of everyday life. Such an intent forms the basis for soundscape study and design: "If we shift our focus from the sound wave and the audio signal as the artifact to the soundscape, where sound mediates relationships between the individual and the environment, we will be able to understand the intricacies of how sound *functions*, not simply how it behaves. Functionality, rather than simply aesthetic quality or the absence of annoyance, becomes the criterion for design" (1984, 12). In *Acoustic Communication*, Truax articulates an orientation also found in works on "acoustemology," "auditory culture," "aurality," and other manifestations of sound studies—that sonic experience is of historical, cultural, contextual, and practical concern.

The problem with Truax's model of acoustic communication, however, is that it casts the listener–environment relationship in terms that are highly cognitivist, semiotic, and informatic, purposefully minimizing the material dimensions of this relation. Truax proposes an "approach to acoustics [that] deals with the exchange of *information*, rather than the transfer of energy," in which the listener "is not engaged in a passive type of energy reception, but is rather part of a dynamic system of information exchange" (1984, 9–10, emphasis in original). Truax draws a sharp distinction between *hearing* as "the processing of acoustic energy" and *listening* as "the processing of sonic information that is useable and potentially meaningful to the brain" (9).

Such a model minimizes the material, affective power of vibration, as well as its cultural meanings and political potentials. It also instates a body/mind dualism in aurality between material *vibration processing* and immaterial *information processing*, discounting the former and privileging the latter. Truax's purpose in making these divisions is to show that the energy transfer and signal processing paradigms are inadequate to the job of designing better sonic environments for people: even the most "transparent" electroacoustic reproduction of a sound will lose that sound's original cultural and contextual "information," while even the complete elimination of noise through soundproofing will not create a meaningful soundscape for the listener. However, there is an irony to Truax's use of information in this argument, in that information theory itself was developed in an effort to eliminate noise in the transmission of voice signals across telephone lines (Shannon and Weaver 1964). In fact, the notions of information and communication that Truax deploys derive in large part from the very noise-eliminating signal processing practices he finds reductive (Mills 2011a, 122–24; Peters 1999, 22–25; Sterne 2012, 20).

What makes information such a powerful concept is that it allows a message to *become independent of its original material context* and thus highly manipulable and circulatable. This makes information a curious paradigm through which to understand cultural and physical context or the embodied subjective experience of sound; indeed, one can see the inherited linear intentionality of audio media practices in Truax's emphasis on what is "useable and potentially meaningful to the brain." Thus, while his paradigm seeks to transcend the limitations of the engineer's perspective, it unintentionally projects an engineering epistemology and intentionality upon the human–environment relationship. While the environmental orientation of the acoustic communication model is a necessary intervention, its reliance on an informatic notion of sound weakens its potential both as an approach to affect and as a model for the critique of media practices. For this reason, I retain Truax's conception of sound-as-medium without reducing the mechanism of its mediation to the transmission of information.

Chapter 1: Tinnitus and Its Aural Remedies

Epigraph: Michel Serres, 2008, *The Five Senses: A Philosophy of Mingled Bodies*, translated by Margaret Sankey and Peter Cowley, 178 (London: Continuum).

1 With the exception of Joel Styzens, who appears later in this chapter and has been very public about his experience with tinnitus, the names of tinnitus sufferers have been changed. The names of tinnitus researchers and clinicians are unchanged.

2 I use the term *tinnitus sufferer* to refer only to a person bothered by tinnitus, not to a person who experiences tinnital sound but does not feel negatively affected by the experience.

3 "In several recent [scientific] publications, tinnitus has been likened to the phenomenon of pain. Because tinnitus can be associated with every known pathology of the entire auditory system, it has often been referred to as the 'pain' signal of the hearing mechanism—that is 'auditory pain'" (Vernon and Møller 1995, xiv).

4 In this study, I follow Jastreboff and Hazell in reserving the term *tinnitus* for sounds that cannot be heard by others. Some subjects hear their own circulatory system or other bodily sounds that can be heard by a clinician with a stethoscope. Jastreboff and Hazell refer to these as "somatosound" (Jastreboff and Hazell 2004, 3).

5 In the past, Mol notes, sociologists of medicine added a social, subjective component, "illness," to the object of disease. Subsequently, sociologists came to see both illness and disease as socially constructed, so that "illness" came to refer to the perspective of the patient and "disease" to the perspective of medical staff. Mol goes further, moving away from epistemology and into ontology with a third step

that "foreground[s] practicalities, materialities, events" (2002, 12–13, emphasis in original).

6   Neuromonics, "How It Works," http://www.neuromonics.com/?page_id=89, accessed March 20, 2013.

Chapter 2: Sleep-Mates and Sound Screens

Epigraph: Charles Babbage, in *Making Noise: From Babel to the Big Bang and Beyond*, by Hillel Schwartz, 2011, 234 (New York: Zone).

1   Though it seemingly hasn't so far. In fact, Pauline Webb and Mark Suggitt's *Gadgets and Necessities: An Encyclopedia of Household Innovations* (2000) makes no mention of sound machines at all.

2   The Buckwalters met just after the end of World War II at the Jacksonville, Florida, USO. After the couple married, James Buckwalter worked for a watch company while earning a degree in accounting at Franklin and Marshall in Pennsylvania, which he completed in 1947. In 1948, they moved to Wooster, Ohio, where he began work for the Wooster Rubber Company as a traveling salesman, eventually becoming sales manager, then vice president of sales, then finally moving into product development. According to his daughter Janet Zimmerman, Buckwalter went through a series of jobs after leaving Wooster in 1957.

3   "Personal Therapy in the U.S.: Electronic Massagers and Other Sensory Devices," MarketResearch.com, August 1, 2007, http://www.marketresearch.com/Packaged -Facts-v768/Personal-Therapy-Electronic-Massagers-Sensory-1432870/view -toc/.

4   Ihde's difference from Deleuze (and Latour, for that matter) is a strong concern with subjects' sensory perspectives. For the purposes of this chapter, this is a feature, not a bug. The orphic media users that I interview do, of course, feel themselves to be individual agents—and it is a basic precept of contemporary ethnography to take subjective experience seriously. In this book, I often take a more Deleuzian approach, examining ontologically how orphic media intercede in the emergence of subjectivity, changing affective relations in ways that individuals are not consciously aware of. Presently, however, I examine how orphic technologies have come to mediate our microperceptual experience of the homes we inhabit within a macroperceptual regime that privileges circulation above all else.

5   Media's status as objects of interactive or attentional focus has long been an area of inquiry and debate in media and cultural studies; just recently, we have seen video game scholar Ian Bogost and other media and art scholars embrace Graham Harman's object-oriented ontology (OOO) as a means of doing a phenomenology from the position of the objects themselves (2011). For Harman, both Foucault's historical analysis and phenomenology are idealisms in materialist

clothing—the former because it explores materiality only in terms of the evolution of subjectivity and the latter because it claims we can only know the world through the filter of human experience. However, I think Harman's critique is too totalizing and his alternative has some troubling potentials. While I do believe that the discursive and postphenomenological approaches offer incomplete pictures, I also think that, taken together, they offer a politically potent view on human–technological relations. Though appreciative of OOO's appreciation of objects and their relations, I find myself among those who question the political consequences of such a radical decentering of the (post)human. It seems to me that there is plenty left to learn about human subjects' interactions with media—and that the stakes of doing so are high. As a white male, I also can't help but notice that my fellow white guys are the group most interested in speaking for objects, and I can't help but see continuities between OOO and a long history of "objectivities" that have redounded to the benefit of white males (Harman 2011).

6 Sound scholar Karin Bijsterveld and her collaborators take Ihde's cocoon on the road, pointing out that automobiles have been molded in such a way as to acoustically seclude the driver from her immediate surroundings through the "acoustic cocooning" of soundproofing and radio while also connecting her to music, news, mobile telephony, and satellite navigation (Bijsterveld et al. 2013).

7 Adolph P. Meisch, message to "PBY Catalina/Canso" group, http://groups.yahoo .com/group/PBY/message/16839.

8 It should be noted that by the 1940s the term *sound conditioning* was being used by the Celotex Corporation to market their sound-absorptive ceiling tiles (Schwartz 2012, 287). I have found no indication that Buckwalter was aware of this.

9 Moreover, the U.S. Patent Office offers a second type of document called the "patent interference," which records efforts by one party to turn another party's patented black box into a contested artifact; such documents have proved more interesting to some historians of technology than patents themselves (e.g., Chapin 1971).

10 Dave Theissen told me of the painstaking and largely fruitless efforts that ensued when Mr. B encouraged him to improve upon the Sleep-Mate design. Though Theissen managed to create substantial sonic improvements in the fan blades and adjustable housing, when it came to size and shape, it seemed that Buckwalter had initially happened upon a near-optimal design. Theissen's changes were no better and many were much worse. "I've often thought that we haven't gotten knocked off on the electromechanical machine because no one can do a better shape," he told me.

11 http://webdesign.about.com/od/webdesignbasics/a/whitespace.htm.

Chapter 3: Cybernetic Soundscapes

Epigraphs: R. Murray Schafer, 1994, *The Soundscape: Our Sonic Environment and the Tuning of the World*, 160 (Rochester, NY: Destiny).

N. Katherine Hayles, summarizing Friedrich Kittler, 1999, *Gramophone, Film, Typewriter*, 48 (Stanford, CA: Stanford University Press).

1 For more on guides, set, and setting in LSD psychotherapy, see Grof (1994). Chapter 1 is online at http://www.druglibrary.org/schaffer/lsd/grofhist.htm.
2 Teibel's promotion and distribution efforts took place before the present era of computerized technological convergence, however. Teibel took and developed photos, did graphic layout, wrote ad copy, and recorded audio in separate physical media that required quite different skill sets and physical channels of supply, production, and distribution.
3 Tony Conrad remembers it as January 1969, while Teibel wrote that it was the winter of 1968 (Teibel 1984, 224).
4 Bruce Lambert, "Louis Gerstman, 61, a Specialist in Speech Disorders and Processes," *New York Times*, March 21, 1992.
5 Teibel never uses Gerstman's name in the essay, though he appears three different times as seemingly different individuals (Teibel uses no names in the essay at all). Miriam Berman confirms that these references are indeed to Gerstman, leaving one with the question of why Teibel would divide and obscure the important roles this individual played. One likely answer is that Teibel did not want Gerstman's role to rival his own in this public account.
6 My reading of Helmholtz's *On the Sensation of Tone* does not bring to light a claim that natural sounds could be psychologically beneficial.
7 The irony is that many genres of minimalist and droning music are designed to cultivate similar states of mind *through* repetition, a fact that underscores the lack of a natural or automatic connection between particular sounds and particular mental states.
8 This professor well may have been Gerstman, but, as the test was not an official research study, there is no record to confirm its existence, let alone any details.
9 These quotes originally included full names and addresses, which I have removed.

Chapter 4: A Quiet Storm

1 http://www.doctoroz.com/episode/dr-ozs-13-miracles-2013?video=16259. Accessed February 27, 2013.
2 Results as of January 15, 2013.

3   http://mashable.com/2010/11/08/jimmy-fallon-gives-late-night-its-first-mobile
    -app-video/. Accessed February 26, 2013.
4   Shannon's "abstract yet measurable" conception of information had precedents
    in the work of his Bell Labs colleague Ralph V. L. Hartley, as well as the British
    statistician and geneticist R. A. Fisher (Byfield 2008, 126–27).
5   I address criticism of this position on p. 235n3.
6   https://www.ted.com/talks/mihaly-csikszentmihalyi_on_flow/. Accessed Janu-
    ary 20, 2013.
7   Indeed, this interpretation of sound app pragmatics fits nicely into the history of
    information theory, which began with the attempt to fight the entropy of noise
    in telephone lines and ended up domesticating noise itself, using its masking
    properties to promote the more efficient transmission of information.
8   https://www.tmsoft.com/white-noise-player/. Accessed May 10, 2016.
9   Sindya N. Bhanoo, "Smartphone Applications Include Health-Care and Fitness
    Options," *Washington Post*, February 3, 2009, http://www.washingtonpost.com/wp
    -dyn/content/article/2009/02/02/AR2009020202203.html?noredirect=on.
10 Issue 18756: "StageFright—setLooping(true) Leaves a Noticeable Gap in Audio,"
    https://code.google.com/p/android/issues/detail?id=18756; accessed January 24,
    2016.
11 "Life of a Bug," https://source.android.com/source/life-of-a-bug.html#resolved
    -issues. Accessed January 24, 2016.

Chapter 5: Bose QuietComfort and the Mobile Production of Personal
Space

Epigraph: Amar Bose, *Cancelling Noise*. Video interview with Amar Bose, 2009, The
Futures Channel, accessed May 3, 2010, http://www.thefutureschannel/dockets
/critical_thinking/bose/.

1   This phrase was used in the marketing copy of the American Bose website until a
    recent update. It can still be found on the Australian Bose website: http://www.bose
    .com/controller?url=/shop_online/headphones/noise_cancelling_headphones
    /index.jsp. Accessed July 20, 2010.
2   For an account of the heroic individual narrative as it relates to another sound-
    scaping technology, see du Gay et al. (1997, 44–46).
3   See, for example, Timothy Mitchell's *Colonising Egypt* (1988), which explains the
    role of a modern and objectifying gaze in European colonialism.
4   For a fascinating exploration of aural architecture, see Barry Blesser and Linda
    Ruth Salter's *Spaces Speak, Are You Listening?* (2007).
5   Morse (1990) sets out to understand the psychology and ontology of subjects whose
    daily lives are lived in the dominant "spaces" of contemporary capitalism: televi-
    sion and its "analogs" such as freeways and malls. She characterizes these as non-

space, a space of flows between two- and three-dimensional realities, virtuality and actuality, and presence and absence of mind; this nonspace forms the ground of our everyday, semiconscious activity. If we follow Morse's logic, QuietComfort users are fighting one nonspace with another.

6 http://www.businesstraveller.com/discussion/topic/The-fattest-person-I-have-ever-sat-next-to, accessed July 22, 2010.

7 A user testimonial video currently on the Bose website, for example, features comments from two women dressed in professional attire, though the great majority of the ad features white professional men.

8 "Bose 'Mimes' by Euro RSCG Singapore," *Campaign*, July 21, 2009, https://www.campaignlive.co.uk/article/bose-mimes-euro-rscg-singapore/921537.

9 Given my subject matter, the irony is, of course, particularly rich in my case.

Chapter 6: Beats by Dre

Epigraphs: Liana M. Silva, 2015, "As Loud as I Want to Be: Gender, Loudness, and Respectability Politics," *Sounding Out!*, February 9, https://soundstudiesblog.com/2015/02/09/as-loud-as-i-want-to-be-gender-loudness-and-respectability-politics/.

Positive K, "I Got a Man," 1992.

1 Randall Roberts, "Aloe Blacc's 'The Man': From Dr. Dre Reject to iTunes Chart-Topper," *Los Angeles Times*, January 23, 2014.

2 Burt Helm, "How Dr. Dre's Headphones Company Became a Billion-Dollar Business," *Inc.*, May 2014, http://www.inc.com/audacious-companies/burt-helm/beats.html.

3 "Colin Kaepernick Explains Why He Won't Stand during National Anthem," https://www.youtube.com/watch?v=ka0446tibig&ab_channel=KTVU. Accessed November 19, 2017.

Conclusion: Wanting What We Hear

1 Tim Ingham, "Spotify Is Making Its Own Records . . . And Putting Them on Playlists," Music Business Worldwide, August 31, 2016, https://www.musicbusinessworldwide.com/spotify-is-creating-its-own-recordings-and-putting-them-on-playlists/.

2 Liz Pelly, "The Problem with Muzak," *The Baffler*, December 2017, https://thebaffler.com/salvos/the-problem-with-muzak-pelly.

3 Andrea Bartz, "How City Noise Is Slowly Killing You," *Harper's Bazaar*, July 25, 2017, http://www.harpersbazaar.com/culture/features/a10295155/noise-detox/; Winnie Hu, "New York Becomes the City That Never Shuts Up," *New York Times*,

July 19, 2017, https://www.nytimes.com/2017/07/19/nyregion/new-york-becomes
-the-city-that-never-shuts-up.html; Jonathan Wolfe, "New York Today: Blocking
Out the City's Noise," *New York Times*, July 24, 2017, https://www.nytimes.com
/2017/07/24/nyregion/new-york-today-blocking-out-the-citys-noise.html.

4   Mike Elgan, *This Week in Tech*, podcast no. 569, July 3, 2016.

5   Philip Jaekl, "Why People Believe Low-Frequency Sound Is Dangerous," *The Atlantic*, June 19, 2017, https://www.theatlantic.com/science/archive/2017/06/wind
-turbine-syndrome/530694/; Anne Gearan, "U.S. Investigating whether American
Diplomats Were Victims of Sonic Attack in Cuba," *Washington Post*, August 10,
2017, https://www.washingtonpost.com/world/national-security/us-investigating
-whether-american-diplomats-were-victims-of-sonic-attack-in-cuba/2017/08/10/.

6   https://hereplus.me, accessed July 21, 2017.

7   Although Oliveros, part of the New Communalist milieu, did sometimes use
informatic language—as in her essay collection *Software for People* (1984, xxiii)—
her techniques of listening are profoundly affective in their orientation and not at
all reducible to an information-transmission model.

References

Alperin, Jordan, Alexander Brown, Jennifer Huang, and Shastri Sandy. 2001. "Bolt, Beranek, and Newman Inc.: A Case History of Transition." *Structure of Engineering Revolutions: Final Project Papers*. Cambridge, MA: MIT Press.

Altman, Rick. 2004. *Silent Film Sound*. New York: Columbia University Press.

Anderson, Chris W. 2011. "Deliberative, Agonistic, and Algorithmic Audiences: Journalism's Vision of Its Public in an Age of Audience Transparency." *International Journal of Communication* 5: 529–47.

Anderson, Reb. 2001. *Being Upright: Zen Meditation and the Bodhisattva Precepts*. Berkeley, CA: Rodmell Press.

Anderson, Tim J. 2006. *Making Easy Listening: Material Culture and Postwar American Recording*. Minneapolis: University of Minnesota Press.

Andersson, Gerhard, David M. Baguley, Laurence McKenna, and Don McFerran. 2005. *Tinnitus: A Multidisciplinary Approach*. London: Whurr.

Atkinson, Niall. 2015. "Thinking through Noise, Building toward Silence: Creating a Sound Mind and Sound Architecture in the Premodern City." *Grey Room* 60: 10–35.

Bailey, Peter. 1996. "Breaking the Sound Barrier: A Historian Listens to Noise." *Body and Society* 2, no. 2: 49–66.

Bandini, Paolo. 2014. "Richard Sherman: Stanford, Seattle and Post-Game Controversies." *The Guardian*, January 28.

Barglow, Raymond. 1994. *The Crisis of the Self in the Age of Information: Computers, Dolphins, and Dreams*. London: Routledge.

Beazley, Charles. 1953. "Acoustic Sleep-Inducing Apparatus." U.S. Patent No. 2644153A.

Becker, Judith. 2004. *Deep Listeners: Music, Emotion, and Trancing*. Bloomington: Indiana University Press.

Beer, Jeff. 2015. "How Beats Tapped the Stories of Sport to Sell the Emotion of Sound." *Fast Company*, February 11.

Beniger, James. 1986. *The Control Revolution: Technological and Economic Origins of the Information Society*. Cambridge, MA: Harvard University Press.

Beranek, Leo. 1971. *Noise and Vibration Control*. New York: McGraw-Hill.

Beranek, Leo. 1989. Interview by William W. Lang. College Park, MD: Niels Bohr Library and Archives, American Institute of Physics. https://www.aip.org /history-programs/niels-bohr-library/oral-histories/5190-1.

Beranek, Leo Leroy. 1949. *Acoustic Measurements*. Hoboken, NJ: John Wiley and Sons.

Berger, Harris M. 2009. *Stance: Ideas about Emotion, Style, and Meaning for the Study of Expressive Culture*. Middletown, CT: Wesleyan.

Berland, Jody. 2009. *North of Empire: Essays on the Cultural Technologies of Space*. Durham, NC: Duke University Press.

Bickford, Tyler. 2014. "Earbuds Are Good for Sharing: Children's Sociable Uses of Headphones at a Vermont Primary School." In *Oxford Handbook of Mobile Music Studies*, edited by S. Gopinath and J. Stanyek. Oxford: Oxford University Press.

Biguenet, John. 2015. *Silence*. New York: Bloomsbury.

Bijsterveld, Karin. 2008. *Mechanical Sound: Technology, Culture, and Public Problems of Noise in the Twentieth Century*. Cambridge, MA: MIT Press.

Bijsterveld, Karin, Eefje Cleophas, Stefan Krebs, and Gijs Mom. 2013. *Sound and Safe: A History of Listening behind the Wheel*. Oxford: Oxford University Press.

Blesser, Barry, and Linda-Ruth Salter. 2007. *Spaces Speak, Are You Listening? Experiencing Aural Architecture*. Cambridge, MA: MIT Press.

Blue V, Alex. 2017. "'Hear What You Want': Sonic Politics, Blackness, and Racism-Canceling Headphones." *Current Musicology* 99–100 (spring): 87–106.

Boettcher, Flint A., and Richard J. Salvi. 1993. "Functional Changes in the Ventral Cochlear Nucleus Following Acute Acoustic Overstimulation." *Journal of the Acoustical Society of America* 94: 2123.

Bolter, J. David. 1984. *Turing's Man: Western Culture in the Computer Age*. Chapel Hill: University of North Carolina Press.

"Bose Corporation." 2010. In *SGA Executive Tracker*. Amsterdam, NY: Sheila Greco Associates.

Brennan, Teresa. 2003. *Globalization and Its Terrors: Daily Life in the West*. London: Routledge.

Brinson, Will. 2016. "Here's How Nate Boyer Got Colin Kaepernick to Go from Sitting to Kneeling." CBS Sports, September 27. https://www.cbssports.com /nfl/news/heres-how-nate-boyer-got-colin-kaepernick-to-go-from-sitting-to -kneeling/.

Bucher, Taina. 2012. "Want to Be on the Top? Algorithmic Power and the Threat of Invisibility on Facebook." *New Media and Society* 14, no. 7: 1164–80.

Buckwalter, James K. 1964. "Sleep-Inducing Sound-Producing Device." U.S. Patent No. 3121220A.

Bull, Michael. 2004. "Thinking about Sound, Proximity, and Distance in Western Experience: The Case of Odysseus's Walkman." In *Hearing Cultures: Essays on Sound, Listening and Modernity,* edited by Veit Erlmann, 173–91. Oxford: Berg.

Bull, Michael. 2007. *Sound Moves: iPod Culture and Urban Experience.* London: Routledge.

Burchell, Graham. 1996. "Liberal Government and Techniques of the Self." In *Foucault and Political Reason: Liberalism, Neo-Liberalism and Rationalities of Government,* edited by T. O. A. Barry and N. Rose. Chicago: University of Chicago Press.

Burnim, Mellonee V., and Portia K Maultsby. 2014. *African American Music: An Introduction.* New York: Routledge.

Byfield, Ted. 2008. "Information." In *Software Studies: A Lexicon,* edited by M. Fuller. Cambridge, MA: MIT Press.

Cecchetto, David. 2013. *Humanesis: Sound and Technological Posthumanism.* Minneapolis: University of Minnesota Press.

Chadabe, Joel. 1997. *Electric Sound: The Past and Present of Electronic Music.* Upper Saddle River, NJ: Prentice Hall.

Chang, Jeff. 2012. "I Gotta Be Able to Counterattack: Rap and the Los Angeles Riots." *Los Angeles Review of Books,* May 3.

Chapin, Seymour L. 1971. "Patent Interferences and the History of Technology: A High-Flying Example." *Technology and Culture* 12, no. 3: 414–46.

Cheney-Lippold, John. 2017. *We Are Data: Algorithms and the Making of Our Digital Selves.* New York: NYU Press.

Chow, Rey. 1990. "Listening Otherwise, Music Miniaturized: A Different Type of Question about Revolution." *Discourse* 13, no. 1: 129–48.

Chun, Wendy Hui Kyong. 2008. *Control and Freedom: Power and Paranoia in the Age of Fiber Optics.* Cambridge, MA: MIT Press.

Clarke, Bruce. 2012. "From Information to Cognition: The Systems Counterculture, Heinz von Foerster's Pedagogy, and Second-Order Cybernetics." *Constructivist Foundations* 7, no. 3: 196–207.

Clarke, Bruce, and Mark N. B. Hansen. 2009. *Emergence and Embodiment: New Essays on Second-Order Systems Theory.* Durham, NC: Duke University Press.

Clifford, James. 1986. "Introduction: Partial Truths." In *Writing Culture: The Poetics and Politics of Ethnography,* edited by J. Clifford and G. E. Marcus. Berkeley: University of California Press.

Clough, Patricia T. 2008. "The Affective Turn: Political Economy, Biomedia, and Bodies." *Theory, Culture and Society* 25, no. 1: 1–22.

Connor, Steven. 2010. "Auscultations." Presentation at the University of Iowa Sound Research Seminar, January 29.

Corbin, Alain. 2005. "Charting the Cultural History of the Senses." In *Empire of the Senses: The Sensual Culture Reader,* edited by D. Howes. New York: Bloomsbury.

Corsello, Andrew. 2016. "Mr. Colin Kaepernick." http://www.mrporter.com/journal/the-look/mr-colin-kaepernick/535.

Cox, Christoph. 2011. "Beyond Representation and Signification: Toward a Sonic Materialism." *Journal of Visual Culture* 10, no. 2: 145–61.

Crary, Jonathan. 2001. *Suspensions of Perception: Attention, Spectacle, and Modern Culture*. Cambidge, MA: MIT Press.

Crary, Jonathan. 2013. *24/7: Late Capitalism and the Ends of Sleep*. London: Verso.

Creed, Roscoe. 1985. *PBY: The Catalina Flying Boat*. Annapolis: U.S. Naval Institute Press, 1985.

Csíkszentmihályi, Mihály. 1990. *Flow: The Psychology of Optimal Experience*. New York: Harper and Row.

Cummings, Jim. 2010. "Irv Teibel Died This Week: Creator of 1970s 'Environments' LPs." *EarthEar*, November 2. http://earthear.com/blog/archives/198.

Dean, Jodi. 2009. *Democracy and Other Neoliberal Fantasies*. Durham, NC: Duke University Press.

De Certeau, Michel. 1988. *The Practice of Everyday Life*. Berkeley: University of California Press.

Deleuze, Gilles. 1978. "Lecture Transcripts on Spinoza's Concept of Affect." https://www.gold.ac.uk/media/images-by-section/departments/research-centres-and-units/research-centres/centre-for-invention-and-social-process/deleuze_spinoza_affect.pdf.

Deleuze, Gilles. 1992. "Postscript on the Societies of Control." *October* 59 (winter): 3–7.

Deleuze, Gilles, and Félix Guattari. 1987. *A Thousand Plateaus: Capitalism and Schizophrenia*. Minneapolis: University of Minnesota Press.

DeNora, Tia. 1999. "Music as a Technology of the Self." *Poetics* 27, no. 1: 31–56.

Descartes, René. [1641] 1951. *Meditations on First Philosophy*. New York: Macmillan.

Doyle, Peter. 2005. *Echo and Reverb: Fabricating Space in Popular Music Recording, 1900–1960*. Middletown, CT: Wesleyan University Press.

Dreher, Tanja. 2009. "Listening across Difference: Media and Multiculturalism beyond the Politics of Voice." *Continuum: Journal of Media and Cultural Studies* 23, no. 4: 445–58.

Du Gay, Paul, Stuart Hall, Linda Janes, Hugh Mackay, and Keith Negus. 1997. *Doing Cultural Studies: The Story of the Sony Walkman*. Thousand Oaks, CA: SAGE.

Ellcessor, Elizabeth, and Bill Kirkpatrick, eds. 2017. *Disability Media Studies*. New York: NYU Press.

Ellis, Katie, and Mike Kent. 2010. *Disability and New Media*. New York: Taylor and Francis.

Erlmann, Veit. 2004. "But What of the Ethnographic Ear." In *Hearing Cultures: Essays on Sound, Listening, and Modernity*, edited by Veit Erlmann. Oxford: Berg.

Fehr, R. O., and R. J. Wells. 1955. "Noise Reduction of Machinery and Vehicles." *Noise Control* 1, no. 1: 30–40.

Feld, Steven. 1990. *Sound and Sentiment: Birds, Weeping, Poetics, and Song in Kaluli Expression*. Philadelphia: University of Pennsylvania Press.

Ferris, Timothy. 1971. "Syntonic Research: Sounds of Silence." *Rolling Stone*, September 30.

Fischer, Kurt W. 1980. "A Theory of Cognitive Development: The Control and Construction of Hierarchies of Skills." *Psychological Review* 87, no. 6: 477–531.

Florida, Richard. 2014. *The Rise of the Creative Class—Revisited: Revised and Expanded*. New York: Basic Books.

Floridi, Luciano. 2010. *Information: A Very Short Introduction*. Oxford: Oxford University Press.

Foucault, Michel. 2002. *The Order of Things: An Archaeology of the Human Sciences*. London: Psychology Press.

Foucault, Michel, Luther H. Martin, Huck Gutman, and Patrick H. Hutton. 1988. *Technologies of the Self: A Seminar with Michel Foucault*. Amherst: University of Massachusetts Press.

Fouché, Rayvon. 2006. "Say It Loud, I'm Black and I'm Proud: African Americans, American Artifactual Culture, and Black Vernacular Technological Creativity." *American Quarterly* 58, no. 3: 639–61.

Foy, George. 2010. *Zero Decibels: The Quest for Absolute Silence*. New York: Scribner.

Fuller, Matthew, ed. 2008. *Software Studies: A Lexicon*. Cambridge, MA: MIT Press.

Galison, Peter. 2004. "Image of Self." In *Things That Talk: Object Lessons from Art and Science*, edited by Lorraine J. Daston. New York: Zone Books.

Galloway, Alexander R. 2004. *Protocol: How Control Exists after Decentralization*. Cambridge, MA: MIT Press.

Galloway, Alexander R. 2012. *The Interface Effect*. Cambridge: Polity.

Geertz, Clifford. 1983. *Local Knowledge: Further Essays in Interpretive Anthropology*. New York: Basic Books.

Gergen, Kenneth J. 1991. *The Saturated Self: Dilemmas of Identity in Contemporary Life*. New York: Basic Books.

Gergen, Kenneth J. 1996. "Technology and the Self: From the Essential to the Sublime." In *Constructing the Self in a Mediated World*, edited by Debra Grodin and Thomas R. Lindlof, 127–40. Thousand Oaks, CA: SAGE.

Gergen, Kenneth J. 2000. "The Self: Death by Technology." *Hedgehog Review* 1: 25–34.

Gerken, George M. 1996. "Central Tinnitus and Lateral Inhibition: An Auditory Brainstem Model." *Hearing Research* 97, no. 1: 75–83.

Gershon, Ilana. 2011. "Neoliberal Agency." *Current Anthropology* 52, no. 4: 537–55.

Gillespie, Tarleton. 2014. "The Relevance of Algorithms." In *Media Technologies: Essays on Communication, Materiality, and Society*, edited by T. Gillespie, P. J. Boczkowski, and K. A. Foot. Cambridge, MA: MIT Press.

Gitelman, Lisa. 2006. *Always Already New: Media, History, and the Data of Culture*. Cambridge, MA: MIT Press.

Gleick, James. 2011. *The Information: A History, A Theory, A Flood*. New York: Vintage.

Goggin, Gerard, and C. J. Newell. 2005. "Foucault on the Phone: Disability and the Mobility of Government." In *Foucault and the Government of Disability*, edited by S. Tremain. Ann Arbor: University of Michigan Press.

Goldsmith, Mike. 2012. *Discord: The Story of Noise*. Oxford: Oxford University Press.

Golumbia, David. 2009. *The Cultural Logic of Computation*. Cambridge, MA: Harvard University Press.

Goodman, Steve. 2010. *Sonic Warfare: Sound, Affect, and the Ecology of Fear*. Cambridge, MA: MIT Press.

Grand View Research, Inc. 2015. "Earphones & Headphones Market Worth $17.55 Billion by 2022: Grand View Research, Inc." *PRNewswire*, August 5. https://www.prnewswire.com/news-releases/earphones-headphones-market-worth-1755-billion-by-2022-grand-view-research-inc-520738251.html.

Gray, Mary. 2009. *Out in the Country: Youth, Media, and Queer Visibility in Rural America*. New York: NYU Press.

Gregory, Sean. 2016. "All Across the Country, Athletes Are Fueling a Debate about How America Defines Patriotism." *Time*, September 22.

Grof, Stanislav. 1994. *LSD Psychotherapy*. Alameda, CA: Hunter House.

Grossberg, Lawrence. 2010. "Rediscovering the Virtual in the Actual." In *The Affect Theory Reader*, edited by M. Gregg and G. J. Seigworth. Durham, NC: Duke University Press.

Grossberg, Lawrence. 2014. *We Gotta Get Out of This Place: Popular Conservatism and Postmodern Culture*. New York: Routledge.

Guenzel, Stephan. 2014. "Deleuze and Phenomenology." *Metodo: International Studies in Phenomenology and Philosophy* 2, no. 2: 31–45.

Hagood, Mack. 2014. "Unpacking a Punch: Transduction and the Sound of Combat Foley in Fight Club." *Cinema Journal* 53, no. 4: 98–120.

Hagood, Mack. 2015. "The Tinnitus Trope: Acoustic Trauma in Narrative Film." *Cine-Files* 8.

Hagood, Mack. 2017. "Disability and Biomediation: Tinnitus as a Phantom Disability." In *Disability Media Studies*, edited by E. Ellcessor and B. Kirkpatrick. New York: NYU Press.

Hagood, Mack. 2018. "Here: Active Listening System Sound Technologies and the Personalization of Listening." In *Appified: Culture in the Age of Apps*, edited by Jeremy Wade Morris and Sarah Murray, 276–85. Ann Arbor: University of Michigan Press.

Hain, Timothy C. 2014. "Malingering of Hearing." https://www.dizziness-and-balance.com/testing/hearing/malingering.html.

Hall, Bronwyn H., Adam Jaffe, and Manuel Trajtenberg. 2006. "Market Value and Patent Citations." *International Library of Critical Writings in Economics* 197, no. 2: 233.

Hall, Stuart. 1999. "Encoding, Decoding." In *The Cultural Studies Reader*, edited by S. During. London: Routledge.

Hansen, Mark B. N. 2004. *New Philosophy for New Media*. Cambridge, MA: MIT Press.

Haring, Kristen. 2003. "The 'Freer Men' of Ham Radio: How a Technical Hobby Provided Social and Spatial Distance." *Technology and Culture* 44, no. 4: 734–61.

Harman, Graham. 2011. *The Quadruple Object*. London: Zero Books.

Harvey, D. 2003. *The Condition of Postmodernity*. Oxford: Blackwell.

Hayles, N. Katherine. *How We Became Posthuman: Virtual Bodies in Cybernetics, Literature, and Informatics*. Chicago: University of Chicago Press.

Heidegger, Martin. 1962. *Being and Time*, translated by John Macquarrie and Edward Robinson. New York: Harper and Row.

Heller, Morris F., and M. Bergman. 1953. "Tinnitus Aurium in Normally Hearing Persons." *Annals of Otology, Rhinology and Laryngology* 62, no. 1: 73–83.

Heller, Natasha. 2014. "Buddha in a Box: The Materiality of Recitation in Contemporary Chinese Buddhism." *Material Religion* 10, no. 3: 294–314.

Helmholtz, Hermann. 1954. *On the Sensations of Tone*. New York: Dover.

Helmreich, Steven. 2007. "An Anthropologist Underwater." *American Ethnologist* 34, no. 4: 621–41.

Hempton, Gordon, and John Grossmann. 2009. *One Square Inch of Silence: One Man's Search for Natural Silence in a Noisy World*. New York: Simon and Schuster.

Hendy, David. 2013. *Noise: A Human History of Sound and Listening*. London: Profile.

Hennion, Antoine. 1989. "An Intermediary between Production and Consumption: The Producer of Popular Music." *Science, Technology and Human Values* 14, no. 4: 400–424.

Henriques, Julian. 2011. *Sonic Bodies: Reggae Sound Systems, Performance Techniques, and Ways of Knowing*. London: Bloomsbury.

Henry, J. A., and M. B. Meikle. 2000. "Psychoacoustic Measures of Tinnitus." *Journal of the American Academy of Audiology* 11, no. 3: 138–55.

Heptinstall, Simon. 2005. "Travel Companion." *Mail on Sunday*, July 17.

Hoffman, Howard J., and George W. Reed. 2004. "Epidemiology of Tinnitus." In *Tinnitus: Theory and Management*, edited by James B. Snow Jr., 16–41. Hamilton, ON: B. C. Decker.

Hogan, Kevin, and Jennifer Battaglino. 2010. *Tinnitus: Turning the Volume Down*. Eagan, MN: Network 3000.

Horkheimer, Max, and Theodor Adorno. [1944] 1972. *Dialectic of Enlightenment*, translated by J. Cumming. New York: Continuum.

Horton, Robert R. 1960. "Infant Pacifying Device." U.S. Patent No. 2932821A.

Hosokawa, Shuhei. 1984. "The Walkman Effect." *Popular Music* 4: 165–80.

Hunn, Nick. 2014. "Hearables—The New Wearables." http://www.nickhunn.com/hearables-the-new-wearables/.

Ibrahim, Awad. 2007. "Operating under Erasure: Hip-Hop and the Pedagogy of Affect." http://awadmibrahim.blogspot.com/2007/11/operating-under-erasure -hip-hop-and.html.

Ihde, Don. 1979. *Technics and Praxis*. Dordrecht: D. Reidel.

Ihde, Don. 1990. *Technology and the Lifeworld: From Garden to Earth*. Bloomington: Indiana University Press.

Ihde, Don. 1993. *Postphenomenology: Essays in the Postmodern Context*. Evanston, IL: Northwestern University Press.

James, Robin. 2014. "Some Philosophical Implications of the 'Loudness War' and Its Criticisms." https://www.its-her-factory.com/2014/12/some-philosophical -implications-of-the-loudness-war-and-its-criticisms/.

Jameson, Fredric. 1991. *Postmodernism, or, The Cultural Logic of Late Capitalism*. Durham, NC: Duke University Press.

Jastreboff, Pawel J. 1990. "Phantom Auditory Perception (Tinnitus): Mechanisms of Generation and Perception." *Neuroscience Research* 8, no. 4: 221–54.

Jastreboff, Pawel J., James F. Brennan, John K. Coleman, and Clarence T. Sasaki. 1988. "Phantom Auditory Sensation in Rats: An Animal Model for Tinnitus." *Behavioral Neuroscience* 102, no. 6: 811–22.

Jastreboff, Pawel J., and Jonathan W. P. Hazell. 2004. *Tinnitus Retraining Therapy: Implementing the Neurophysical Model*. Cambridge: Cambridge University Press.

Jenkins, Eric. 2014. *Special Affects: Cinema, Animation and the Translation of Consumer Culture*. Edinburgh: Edinburgh University Press.

Josephson, E. M. 1931. "A Method of Measurement of Tinnitus Aurium." *Archives of Otolaryngology* 14, no. 3: 282–83.

Kane, Brian. 2015. "Sound Studies without Auditory Culture: A Critique of the Ontological Turn." *Sound Studies* 1, no. 1: 2–21.

Kassabian, Anahid. 2013. *Ubiquitous Listening*. Berkeley: University of California Press.

Katz, Jack. 2002. "Clinical Audiology." In *Handbook of Clinical Audiology*, 5th ed. Baltimore: Williams and Wilkins.

Katz, Mark. 2004. *Capturing Sound: How Technology Has Changed Music*. Berkeley: University of California Press.

Kearney, Richard. 2015. "What Is Carnal Hermeneutics?" *New Literary History* 46, no. 1: 99–124.

Keightley, Keir. 1996. "'Turn It Down!' She Shrieked: Gender, Domestic Space, and High Fidelity, 1948–59." *Popular Music* 15, no. 2: 149–77.

Keizer, Garret. 2010. *The Unwanted Sound of Everything We Want: A Book about Noise*. New York: Public Affairs.

Kellner, Mark A. 2009. "Your Tech: Heavenly Non-Sound; Noise Out, Music Clear in Latest Bose Headset." *Washington Times*, September 2.

Kittler, Friedrich A. 1999. *Gramophone, Film, Typewriter*. Translated, with an introduction by Geoffrey Winthrop-Young and Michael Wutz. Stanford, CA: Stanford University Press.

Klett, Joseph. 2016. "Baffled by an Algorithm." In *Algorithmic Cultures: Essays on Meaning, Performance and New Technologies,* edited by R. Seyfert and J. Robberge. New York: Routledge.

Kosko, Bart. 2006. *Noise.* New York: Penguin.

Kryter, K. D. 1994. *The Handbook of Hearing and the Effects of Noise: Physiology, Psychology, and Public Health.* New York: Academic Press.

LaBelle, Brandon. 2010. *Acoustic Territories: Sound Culture and Everyday Life.* New York: Bloomsbury.

Lacey, Kate. 2013. *Listening Publics: The Politics and Experience of Listening in the Media Age.* New York: John Wiley and Sons.

Lang, William W., and George C. Maling. 2014. "Leo Beranek's Contributions to Noise and Vibration Control." *Acoustics Today* (fall): 21–27.

Lanza, Joseph. 1994. *Elevator Music: A Surreal History of Muzak, Easy-Listening and Other Moodsong.* New York: St. Martin's.

Latour, Bruno. 1987. *Science in Action: How to Follow Scientists and Engineers through Society.* Cambridge, MA: Harvard University Press.

Latour, Bruno. 2005. *Reassembling the Social: An Introduction to Actor-Network-Theory.* New York: Oxford University Press.

Lefebvre, Henri. 1991. *The Production of Space.* London: Wiley-Blackwell.

Leydesdorff, Loet. 2007. "Patents and Patent Citations." http://www.leydesdorff.net/indicators/lesson5.htm.

Leys, Ruth. 2011. "The Turn to Affect: A Critique." *Critical Inquiry* 37, no. 3: 434–72.

Lipari, Lisbeth. 2014. *Listening, Thinking, Being: Toward an Ethics of Attunement.* University Park: Pennsylvania State University Press.

Lockwood, Alan H., R. J. Salvi, M. L. Coad, M. L. Towsley, D. S. Wack, and B. W. Murphy. 1998. "The Functional Neuroanatomy of Tinnitus: Evidence for Limbic System Links and Neural Plasticity." *Neurology* 50, no. 1: 114–20.

Lyles, Harry, Jr. 2017. "Richard Sherman Stands Up for Colin Kaepernick, despite Disagreeing with How He Protested." SBNation, September 6. https://www.sbnation.com/2017/9/6/16264158/richard-sherman-colin-kaepernick-michael-bennett-protest.

Lyman, Kenneth E. 1951. "Warning Signal for Vehicles." U.S. Patent No. 2564984A.

Lyotard, Jean-François. 1984. *The Postmodern Condition: A Report on Knowledge.* Minneapolis: University of Minnesota Press.

Macatee, Rebecca. 2014. "NFL Fines Colin Kaepernick $10,000 for Wearing Beats by Dre Headphones." *ENews,* October 10. https://www.eonline.com/news/587237/nfl-fines-colin-kaepernick-10-000-for-wearing-beats-by-dre-headphones.

Manovich, Lev. 2001. *The Language of New Media.* Cambridge, MA: MIT Press.

Martin, Jill. 2017. "Michael Bennett: 'I Can't Stand for the National Anthem.'" CNN, August 17. https://www.cnn.com/2017/08/16/sport/seahawks-michael-bennett-not-standing-for-national-anthem/index.html.

Massumi, Brian. 1995. "The Autonomy of Affect." *Cultural Critique* 31: 83–109.

Massumi, Brian. 1998. "Sensing the Virtual, Building the Insensible." *Architectural Design* 68: 16–25.

Massumi, Brian. 2002. *Parables for the Virtual: Movement, Affect, Sensation*. Durham, NC: Duke University Press.

Massumi, Brian. 2015. *Politics of Affect*. New York: John Wiley and Sons.

Maturana, Humberto. 2007. "Interview on von Foerster, Autopoiesis, the BCL and Augusto Pinochet." In *An Unfinished Revolution? Heinz Von Foerster and the Biological Computer Laboratory, BCL 1958–1976*, edited by A. Müller and K. H. Müller, 37–51. Vienna: Ed. Echoraum.

Maturana, Humberto R., and Francisco J. Varela. [1987] 1998. *The Tree of Knowledge: The Biological Roots of Human Understanding*. Boston: Shambhala.

McKenna, Laurence, and Gerhard Andersson. 2008. "Changing Reactions." In *The Consumer Handbook on Tinnitus*, edited by R. S. Tyler. Sedona, AZ: Auricle Ink.

Mehta, Ravi, Rui Zhu, and Amar Cheema. 2012. "Is Noise Always Bad? Exploring the Effects of Ambient Noise on Creative Cognition." *Journal of Consumer Research* 39, no. 4: 784–99.

Melley, Timothy. 2000. *Empire of Conspiracy: The Culture of Paranoia in Postwar America*. Ithaca, NY: Cornell University Press.

Merton, Robert K. 1963. "Resistance to the Systematic Study of Multiple Discoveries in Science." *European Journal of Sociology/Archives Européennes de Sociologie* 4, no. 2: 237–82.

Millard, Frederick C. 1945. "Siren." U.S. Patent No. 2462862A.

Mills, Mara. 2011a. "Deafening: Noise and the Engineering of Communication in the Telephone System." *Grey Room* 43: 118–43.

Mills, Mara. 2011b. "On Disability and Cybernetics: Helen Keller, Norbert Wiener, and the Hearing Glove." *differences* 22, nos. 2–3: 74–111.

Mills, Mara. 2012. "What Should We Call Reading?" *Flow* 3. https://www.flowjournal.org/2012/12/what-should-we-call-reading/.

Mills, Mara. 2015. "Deafness." In *Keywords in Sound*, edited by David Novak and Matt Sakakeeny, 45–54. Durham, NC: Duke University Press.

Mintel. 2008. "Business and Conference Travel—US." Mintel database.

Mintel. 2010. "US Travel Market." Mintel database.

Mishima, Yukio. 1958. *Confessions of a Mask*, translated by M. Weatherby. New York: New Directions.

Mitchell, Timothy. 1988. *Colonising Egypt*. Berkeley: University of California Press.

Mol, Annemarie. 2002. *The Body Multiple: Ontology in Medical Practice*. Durham, NC: Duke University Press.

Morse, Margaret. 1990. "An Ontology of Everyday Distraction: The Freeway, the Mall and Television." In *Logics of Television: Essays in Cultural Criticism*, edited by P. Mellencamp. Bloomington: Indiana University Press.

Nakamura, Lisa. 2009. *Digitizing Race: Visual Cultures of the Internet*. Minneapolis: University of Minnesota Press.

Narse, Rohan. 2011. *In Search of Silence*. St. Albans, UK: Ecademy Press.

"NASEM Committee Looks into OTC Hearing Device Regulations." 2017. *Hearing Review*, June 12. http://www.hearingreview.com/2017/06/nasem-committee-looks-regulations-otc-hearing-devices/.

Ng, Serena, Eva Dou, and Hannah Karp. 2013. "Beats by Dre Looks to Drop HTC." *Wall Street Journal*, August 19.

Novak, David. 2013. *Japanoise: Music at the Edge of Circulation*. Durham, NC: Duke University Press.

Novak, David. 2015. "Noise." In *Keywords in Sound*, edited by D. Novak and M. Sakakeeny. Durham, NC: Duke University Press.

Novak, David, and Matt Sakakeeny. 2015. *Keywords in Sound*. Durham, NC: Duke University Press.

Oliveros, Pauline. 1984. *Software for People: Collected Writings 1963–80*. Rochester, NY: Writers and Books.

Oliveros, Pauline. 2005. *Deep Listening: A Composer's Sound Practice*. Lincoln, NE: iUniverse.

Pais, Arthur J. 1996. "Amar Bose: The Sound of Success." *India Today Plus*, January 1.

Pallotta, Frank. 2017. "Yes, the NFL's TV Ratings Are Down, but So Is the Rest of Network Television." CNN, October 26. http://money.cnn.com/2017/10/26/media/nfl-ratings-tv-networks/index.html.

Pan, Tao, Richard S. Tyler, Haihong Ji, Claudia Coelho, Anne K. Gehringer, and Stephanie A. Gogel. 2009. "The Relationship between Tinnitus Pitch and the Audiogram." *International Journal of Audiology* 48, no. 5: 277–94.

Pariser, Eli. 2011. *The Filter Bubble: How the New Personalized Web Is Changing What We Read and How We Think*. New York: Penguin.

Perlman, Marc. 2004. "Golden Ears and Meter Readers." *Social Studies of Science* 34, no. 5: 783–807.

Peters, John Durham. 1999. *Speaking into the Air: A History of the Idea of Communication*. Chicago: University of Chicago Press.

Peters, John Durham. 2015. *The Marvelous Clouds: Toward a Philosophy of Elemental Media*. Chicago: University of Chicago Press.

Pettman, Dominic. 2017. *Sonic Intimacy: Voice, Species, Technics (or, How to Listen to the World)*. Stanford, CA: Stanford University Press.

Phua, Peter. 2015. "Guest Article: What Are the Most Common Tinnitus Frequencies?" *The Hearing Blog*. http://thehearingblog.com/archives/4784.

Piaget, Jean. 1951. *The Child's Conception of the World*. Lanham, MD: Rowman and Littlefield.

Piaget, Jean, and Bärbel Inhelder. 1969. *The Psychology of the Child*. New York: Basic Books.

Picker, John M. 2000. "The Soundproof Study: Victorian Professionals, Work Space, and Urban Noise." *Victorian Studies* 42, no. 3: 427–53.

Pinch, Trevor, and Karin Bijsterveld. 2004. "Sound Studies: New Technologies and Music." *Social Studies of Science* 34, no. 5: 635–48.

Pogue, David. 2007. "What Price to Shut Out the World?" *New York Times*, June 14.

Pogue, David. 2009. "Ho Ho Ho? You Won't Hear a Thing." *New York Times*, December 3.

Prochnik, George. 2011. *In Pursuit of Silence: Listening for Meaning in a World of Noise*. Garden City, NJ: Doubleday.

Protevi, John. 2009. *Political Affect: Connecting the Social and the Somatic*. Minneapolis: University of Minnesota Press.

Protevi, John. 2013. *Life, War, Earth: Deleuze and the Sciences*. Minneapolis: University of Minnesota Press.

Quashie, Kevin. 2012. *The Sovereignty of Quiet: Beyond Resistance in Black Culture*. New Brunswick, NJ: Rutgers University Press.

Quinn, Eithne. 2013. *Nuthin' but a "G" Thang: The Culture and Commerce of Gangsta Rap*. New York: Columbia University Press.

Rauschecker, Josef P., Amber M. Leaver, and Mark Mühlau. 2010. "Tuning Out the Noise: Limbic-Auditory Interactions in Tinnitus." *Neuron* 66, no. 6: 819–26.

Rauschecker, Josef P., Elisabeth S. May, Audrey Maudoux, and Markus Ploner. 2015. "Frontostriatal Gating of Tinnitus and Chronic Pain." *Trends in Cognitive Sciences* 19, no. 10: 567–78.

Richter, Felix. 2014. "U.S. Teens Love Beats Headphones." *Statistica*. https://www.statista.com/chart/2227/preferred-headphone-brands-among-us-teens/.

Rodman, Gilbert B. 2015. "Waiting for the Great Leap Forwards: Mixing Pop, Politics and Cultural Studies." In *The SAGE Handbook of Popular Music*, edited by A. Bennett and S. Waksman. Los Angeles: SAGE.

Rogers, Kenneth. 2014. *The Attention Complex: Media, Archeology, Method*. New York: Palgrave Macmillan.

Roquet, Paul. 2016. *Ambient Media: Japanese Atmospheres of Self*. Minneapolis: University of Minnesota Press.

Rose, Nikolas. 1999. *Governing the Soul: The Shaping of the Private Self*. New York: Free Association.

Rose, Tricia. 1994. *Black Noise: Rap Music and Black Culture in Contemporary America*. Hanover, NH: Wesleyan University Press.

Rosenblith, Walter A., and Kenneth N. Stevens. 1953. *Handbook of Acoustic Noise Control*, vol. 2: *Noise and Man*. Wright-Patterson Air Force Base, OH: Defense Technical Information Center.

Russolo, Luigi. 2004. "The Art of Noises: Futurist Manifesto." In *Audio Culture: Readings in Modern Music*, edited by C. Cox and D. Warner. New York: Continuum.

Saltzman, Mark. 2006. "A Bubble of Silence amid Babel: Noise-Cancelling Headphones Aim to Create an Oasis of Quiet." *Gazette*, September 2.

Samuels, David W., and Thomas Porcello. 2015. "Language." In *Keywords in Sound*, edited by D. Novak and M. Sakakeeny. Durham, NC: Duke University Press.

Samuels, Ellen Jean. 2003. "My Body, My Closet: Invisible Disability and the Limits of Coming-Out Discourse." *GLQ: A Journal of Lesbian and Gay Studies* 9, no. 1: 233–55.

Sassen, Saskia. 1996. "Whose City Is It? Globalization and the Formation of New Claims." *Public Culture* 8, no. 2: 205–23.

Scarry, Elaine. 1985. *The Body in Pain: The Making and Unmaking of the World*. New York: Oxford University Press.

Schafer, R. Murray. 1994. *The Soundscape: Our Sonic Environment and the Tuning of the World*. Rochester, NY: Destiny.

Schmidt, Leigh Eric. 2000. *Hearing Things: Religion, Illusion, and the American Enlightenment*. Cambridge, MA: Harvard University Press.

Schüll, Natasha Dow. 2012. *Addiction by Design: Machine Gambling in Las Vegas*. Princeton, NJ: Princeton University Press.

Schwartz, Hillel. 2011. *Making Noise: From Babel to the Big Bang and Beyond*. New York: Zone.

Schwartz, Hillel. 2012. "Inner and Outer Sancta: Earplugs and Hospitals." In *The Oxford Handbook of Sound Studies*, edited by Trevor Pinch and Karin Bijsterveld. Oxford: Oxford University Press.

Serres, Michel. 2007. *The Parasite*, translated by L. R. Schehr. Minneapolis: University of Minnesota Press.

Serres, Michel. 2008. *The Five Senses: A Philosophy of Mingled Bodies*, translated by Margaret Sankey and Peter Cowley. London: Continuum.

Shannon, Claude E., and Warren Weaver. [1949] 1964. *The Mathematical Theory of Communication*. Urbana: University of Illinois Press.

Sharp, Hasana. 2005. "Why Spinoza Today? Or, 'A Strategy of Anti-Fear.'" *Rethinking Marxism* 17, no. 4: 591–608.

Sheppard, Ben. 2017. "Affect." Chicago School of Media Theory. https://lucian.uchicago.edu/blogs/mediatheory/keywords/affect/.

Siddiqi, Asif. 2003. "Deregulation and Its Consequences." Centennial of Flight Commission. http://www.centennialofflight.gov/essay/Commercial_Aviation/Dereg/Tran8.htm.

Siebers, Tobin. 2008. *Disability Theory*. Ann Arbor: University of Michigan Press.

Silva, Liana M. 2015. "As Loud as I Want to Be: Gender, Loudness, and Respectability Politics." *Sounding Out!* February 9. https://soundstudiesblog.com/2015/02/09/as-loud-as-i-want-to-be-gender-loudness-and-respectability-politics/.

Skinner, B. F. 1953. *Science and Human Behavior*. New York: Macmillan.

Smith, David Woodruff, and Ronald McIntyre. 1982. *Husserl and Intentionality: A Study of Mind, Meaning, and Language*. Dordrecht: D. Reidel.

Spinoza, Benedict. 1970. *Ethics*. New York: Simon and Schuster.

Spinoza, Benedict. 1994. *A Spinoza Reader*. Princeton, NJ: Princeton University Press.

Starosielski, Nicole. 2015. *The Undersea Network*. Durham, NC: Duke University Press.

Sterne, Jonathan. 1997. "Sounds Like the Mall of America: Programmed Music and the Architectonics of Commercial Space." *Ethnomusicology* 41, no. 1: 22–50.

Sterne, Jonathan. 2003. *The Audible Past: Cultural Origins of Sound Reproduction*. Durham, NC: Duke University Press.

Sterne, Jonathan. 2006. "The MP3 as Cultural Artifact." *New Media and Society* 8, no. 5: 825–42.

Sterne, Jonathan. 2012. MP3: *The Meaning of a Format*. Durham, NC: Duke University Press.

Stiegler, Bernard. 1998. "The Time of Cinema: On the 'New World' and 'Cultural Exception.'" *Tekhnema* 4: 62–113.

Stoever, Jennifer Lynn. 2016. *The Sonic Color Line: Race and the Cultural Politics of Listening*. New York: NYU Press.

Stoute, Steve, with Mim Eichler Rivas. 2012. *The Tanning of America: How Hip-Hop Created a Culture That Rewrote the Rules of the New Economy*. New York: Gotham.

Striphas, Ted. 2015. "Algorithmic Culture." *European Journal of Cultural Studies* 18, nos. 4–5: 395–412.

Swade, Doron. 2001. *The Difference Engine: Charles Babbage and the Quest to Build the First Computer*. New York: Viking.

Sweetow, Robert W. 2012. "A Critical Analysis of Tinnitus Theories and Therapies." Paper delivered at American Academy of Audiology Annual Meeting.

Teibel, Irving S. 1969a. *Environments: New Concepts in Stereo Sound, Disc 1*. New York: Syntonic Research Inc.

Teibel, Irving S. 1969b. *Features of Environments*. New York: Syntonic Research Inc.

Teibel, Irving S. 1969c. *Progress Report: Environments Disc One*. New York: Syntonic Research Inc.

Teibel, Irving S. 1970. "I. S. Teibel, President, Syntonic Research Inc., Brief Biography." New York: Syntonic Research Inc.

Teibel, Irving S. 1984. "Mother Nature Goes Digital." In *Digital Deli: The Lunch Group*, edited by S. Ditlea. New York: Workman.

Thacker, Eugene. 2004. *Biomedia*. Minneapolis: University of Minnesota Press.

Theberge, P. 1997. *Any Sound You Can Imagine: Making Music/Consuming Technology*. Hanover, NH: Wesleyan University Press.

Thomas, P. L. 2014. "Richard Sherman's GPA and 'Thug' Label: The Codes That Blind." *Truthout*, January 27. http://www.truth-out.org/speakout/item/21471 -richard-shermans-gpa-and.

Thompson, Emily Ann. 2002. *The Soundscape of Modernity: Architectural Acoustics and the Culture of Listening in America, 1900–1933*. Cambridge, MA: MIT Press.

Thompson, Evan. 2015. *Waking, Dreaming, Being: Self and Consciousness in Neuroscience, Meditation, and Philosophy*. New York: Columbia University Press.

Thompson, Marie. 2017. *Beyond Unwanted Sound: Noise, Affect and Aesthetic Moralism*. New York: Bloomsbury.

Todes, Daniel Philip. 2014. *Ivan Pavlov: A Russian Life in Science*. Oxford: Oxford University Press.

Tompkins, Dave. 2010. *How to Wreck a Nice Beach: The Vocoder from World War II to Hip-Hop*. Chicago: Stop Smiling.

Trajtenberg, Manuel. 1990. "A Penny for Your Quotes: Patent Citations and the Value of Innovations." *Rand Journal of Economics* 21, no. 1: 172–87.

Truax, Barry. 1984. *Acoustic Communication*. Norwood, CT: Ablex.

Tsuji, Alysha. 2017. "Richard Sherman Responds to Trump in Video: 'It's Time for the Racism and Bigotry to Go Away.'" *USA Today*, September 23. https://ftw .usatoday.com/2017/09/richard-sherman-seahawks-president-donald-trump -nfl-comments-anthem-protest-white-supremacists-video-reaction.

Turkle, Sherry. 1997. *Life on the Screen: Identity in the Age of the Internet*. New York: Touchstone Books.

Turner, Fred. 2006. *From Counterculture to Cyberculture: Stewart Brand, the Whole Earth Network, and the Rise of Digital Utopianism*. Chicago: University of Chicago Press.

Turner, Fred. 2013. *The Democratic Surround: Multimedia and American Liberalism from World War II to the Psychedelic Sixties*. Chicago: University of Chicago Press.

Tyler, Anne. 2002. *The Accidental Tourist: A Novel*. New York: Random House.

Tyler, Richard S. 2005. *Tinnitus Treatment: Clinical Protocols*. New York: Thieme.

Tyler, Richard S. 2008. *The Consumer Handbook on Tinnitus*. Sedona, AZ: Auricle Ink.

Uchiyama, Kosho. 2004. *Opening the Hand of Thought: Foundations of Zen Buddhist Practice*, translated by J. W. Tom Wright and Shohaku Okumura. Boston: Wisdom.

Urban, Greg. 2001. *Metaculture: How Culture Moves through the World*. Minneapolis: University of Minnesota Press.

Varela, Francisco J., Evan Thompson, and Eleanor Rosch. 1991. *The Embodied Mind: Cognitive Science and Human Experience*. Cambridge, MA: MIT Press.

Verbeek, P. P. 2005. *What Things Do: Philosophical Reflections on Technology, Agency, and Design*. University Park: Pennsylvania State University Press.

Vernon, Jack A., and Aage R. Møller, eds. 1995. *Mechanisms of Tinnitus*. Boston: Allyn and Bacon.

Virilio, Paul. 1986. *Speed and Politics*. New York: Columbia University Press.

Wagner, Kyle. 2014. "The Word 'Thug' Was Uttered 625 Times on TV on Monday. That's a Lot." *Deadspin*, January 21. https://deadspin.com/the-word-thug-was -uttered-625-times-on-tv-yesterday-1506098319.

Walker, Rob. 2008. "The Silence Generation." *New York Times*, June 8.

Ward, W. Dixon, Aram Glorig, and Diane L. Sklar. 1959. "Temporary Threshold Shift from Octave-Band Noise: Applications to Damage-Risk Criteria." *Journal of the Acoustical Society of America* 31, no. 4: 522–28.

Webb, Pauline, and Mark Suggitt. 2000. *Gadgets and Necessities: An Encyclopedia of Household Innovations*. London: ABC-CLIO.

Werner, Hans U. 1987. "Interview with Irv Teibel." New York: Syntonic Research Inc.

Whitley, David. 2012. "Colin Kaepernick Ushers in an Inked-Up NFL Quarterbacking Era." *Sporting News*, November 28. http://www.sportingnews.com/nfl/news

/4351417-colin-kaepernick-tattoos-49ers-qb-start-alex-smith-stats-contract
-draft.

Wiener, Norbert. 1948. *Cybernetics: Or Control and Communication in the Animal and the Machine*. Cambridge, MA: MIT Press.

Wiener, Norbert. [1950] 1988. *The Human Use of Human Beings: Cybernetics and Society*. Cambridge, MA: Da Capo.

Wiesman, Frank H. 1953. "Device for Inducing Sleep and Rest." U.S. Patent No. 2659073A.

Williams, Raymond. [1974] 2003. *Television: Technology and Cultural Form*. London: Routledge.

Williams, Raymond. 1977. *Marxism and Literature*. Oxford: Oxford University Press.

Wroe, Ann. 2011. *Orpheus: The Song of Life*. New York: Overlook.

Wyche, Steve. 2016. "Colin Kaepernick Explains Why He Sat during National Anthem." NFL.com, August 27. http://www.nfl.com/news/story /0ap3000000691077/article/colin-kaepernick-explains-why-he-sat-during -national-anthem.

Zieliński, Kazimierz. 2006. "Jerzy Konorski on Brain Associations." *Acta Neurobiologiae Experimentalis* 66: 75–84.

Index

Page numbers followed by *f* indicate figures.

ontogenic structural drift, 165

ontology, 83, 159, 173, 238n5, 243n5; informatic, 156; neocybernetic, 166; object-oriented (OOO), 239n5; vibrational, 27

Orientalism, 182

Orpheus, 2–3, 3f, 5, 9, 12–13, 18, 23–24, 24f, 77, 104, 153, 163, 228–29, 233–34

orphic media, 8–9, 14, 21, 78, 88, 119, 155–56, 158, 185–86, 201, 220, 229–34, 235n2, 239n4; control and, 4, 6, 16–17, 23, 150, 198, 223; definition, 23–28; infocentrism and, 10; intentionality of, 104; representation and, 22; shaping social relations, 179; sleep/concentration binary and, 111f, 139; as technologies of the self, 16; tinnitus and, 7, 34–38, 46, 56, 63–64, 71, 168

oscilloscopes, 26

pain, 42, 191, 238n3; chronic, 49; phantom, 34. See also suffering

Panasonic, 199

Pandora, 69

Pariser, Eli, 158, 226

patents, 76, 79, 89, 94f, 95–97, 100–103, 107–8, 124, 167; patent citations, 91–93, 98–99; patent interference, 240n9; patent law, 80

Pavlov, Ivan, 44–45, 49

P. Diddy, 202

Peace Noise Generator, 153

Pelly, Liz, 221

Pence, Mike, 213

Penn, Irving, 128

Pennsylvania, 111, 239n2; Philadelphia, 181

Pentagon, 193

perceptual coding, 137, 157

performance studies, 236n10

personal responsibility, 37, 39–40, 189

personal sensory therapy, 102, 146f, 147

personal stereo scholarship, 12

personal therapy sensory devices, 80

perturbations, 23, 164–66, 228, 232

Peters, John Durham, 4

Pettman, Dominic, 233

phantom sound, 7, 32–34, 37, 41–42, 44–45, 50–51, 53, 57, 61–62, 66

phase cancellation, 7–8, 177, 188, 222, 225, 230. See also fighting sound with sound; noise; noise-canceling headphones

phenomenology, 5, 22, 43–44, 50–51, 55, 82–84, 155, 159, 178, 189, 195, 229, 239n5. See also postphenomenology

Philips, 199

philosophy, 4, 9, 10, 12, 20, 156, 167, 216. See also individual traditions

phonograph, 8, 12, 27, 77, 82, 120, 123–24, 127, 142

physiology, 34, 43, 89, 143; neurophysiology, 7, 37, 44–47, 49, 65, 84, 231, 235n4

Piaget, Jean, 163–64

Picker, John, 14

Pierce, John, 138

Pioneer Corporation, 199

Piskosz, Michael, 62–63

pitch, 50, 55, 58–62, 64–66, 72, 101, 125, 220

Platonic ideal, 114, 136

playlists, 221, 227

Pogue, David, 188, 190

Poland: Warsaw, 44

police, 102, 230; police violence, 203, 210–11

Popular Photography, 121

Positive K, 198

postmodernism, 184, 230

postphenomenology, 82, 239n5

practice theory, 236n10

praxiology, 38, 57

prescription media, 64, 224–25

Primitives (band), 128

privacy, 16–17, 84, 110, 114, 218; acoustic, 101–3; public/private divide, 4

progressive tinnitus management (PTM), 66

Protevi, John, 42, 50, 167–68

psychiatry, 14, 102, 139, 145

psychoacoustics, 54, 102, 125, 137–39, 143, 145, 157, 181

"The Psychologically Ultimate Seashore,"
123, 126–30, 133–36, 139, 145, 153

psychology, 89, 102, 159, 163, 180, 187,
194, 220, 241n6; behaviorism, 44, 49;
capitalism and, 243n5; *environments*
albums and, 117, 123, 125–29, 135, 139–
40, 142–43, 145; information science
and, 235n3, 242n5; tinnitus and, 70

Quashie, Kevin: *The Sovereignty of Quiet*,
217

quiet, 12, 28, 73, 90, 168, 210, 217–18, 230;
headphones and, 180, 187; tinnitus
and, 7, 32–33, 35, 37, 46, 55, 63, 65; white
noise machines and, 149, 152, 157.
See also silence

Quiet Mark, 221

Quinn, Eithne, 203

race, 38, 144, 185, 194; 2016–17 racial justice protest in NFL, 1, 200–201, 210–15,
219; Beats headphones and, 8, 190, 195,
197, 199–219; Bose headphones and, 8,
179–82, 189, 199, 224, 243n7; digital racial formation, 195; in object-oriented
ontology, 239n5; racialized loudness,
198, 216–17; sonic color line, 180,
195–97, 199, 215. *See also* black noise

racial justice, 210–11, 213

racism, 8, 15, 181–82, 196, 201, 204; Donald Trump's, 211–12; in NFL, 205–12,
215–17. *See also* Unite the Right Rally;
white supremacists

Rainy Mood, 153

rainymood.com, 22

ready-to-hand (Heideggerian), 83, 86

Reagan, Ronald, 179

realism, 120, 136–38

Reed, Lou, 128

Refrain (Deleuzian/Guattarian), 18–19

Relax and Sleep, 153

Relax Forest, 153

remediation, 36–37, 77, 79, 85, 149, 166,
168, 179, 223; of affect, 5–9, 13, 22–28,
35, 80, 89, 91, 97, 103–4, 189, 198; of the

sonic color line, 180, 196, 199, 215; of
tinnitus, 35, 43, 62–66, 68, 71–72.
See also mediation

representation (media), 8, 10, 13, 26–27,
78, 111, 166, 180, 189, 205, 220, 229,
236nn5–6, 236n9; disability and, 35, 51;
gendered, 104–9; nonrepresentational
media, 5, 19, 21–22, 163–65; racialized,
209–17; tinnitus and, 58, 63, 65

representationalism, 20–21

Republican Party, 213

ReSound, 62, 70–71

responsibilization, 102, 114, 142

Rodman, Gil, 214

Rolling Stone, 118, 134, 141

Roquet, Paul, 5–6, 233

Rorschach ink blot test, 126

Rose, Axl, 153

Rose, Nikolas, 102, 188

Rose, Tricia, 199–200

Rosenblith, Walter A., 148

Ross, Diana, 145

Rousseau, Jean-Jacques, 42

Rubbermaid, 76. *See also* Wooster Rubber
Company

Russolo, Luigi: "Art of Noises," 119

Saint Teresa of Avila, 53

Sakakeeny, Matt, 27

Samsung Galaxy S2, 170

Samuels, Ellen, 42

San Francisco 49ers, 1, 210, 215

San Quentin State Prison, 206

Sartre, Jean-Paul, 82

Sasaki, Clarence, 44

Sassen, Saskia, 183–85

Satie, Eric, 12, 233

Scarry, Elaine, 42

Schafer, R. Murray, 9, 116, 133, 134, 184;
The Soundscape, 149

schizophonia, 133

Schmidt, Leigh Eric, 62, 184

Schüll, Natasha Dow, 3–4

Schwartz, Hillel, 9, 75

Science and Invention, 10–11, 11f

Xerox, 125

Yale University, 44–45
Young, Andre. *See* Dr. Dre
Young and Rubicam, 121

Zero Decibels: The Quest for Absolute Silence, 9
Zhang Jian: Buddha Machine, 19–20, 20*f*, 22, 236n5
Zimmerman, Janet, 79, 239n2